SCHOOL DESEGREGATION PLANS THAT WORK

Recent Titles in
Contributions to the Study of Education

Black Students in Higher Education:
Conditions and Experiences in the 1970s
Edited by Gail E. Thomas

The Scope of Faculty Collective Bargaining:
An Analysis of Faculty Union Agreements
at Four-Year Institutions of Higher Education
Ronald L. Johnstone

Brainpower for the Cold War:
The Sputnik Crisis
and National Defense Education Act of 1958
Barbara Barksdale Clowse

In Opposition to Core Curriculum:
Alternative Models for Undergraduate Education
Edited by James W. Hall with Barbara L. Kevles

Peer Teaching: Historical Perspectives
Lilya Wagner

School Law for the Practitioner
Robert C. O'Reilly and Edward T. Green

The Search for Quality Integrated Education:
Policy and Research on Minority Students in School and College
Meyer Weinberg

From Little Rock to Boston:
The History of School Desegregation
George R. Metcalf

American Higher Education:
Servant of the People or Protector of Special Interests?
E. C. Wallenfeldt

SCHOOL DESEGREGATION PLANS THAT WORK

CHARLES VERT WILLIE

Contributions to the Study of Education, Number 10

GREENWOOD PRESS
Westport, Connecticut • London, England

Library of Congress Cataloging in Publication Data

Willie, Charles Vert, 1927-
    School desegregation plans that work.

    (Contributions to the study of education, 0196-707X ;
no. 10)
    Bibliography: p.
    Includes index.
    1. School integration—United States—Case studies
—Addresses, essays, lectures. 2. Discrimination in
education—Law and legislation—United States—
Addresses, essays, lectures. I. Title. II. Series.
LC212.52.W54 1984   370.19'342   83-12685
ISBN 0-313-24051-5 (lib. bdg.)

Library of Congress Catalog Card Number: 83-12685
ISBN: 0-313-24051-5
ISSN: 0196-707X

First published in 1984

Greenwood Press
A division of Congressional Information Service, Inc.
88 Post Road West
Westport, Connecticut 06881

Printed in the United States of America
10 9 8 7 6 5 4 3 2 1

Contents

Tables and Figure

Preface

In destroying the old and making way for the new, social change is both destructive and constructive. With reference to school desegregation, educational planners, analysts, and policy makers have been preoccupied with its destructive features and have given only limited attention to the constructive aspects of this revolutionary event. Whether the school desegregation struggle occurs in Pontiac, Michigan, Boston, Massachusetts, or Richmond, California, as sociologist Lillian Rubin said, "the response is the same—a cry of outrage and pain."

"We don't want our city to become another Boston" is the rallying call by public-spirited citizens across the nation. A litany of negative outcomes usually accompanies this declaration. The violence in Boston distracted the public from seeing many of the fine accomplishments of school desegregation.

One suspects that the citizens of any community would be pleased with a public school system that had "a rating process for appointment of principals . . . a personnel evaluation system, improved budget and personnel management . . . a citywide curriculum, the beginning of a systemwide testing program and a new alliance between the schools and business," and an organized data system. These are precisely what reporter Muriel Cohen found in her assessment of the school desegregation process in Boston ten years after litigation began in the federal court.

Moreover, in her article in the December 9, 1982, *Boston Globe*, Cohen reported that patronage in the school system had been substantially reduced and that parent councils had assumed a strong role in school decisions. The Boston School Committee, a public policy-making body once described as intransigent and now classified as progressive, has become more diversified with minority and majority members since the school-desegregation court order.

In addition to neighborhood attendance zones, a citywide magnet-school district has been added that includes schools with enriched educational offerings, facilitated in part by pairing arrangements between individual schools and local colleges and universities. The recently announced Boston Compact, an alliance between the public education system and major area businesses, guarantees high school graduates jobs in exchange for continued improved performance on the part of the public schools. These added attractions including programs for bilingual and special needs students and an occupational resource center coexist with a program for the conservation of resources ordered by the court that has resulted in the closing of at least twenty-seven schools as enrollments have declined.

The public school system in Boston has been significantly altered, according to the *Boston Globe* newspaper reporter, because of "a series of orders" issued by U.S. District Court Judge W. Arthur Garrity, Jr. Despite the trauma and agony, some Bostonians have described court-ordered school desegregation in their city as contributing to "positive changes."

It is possible that people in Boston and in other communities of the United States do not know about the positive changes associated with school desegregation and cannot appreciate them because the media have been slow to inform and deficient in their interpretation.

Florence Levinsohn said that "television news," for example, "has gone for the violent." Notwithstanding that there has been "much more peaceful school desegregation than violent," reports of this have been missing in favor of a theme of "social discord," according to Levinsohn.

Assessing blame is of limited value if efforts are not undertaken to reverse the situation by linking information about the positive outcomes of school desegregation to the plentiful supply of negative events reported. With the assistance of a grant from the Danforth Foundation, this study has accepted the challenge. It shares with the public detailed information about school desegregation plans that work—*what* their significant components are, *how* they work, and *why*.

This report of workable desegregation plans and their analysis should be of particular benefit to educational administrators, planners, and analysts. School board members, city councilors, and state legislators will find these model plans of value as will members of community groups who wish to propose alternatives to official school desegregation policies. Attorneys will also find a review of the various desegregation strategies helpful in suggesting ways by which schools may comply with the constitutional requirement for a unitary system, with or without litigation. Several plans are described so that the reader may select one that is more suitable to the circumstances of his or her local community.

The author is particularly grateful to Dr. John B. Ervin of the Danforth Foundation who recognized the need for a policy study like this one on model school desegregation plans. The author is also grateful to his consultants in Atlanta, Boston, Milwaukee, and Seattle who enhanced his knowledge of these communities. Their names are mentioned in the chapters that describe and analyze the desegregation process in each city. Finally the author acknowledges with appreciation Michael Fultz, research assistant, Betty Blake, project secretary, and his family, Mary Sue, Sarah, Martin, and James—who create a loving, learning, and living environment that supports and sustains him.

Part I

INTRODUCTION

Chapter 1

A Recent History of Court-Ordered School Desegregation Planning

In a free, open, and pluralistic society, it is difficult to read aright the signs of the time. In a democracy no single sector has the ultimate right and responsibility to determine what is good or bad for all. With no ultimate authority other than the people and their conflicting interests, there is everywhere flexibility and, of course, ambiguity. Benjamin Franklin is reported to have observed that painters have difficulty distinguishing in their art a rising and a setting sun. As the debate in the Constitutional Convention dragged on for months in 1787, Franklin said he continued to look at the painting behind the chair of the president of the convention and wondered whether the sun was indeed rising or setting. At the happy conclusion of the convention that resulted in consensus on a constitution for the new nation-state, Franklin declared the painting was of a rising sun (quoted in Dahl, 1967:3).

And so it is with school desegregation in the United States. In the final quarter of the twentieth century, parents, professors and politicians among others are trying to figure out the actual accomplishments of court-ordered school desegregation. Some public officials assert that it has been a failure. In a foreword to Ray Rist's study of school integration in American society, I assert that "school desegregation has been the best thing that has happened to public education in this century" (Willie, 1978:viii). Obviously there is conflict in the assessment of the outcome. Different assessments lead to different conclusions—"ain't it awful!" or "ain't it good!"

The "ain't-it-awful" orientation is most frequently expressed by members of the majority who attempt to avoid conflict as a destabilizing experience and use the future as a reference point, indicating how far we must go to achieve preeminence. The "ain't-it-good" orientation is most frequently expressed by members of the minority who embrace conflict as a change-inducing experience and use the past as a point of reference indicating how far we have traveled from adversity. Having declared myself in favor of desegregation, I nevertheless try to avoid both orientations in my research, for I recognize the twin dangers of arrogance in striving only for the future and preeminence, and self-obsession in looking only to the past and its adversity. Polybius, who recorded the histories of Rome, reported that those who strive for supremacy eventually bring their own freedom into danger; they often forget and deny the flexibility that is necessary in a democracy and cannot tolerate failure. Also, those with single-minded determination to overcome the adversity of the past often struggle with fury and obstinate resolution, sometimes forgetting the harm they cause others; they, too, may become rigid, inflexible, and sometimes self-centered (Polybius, "Histories VI," in Thompson, 1971:8-17).

A view that is "clear and complete," said Polybius, "is obtained only by comparison of the separate parts of the whole, by observing their likenesses and their differences" (Polybius, "Histories I," in Thompson, 1971:4-8). In this connection, I examine the history of school desegregation not as victory for the minority or as defeat for the majority but as a series of unfolding events consisting of effective and ineffective actions.

To be declared effective an action must meet the twin tests of morality and ethics. That which is moral is in accord with principles of the group with which an individual identifies. That which is ethical fulfills collective need in a way that is fair. Achieving a just and fair outcome for the multitude that is ethical should not require immoral behavior that is harmful to an individual. And personal morality should not foster unethical arrangements. Thus, effective actions are morally correct and ethically fair. When school desegregation is effective, it helps some and harms none; as such, it is both moral and ethical. A brief review of school desegregation in the United States reveals this outcome.

"Since 1954," according to Florence Levinsohn, "there has been more peaceful integration of schools than violent" (Levinsohn and Wright, 1976:93). This also is the conclusion of the United States Commission on Civil Rights, which further states, in a staff report reviewing the second decade of court-ordered desegregation in the 1960s and 1970s, "desegregation actions . . . were effective" and "a majority of school staff, students, parents, and community leaders accept school desegregation" (U.S. Civil Rights Commission, 1977:3).

Evidence that the entire population has been helped and not harmed by school desegregation is found in these current facts:

- 90 to 95 percent of all school-age children 5 through 17 years of age are in school (U.S. Bureau of the Census, 1982-83:140)
- two-thirds of the adult population (over 25 years) are high school graduates (U.S. Bureau of the Census, 1982-83:142)
- one-third of the adult population (over 25 years) has attended college (U.S. Bureau of the Census, 1982-83:143)

- one-sixth of the adult population (over 25 years) has graduated from college (U.S. Bureau of the Census, 1982-83:143)
- less than 1 percent of the population (over 14 years) is illiterate (U.S. Bureau of the Census, 1982-83:145).

These achievements were substantially different in 1950 before school desegregation began when the disparity between the races in educational opportunity was much greater. For example, 9.7, the median school year completed by white adults (over 25 years), was 40 percent higher than the median of 6.9 years completed by black adults and other racial minorities in 1950 (National Center for Educational Statistics, 1980:16). Today, however, the difference in the medians for these populations is less than 1 percent (U.S. Bureau of the Census, 1982-83:143). Thus, the United States, largely with the aid of school desegregation, has brought about a reasonable degree of parity between minority and majority populations in level of educational attainment as reflected in median years of school completed while virtually wiping out illiteracy and providing universal education.

This achievement has resulted from a fifty-year struggle of minority and majority populations acting and reacting with one another in conflict and in cooperation. The specifics of the struggle that show the symbiotic interrelationship of minority and majority populations are presented in detail in a chapter entitled "New Learnings for Sociology from the Civil Rights Movement" that is published elsewhere (Willie, 1983:229-246).

The civil rights movement in the United States has been closely identified with efforts to achieve equity in educational opportunities. The movement may be divided into four stages: (I) the period of litigation from 1930 to 1954, (II) the period of demonstration from 1955 to 1964, (III) the period of legislation from 1964 to 1968, and (IV) the period of implementation from 1968 to the present (Willie, 1983:229).

In the federal court, the legal attack upon the 1896 separate-but-equal doctrine enunciated by the Supreme Court in the *Plessy* case began in earnest in 1938. Before this attack, southern states had provided substitute arrangements for graduate education for their black citizens. They could do so legally if these arrangements, although separate, were equal to the graduate educational opportunities provided for whites. The National Association for the Advancement of Colored People (NAACP) brought most of the cases against state authorities on behalf of local clients, proving that the separate educational arrangements were unequal. In *Missouri ex rel Gains v. Canada* (1938), the Supreme Court invalidated a Missouri plan to bar black citizens from the state law school and finance their legal education at out-of-state institutions in the North. By 1950 in *Sweatt v. Painter* and in *McLaurin v. Oklahoma,* the Supreme Court ruled that even an in-state segregated school for blacks was insufficient in that both the tangible and intangible attributes of the established state school that had existed for years could not be duplicated in a new segregated facility. The Court also ruled that a black student could not be admitted to a predominantly white publicly supported graduate school but then restricted to a limited area of the classroom.

Some legal experts believed that the cumulative impact of these rulings pertaining to Missouri, Texas, and Oklahoma cases left no other option for the NAACP but to make a frontal attack on the separate-but-equal doctrine.

The court cases pertaining to graduate education in the decades before the *Brown* decision were for the purpose of forcing states to provide equal educational opportunities for minorities. In the record that was made, the Supreme Court had clear and present evidence that no state had ever provided a separate arrangement for the education of blacks that was equal to the arrangements that existed for whites. On the basis of this evidence, there was reason to question whether a segregated arrangement could ever be equal.

Thus, the Supreme Court combined four separate cases from the states of Kansas, South Carolina, Virginia, and Delaware in its 1954 ruling entitled *Brown v. Board of Education*. In each of these cases, black students sought admission to the public schools of their community on a nonsegregated basis. State law in Kansas permitted but did not require segregated schools. But state constitutions and other statutes in the other three states mandated the education of black students in separate schools. Courts in all jurisdictions except Delaware had rejected desegregated admissions requests based on the separate-but-equal doctrine of the *Plessy v. Ferguson* case of 1896. The Delaware court had granted relief to the black students because it found the segregated schools for blacks substantially inferior. However, the Supreme Court declared that segregation solely on the basis of race was illegal because it deprived minority children of equal educational opportunities guaranteed by the Fourteenth Amendment (Zirkel, 1978:79-80).

The Supreme Court returned the cases to the federal district courts for action in accordance with guidelines issued in *Brown II* in 1955. The Court took this action because of the complexities involved in dismantling dual school systems. The federal district courts were closer to local situations and were assigned the responsibility of determining whether local school boards were acting in good faith in formulating and implementing school desegregation plans, which was the responsibility assigned to them by the Supreme Court (Zirkel, 1978:81).

Thus, the Supreme Court recognized that no single plan was appropriate for all communities. For this reason, in my search for school desegregation plans that work, I examine a variety of communities with a number of different plans.

Because demonstrations in several communities followed the refusal of local school authorities to implement the letter and spirit of the law, a variety of federal and state desegregation laws were enacted during stages II and III of the civil rights movement. During this period the Supreme Court also clarified its guidelines in a number of cases that reached it through appeal. Action to secure judicial refinements and the establishment of administrative guidelines emerged in part because of the pressure that the attorney general and the United States Department of Health, Education, and Welfare could bring to bear on localities in accordance with provisions of the 1964 Civil Rights Act.

In the *Green v. School Board* case of 1968 in New Kent County, Virginia, the Court ruled that segregated school systems have an affirmative obligation to achieve desegregation, not merely to refrain from enforcing segregation. Moreover, any plan proposed was permissible only if it offered real promise of contributing to desegregation (Viera, 1978:70).

A year later, in 1969, the Court in *United States v. Montgomery County Board of Education* in Virginia ordered the nonracial assignment of faculty as an essential part of a desegregation plan and numerical ratios of minority and majority students to overcome patterns of tokenism in earlier plans (Zinkel, 1978:86).

Also in 1969, in *Alexander v. Holmes County Board of Education* in Mississippi and *Dowell v. Board of Education,* the Court stated that partial desegregation of a system may proceed, pending formulation of a comprehensive plan, so that the rights of black children may be upheld. In 1970, the Court in *Carter v. West Feliciana Parish School Board* (Louisiana) required immediate and complete compliance with the constitutional mandate to desegregate.

Then, in 1971, the Court in *Swann v. Charlotte-Mecklenburg Board of Education* (North Carolina) ruled that federal district courts had the authority to order the assignment of teachers on a nonsegregative basis, forbid school construction and school closings that perpetuate segregation, impose flexible racial quotas as a starting point in the shaping of a workable desegregation plan, alter school attendance zones, and require the use of transportation to achieve a unitary system. These broad powers were given to district courts, so that they could act to uphold the rights of minority children when school authorities defaulted on their obligation to provide acceptable desegregation plans (Zirkel, 1978:90).

Further clarification the same year on the use of transportation to dismantle a dual school system was provided in *Davis v. Board of School Commissioners* (1971) in Mobile, Alabama. The Court clearly stated that plans to create a unitary school system cannot be limited by the neighborhood school concept and that bus transportation must be given adequate consideration in formulating an effective plan. The same message about busing was given in a Court ruling pertaining to Georgia in the case of *McDaniels v. Barresi* (1971) (Zirkel, 1978:91-92).

While the Court in a New Jersey case in 1971 permitted some racial segregation in schools that clearly was unintentional on the part of school authorities and that resulted largely from housing patterns and population shifts, it would not permit the disaggregation of a consolidated school district when one or more of the withdrawing communities would impede the establishment of a desegregated school system. The Court took a position on maintaining consolidated districts in 1972 in *Wright v. Council of City of Emporia* and in *United States v. Scotland Neck City Board of Education.*

A major refinement in the Court's opinion about desegregation was rendered in 1973 in the Denver case of *Keyes v. School District No. 1.* In that case, the Court held that proof of intentional segregation in a substantial part of a system is sufficient evidence that the entire system is segregated and, therefore, is obligated to prepare a district-wide desegregation plan. In this case, the Court also ruled that Hispanics are minorities and cannot be counted as members of the majority population in a plan to desegregate the public schools.

The opinion that school authorities were not obligated to desegregate a system further that had experienced a measure of resegregation due to changing residential patterns was reaffirmed by the Court in the *Pasadena City Board of Education v. Spangler* case of 1976. This ruling opened the door for some formerly segregated school systems that had experienced court-ordered desegregation to fall back into racially isolated patterns if they could prove that the racial separation was "wholly adventitious" (Viera, 1978:87).

Earlier, I indicated that the Court had looked with disfavor on and indeed had prohibited the disaggregation of a consolidated school district when such action would render ineffective a school desegregation plan because of the absence of diversity in the school population of the remaining district. Equally, the Court looked with disfavor on a plan proposed by one district that involved union with another for the purpose of increasing the racial diversity of the school-age population and the possibility of achieving meaningful desegregation, if no history of segregative action on the part of the other district had been proven. Although the other district not involved in litigation is a unit of the state, it may be incorporated in a multidistrict remedy only if the government of that district committed segregative acts. Thus, in the *Milliken v. Bradley* case in Detroit in 1974, the multidistrict remedy that would have united Detroit with outlying districts was disallowed (Zirkel, 1978:103). However, in instances in which the state board of education has been required by the Court to devise a plan to remedy existing segregation, the consolidation of multiple districts to achieve racial diversity and meaningful desegregation is possible as the Court held in *Evans v. Buchanan* in Delaware in 1975.

The *Milliken II* case in 1977 in Detroit introduced a new liability source, however. Recognizing that the state is the ultimate educational authority and that local school districts are subdivisions of it, the Court ordered that half the cost for remedial educational programs designed to combat the effects of prior *de jure* segregation in Detroit should be borne by the state. This ruling linked the state with the locality as a partner in the payment for desegregation programs that granted relief to minority children whose harm in the local district the state was ignoring.

Finally in the *Dayton* case of 1977 (*Dayton Board of Education v. Brinkman*), the Court pulled back somewhat from its position in the *Keyes* case of Denver that a finding of intentional segregation in part of a system is presumptive evidence of systemwide segregation requiring a systemwide remedy. In the *Dayton* case, the Court declared that where the segregative acts of a school board are not shown to have systemwide effect, a systemwide remedy cannot properly be imposed.

In the light of this review our study of school desegregation plans that work will feature not one but several models that deal with the range of issues discussed. The plans presented are of bi-ethnic and tri-ethnic communities, communities with relatively large and relatively small black student populations. Also examined are plans that are comprehensive and plans of a more limited scope. Some plans are formulated by the community and others by the court or its agents. Some plans are exclusively concerned with race mixing in the public school while others introduce new educational programs and curriculum reform. Some plans also require extensive faculty desegregation while others do not. Some plans require extensive transportation while others retain many walk-in schools. Some plans encourage community and parent participation; others incorporate these components minimally. In summary, this study provides a range of examples of effective school desegregation plans that meet requirements mandated by the court.

References

Dahl, Robert A.
    1967   *Pluralistic Democracy in the United States: Conflict and Consent.* Chicago; Rand McNally.
Levinsohn, Florence H. and Benjamin D. Wright
    1976   *School Desegregation, Shadow and Substance.* Chicago: University of Chicago Press.
National Center for Education Statistics
    1980   *Digest of Education Statistics,* Washington, D.C.: U.S. Government Printing Office.
Polybius
            In David Thompson (ed.), *The Idea of Rome.* Albuquerque, N.M.: University of New Mexico Press, 1971.
U.S. Bureau of the Census
    1982-   *Statistical Abstract of the United States,* Washington, D.C.: U.S. Gov-
    83   ernment Printing Office.

U.S. Civil Rights Commission

1977   *Reviewing a Decade of School Desegregation, 1966-1975*. Washington, D.C.: U.S. Government Printing Office.

Viera, Norman

1978   *Civil Rights in a Nutshell*. St. Paul, Minn.: West Publishing Co.

Willie, Charles V.

1978   "Foreword," in Ray Rist, *The Invisible Children*. Cambridge, Mass.: Harvard University Press.

1983   *Race, Ethnicity, and Socioeconomic Status*. Bayside, N.Y.: General Hall.

Zirkel, Perry

1978   *A Digest of Supreme Court Decisions Affecting Education*. Bloomington, Ind.: Phi Delta Kappa.

Chapter 2

Features of Good School Desegregation Plans

In a sample survey of school districts representative of those with 5 percent or more minority students, the United States Commission on Civil Rights reported "substantial steps to desegregate schools" during the decade from 1966 to 1975. The sample districts encompassed about half of all minority public school students in the nation. Desegregation action was found in communities in southern, northern, and western states, and resulted from multiple sources: superintendents in 37 percent of these districts attributed the pressure to desegregate public schools as coming primarily from the courts; 26 percent acted as a result of desegregation pressure from administrative agencies of the federal government; and 37 percent experienced local or state pressures that motivated desegregation action (U.S. Commission on Civil Rights, 1977:4).

It is important to state without equivocation that school desegregation is proceeding in all regions of the nation, that a substantial population of racial and ethnic minorities has known the advantages resulting from desegregation, and that the pressure to desegregate has come largely from the courts and the federal government but that state and local authorities are beginning to participate in the formulation of desegregation plans and to press for their implementation.

Despite significant movement toward the development of unitary school districts, one-sixth of all minorities (blacks, American Indians, Alaskan Natives, Asians, Pacific Islanders, and Hispanics) continue to be educated in racially isolated or segregated schools in which minority-group enrollment is 99 to 100 percent of the student body. This was the extent of racial isolation in education in this nation as recently as 1978 (U.S. Bureau of the Census, 1981:149).

This limited progress in desegregation is accompanied by significant accomplishments in level of educational attainment in the majority as well as the minority population. The median school year completed by black adults over the age of 25 years, for example, increased from 5.7 years in 1940 before the Supreme Court's *Brown* decision to 12.1 years in 1979, 25 years after *Brown*. This is a 110 percent increase in less than a half century. From a disparate condition in which whites had a median year of educational attainment 53 percent higher than that for blacks, the gap has, since segregated education was ruled unlawful and not in the public interest, narrowed to a difference of only 3 percent. While blacks and other minorities have been increasing their levels of educational attainment, whites have been progressing, too. Before the *Brown* decision, only one-third of white adults 25 years of age and over had graduated from high school; in 1979, a quarter of a century after *Brown*, the proportion of white high school graduates had doubled to almost two-thirds of the age group mentioned. During the same period, blacks changed from a population group in which a minority of adults were high school graduates to one in which a majority had attained that level of education (National Center for Educational Statistics, 1980:16).

Such progress is due to a number of factors and cannot all be attributed to *Brown* and the school desegregation activity that it set in motion. However, one can say that school desegregation has not harmed the minority or the majority in terms of educational attainment. David Cohen and Barbara Neufeld state that "perhaps the most single success of American public education has been providing nearly equal access to elementary and secondary schools for all, an achievement quite distinct in human history" (Cohen and Neufeld, 1981:69). Of all young people from 5 through 17 years of age 95 percent are in school. This proportion refers to the experience of minority groups and the majority group (National Center for Educational Statistics, 1980:9). This high level of educational attainment is directly associated with desegregation efforts. Willis Hawley discovered a "dramatic 50 percent decline in the dropout rate of black students from 1967 to 1977, the period during which desegregation had its greatest import" (Hawley, 1981:148).

These level-of-attainment outcomes indicate that demonstrations, litigation, and legislation for school desegregation have had a beneficial effect. On the basis of these data, it is difficult to understand why some people insist on tarnishing the victory of nearly universal education that the United States has achieved with the propaganda that busing has failed. It is particularly difficult to understand the fixation on busing by opponents of desegregation, since one out of every two students in this country uses bus transportation to go to and from school. Cessation of desegregation would not change this ratio substantially.

There is a tendency in American society to move from one crisis to another without reflecting upon how we overcame them. As a result of this practice, we have missed significant learnings of the past that could guide us in the future. Of school desegregation, Richard Kluger said that "probably no case ever to come before the nation's highest tribunal affected more directly the minds, hearts, and daily lives of so many Americans." He said that "scholars have assigned the cases known collectively as *Brown* v. *Board of Education of Topeka* a high place in the literature of liberty." The decision marked the turning point in America's willingness to face the consequences of centuries of racial discrimination (Kluger, 1975:x). As the nation increasingly accepts school desegregation as inevitable, we should learn from the various ad hoc arrangements to implement the *Brown* decision in our various communities.

The turbulence experienced in public education since mid-century is directly attributable to the fact that we did not make the necessary changes required to implement the 1896 *Plessy* decision of the Court that sanctioned separate but equal treatment in public places. We did not make separate facilities for the races equal. Incidentally, if we had implemented that decision according to the letter of the law, segregation in public education would have ended before 1954 because it would have been too expensive to maintain in a separate-but-equal fashion. We have reaped a whirlwind because of our failure to implement the requirement of the 1896 Court decision lawfully and did not reflect upon what we did that was wrong.

Again we are faced with a Supreme Court requirement, the *Brown* decision. This time, localities are required to achieve a unitary desegregated school system where resources for education are distributed in a way that is equitable and fair for all racial populations. As in the past, the Court has not provided clear guidelines on implementation. If the nation ignores this requirement as it did during the years following the *Plessy* decision, it can expect a troublesome future.

There is value in a study on alternative ways of achieving unitary school systems at this point in history. The desegregation of schools is far from complete. The federal government has been involved in more than 500 cases (Wise, 1977:200-201). Many of these cases are approaching or have already entered the stage for implementing a plan to redress the grievances of the plaintiffs.

Courts have retained jurisdiction in school desegregation cases for extended periods of time but seldom have had appropriate planning advice. Asking local school authorities to develop adequate school desegregation plans as suggested by the Supreme Court in *Brown II* is like asking the fox (the defendant school board) found guilty of stealing chickens (operating racially segregated schools) to develop a plan to secure the chicken house against further theft (to plan for a unitary system). Federal and state courts have operated as if they were courts of equity in school desegregation cases without objective planning information, since they often must rely upon the good offices of the defendants to devise workable desegregation plans.

This study of model school desegregation plans should be of assistance to courts, school authorities, and community groups concerned with quality, desegregated education. In addition to helping individuals responsible for developing and implementing school desegregation plans, this study has a preventive function. The information presented, if acted upon appropriately, could reduce the possibility of future gyrations in local communities that stem from frustration among minorities associated with ineffective enforcement of court decisions and consequently insufficient redress of grievances.

This study is an attempt to learn from the many different ad hoc desegregation plans that sprang into existence without adequate preparation or thought, so that education planners in the future will have more guidance regarding appropriate ways of fashioning school desegregation remedies. Such future remedies, informed by the past, increase their chances of being mutually beneficial for minority and majority populations.

Hawley, relying very much upon deliberations of the scholars who participated in the National Review Panel on School Desegregation Research, said that "desegregated schools seem most likely to improve race relations, enhance achievement, increase self-esteem, and improve students' life chances," if they do these things:

1. "Assign students so that schools and classrooms are neither [overwhelmingly] white nor [overwhelmingly] black"

2. "Assign to each classroom a sizable number of children who perform at or above grade level"

3. "Encourage substantial interaction among races both in academic settings and in extracurricular activities"

4. "Eschew academic competition, rigid forms of tracking, and ability grouping that draw attention to individual and group achievement differences correlated with race"

5. "Recruit and retain teachers who are relatively unprejudiced, supportive, and insistent on high performance and racial equality"

6. "Recruit and retain principals who are supportive of desegregation and exert leadership in that direction"

7. "Involve parents at the classroom level in actual instructional or learning activities"

8. "Initiate programs of staff development that emphasize the problems relating to successful desegregation"

9. "Maintain a relatively stable student body over time"

10. "Desegregate students early, in kindergarten if possible"

11. "Desegregate the faculty"

12. "Develop a multiethnic curriculum [and] multiethnic materials . . . that . . . foster interaction across racial lines and get to issues that divide youngsters from different backgrounds" (Hawley, 1981:154-157)

Robert Dentler said that recommendations like these are "linked plainly to the wrong of segregation which is the crucial defect to be remedied" (Dentler, 1976:127). This study investigates school desegregation plans that were developed by professional educators and social scientists and that were designed to achieve several of the goals that Hawley and his colleagues identified as embracing the twofold goal of educational enhancement and racial diversity.

The communities studied are Atlanta, Boston, Milwaukee, and Seattle. These major urban areas are located in different regions of the country and use different approaches to achieve a unitary system.

Community dynamics in these four cities varied from Boston, where the resisting school committee informed the court that it would do no more than it was ordered to do to achieve desegregation, to Seattle, where the school board initiated school desegregation on its own authority rather than contest allegations about segregation in the court and risk coming under its jurisdiction in fashioning remedies. In Atlanta, the plaintiffs and defendant remained in sufficiently meaningful communication to work out a consensus, which the court ordered. Milwaukee school administrators seized the leadership and marshaled community support on behalf of the administration and desegregation, while Boston lost six superintendents in ten years during the height of the desegregation controversy. Milwaukee and Seattle have white majority populations as city residents. Atlanta has a majority black population. Seattle has a significant Asian population three-fourths the size of the black minority. Milwaukee and Boston are heavily populated with white ethnic groups of European origin. The Boston Plan is comprehensive. The Milwaukee Plan emphasizes magnet educational opportunities. The Atlanta Plan redistributes decision-making power between the races. The Seattle Plan emphasizes community participation.

Although individually different, these four cities together have several characteristics that are similar to those found in many other communities of this nation. The divergent routes by which the common goal of a good school desegregation plan was achieved is what makes Atlanta, Boston, Milwaukee, and Seattle interesting communities to study. They were chosen for this analysis because their plans are different but incorporated most of the features of a good school desegregation plan identified by the National Review Panel on School Desegregation Research.

This study analyzes state and local responsibility in school desegregation planning and the ways in which these two levels interrelated in four different cities, and then identifies the best features in each plan.

References

Cohen, David, and Barbara Neufeld
    1981   "The Failure of High Schools and the Progress of Education," *Daedalus*
            110 (Summer): 69-89.

Dentler, Robert
  1976   "Urban School Desegregation," in Marvin B. Scott (ed.), *The Essential Profession*. Stamford, Conn.: Greylock Publishers.
Hawley, Willis D.
  1981   "Increasing the Effectiveness of School Desegregation: Lessons from the Research," in Adam Yarmolinsky, Lance Liebman, and Corinne S. Schelling (eds.), *Race and Schooling in the City*. Cambridge, Mass.: Harvard University Press, pp. 145-162.
Kluger, Richard
  1975   *Simple Justice*. New York: Vintage Books.
National Center for Educational Statistics
  1980   *Digest of Educational Statistics, 1980*. Washington, D.C.: U.S. Government Printing Office.
U.S. Bureau of the Census
  1981   *Statistical Abstract of the United States*. Washington, D.C.: U.S. Government Printing Office.
U.S. Commission on Civil Rights
  1977   *Reviewing a Decade of School Desegregation*. Washington, D.C.: U.S. Government Printing Office.
Wise, Michael B. (ed.)
  1977   *Desegregation in Education: A Directory of Reported Federal Decisions*. Notre Dame, Ind.: Center for Civil Rights, University of Notre Dame Law School.

Chapter 3

Data and Methods of Study

This is a policy study, not an experimental and controlled investigation. The purpose is to analyze the ongoing process of school desegregation in four relatively large urban communities. The investigation seeks to determine *what* are the basic features of good school desegregation plans designed for different kinds of communities, *how* these plans vary, and *why* specific features are included in a plan. Beyond answering the three questions—what, how, and why—for specific plans, this study also will analyze four communities and their plans comparatively to determine those aspects of desegregation planning that may be implemented in a similar way notwithstanding community differences and those that must be tailored to specific situations.

This study, therefore, should make a contribution to situation and general sociology by discovering community situations and social contexts that significantly influence desegregation planning as well as those that transcend local circumstances.

The study investigates relatively large communities because a report of the United States Commission on Civil Rights revealed that such communities tend to be most resistant to the enforcement efforts of federal administrative agencies (U.S. Commission on Civil Rights, 1977:28). To discover why these communities designed the kinds of school desegregation plans that they did, what their basic components were, and how they were implemented should be something of value.

We have studied communities similar in size and their success in designing and implementing school desegregation plans. The criteria of a successful school desegregation plan are those identified by the National Panel on Desegregation Research and listed in chapter 1. A community with a plan that fulfills most of those criteria is eligible for inclusion in this study. Finally, we have studied relatively large communities with effective but different types of school desegregation plans that also vary in population characteristics. The latter variable should enable us to examine the association, if any, between school desegregation planning and special characteristics of communities.

After several relatively large communities were examined, Atlanta, Boston, Milwaukee, and Seattle were selected because of their unique school desegregation plans (which will be described in the chapters that follow), and because of their similarities in size of total city population and public school student population.

As Table 3-1 shows, each of these cities has accommodated more than a half million people within the past decade or so of its history, but all have declined in recent years. In 1980 these cities varied from a low of 425,022 in Atlanta to a high of 636,212 in Milwaukee. Public school student populations reported in 1979 were similarly above 50,000 in all four cities, varying from 54,757 in Seattle to 95,502 in Milwaukee. The size of the physical plant in each school district was similar, ranging from approximately 131 school buildings in Atlanta to 153 in Boston and Milwaukee, according to a 1979 count.

Table 3-2 presents data on the racial and ethnic composition of city populations in Atlanta, Boston, Milwaukee, and Seattle. An analysis of this table reveals substantial differences among the study communities. The more influential racial and ethnic groups in these communities in terms of population size are white Americans, black Americans, Hispanics, Asian Americans, and Native Americans, according to the 1980 census.

Whites are the majority population in all of the communities except Atlanta, where they are one-third of the population. Blacks are two-thirds

Table 3-1 Total Population (1980 and 1970) and Public School Students (1978-79) in Four Cities

City	Total Population[a]				Public School Students[b]		1979 Number of Schools
	1980	*1970*	*Difference*	*% of Change*	*1978-79*	*% of 1980 Population*	
Atlanta	425,022	595,039	170,017	− 29	76,625	18	131
Boston	562,994	641,071	78,077	− 12	71,303	13	153
Milwaukee	636,212	717,372	81,160	− 11	95,502	15	153
Seattle	493,846	530,831	36,985	− 7	54,757	11	147

[a]*Source: The World Almanac and Book of Facts, 1982* (New York: Newspaper Enterprise Associates, Inc.), pp. 207-232.

[b]*Source: Directory of Elementary and Secondary School Districts, in Selected School Districts, School Year, 1978-79* (Washington, D.C.: U.S. Department of Education, Office of Civil Rights, 1980), pp. 282, 614, 1580, 1542.

Table 3-2 **Percentage Distribution of Total Population by Race and Ethnicity in Four Cities, 1980**

City	Total[a] Number	%	White	Black	Hispanic	Asian*	Native American*
Atlanta	425,022	100	32	67	1	—	—
Boston	562,994	100	70	22	6	2	—
Milwaukee	636,212	100	73	23	4	—	—
Seattle	493,846	100	80	10	3	7	—

[a]*Source: The World Almanac and Book of Facts, 1982* (New York: Newspaper Enterprise Associates, Inc.), pp. 207-232.

*Percentage not shown for group comprising less than 1 percent of total.

of the Atlanta population, and Hispanics are about 1 percent. In terms of the racial characteristics of the majority population in numbers, Atlanta is radically different from the three other relatively large cities in this study. Blacks in Seattle, Milwaukee, and Boston vary from 10 to 23 percent of total populations. Whites make up 70 to 80 percent of the total population. Boston and Seattle are significantly different from the other two cities in that they have tri-racial-ethnic populations with 8 to 10 percent, respectively, consisting of identifiable minority groups classified as neither black nor white. In Seattle, Asians are the third largest group, about 7 percent of the total population. And in Boston, Hispanics are the third largest group, representing approximately 6 percent of the population. Although both are tri-racial-ethnic cities, the Asians are only 3 percentage points less than black Americans in Seattle; but the black American population is 16 percentage points larger than Hispanics in Boston.

Basically Milwaukee and Atlanta are numerically biracial communities with the percentage of white Americans three times larger than that of black Americans in the midwestern city and the percentage of black Americans twice as large as that of white Americans in the southern city.

The public school student populations differ from total populations, according to the data in Table 3-3. White Americans are the majority population of public school students in only two of the four cities—Milwaukee and Seattle; the 51 percent majority in Milwaukee is a tenuous lead that could change in the near future.

Black Americans make up 90 percent of the public school population in Atlanta; in this respect, their prevailing numbers in the school population are not unlike their majority status in the total population.

In Boston, however, the public school student population differs

Table 3-3 Percentage Distribution of Public School Students in Four Cities, 1978-79

City	Total[a]		Percent of Public School Students				
	Number	%	White	Black	Hispanic*	Asian*	Native American*
Atlanta	76,625	100	10	90	—	—	—
Boston	71,303	100	40	44	12	3	1
Milwaukee	95,502	100	51	42	5	1	1
Seattle	54,757	100	62	20	4	11	3

[a]*Source:* National Center for Education Statistics, *Digest of Education Statistics* (Washington, D.C.: U.S. Government Printing Office, 1980), p. 41.

*Percentage not shown for group less than 1 percent of total.

radically from the citywide population. Black Americans, Hispanics, Asian Americans, and Native Americans, the minorities in the population at large, have become a new majority in the public school system. Collectively, they outnumber white public school students by 60 to 40 percent, respectively.

The Milwaukee experience is not very different from that of Boston. Although white Americans were reported to be the majority public school population in 1979, only 2 percentage points separated the size of their population from the size of the combined minority populations. If together black Americans, Hispanics, Asian Americans, and Native Americans eventually become a new majority in Milwaukee, three of the four cities in this study will have public school student populations with predominant racial or ethnic populations classified other than white American.

The significance of this extended discussion of the citywide and public school populations is to identify and describe important contextual phenomena. Further analysis in the chapters that follow will determine the impact, if any, of these phenomena upon school desegregation planning and the plan-designs that emerge therefrom.

These four cities have cultural, historical, and geographical characteristics that further differentiate them. A brief summary as derived from *The New Columbia Encyclopedia* (1975) and elsewhere follows. Unless otherwise indicated, the encyclopedia is the source of the cultural, historical, and geographical data.

Founded in 1837, Atlanta incorporated as a city in 1847 and has become a transportation hub of the Southeast. Situated near the Appalachian foothills, Atlanta is a leading city of the South and the industrial, financial, and political center of the state of Georgia, of which it is the capital city. Manufactured in the metropolitan areas are textiles, furniture, chemicals, glass, and paper; also produced are steel, aluminum, leather, and electrical products. Atlanta has automobile and aircraft assembly plants, flour mills, and printing industries.

After being burned during the Civil War, Atlanta was rebuilt and became not only an industrial and commercial center but also an educational center. Its best known institutions of higher education are Emory University, Georgia Institute of Technology, and the Atlanta University Center—"the largest predominantly black educational complex in the country" (*Afro-American*, July 17, 1982:12), including Atlanta University, the Interdenominational Theological Center, Morris Brown, Clark, Morehouse and Spelman colleges, and the Morehouse School of Medicine.

Atlanta has "a black middle class whose economic position came from banking, insurance, and construction as well as higher education." A comfortable relationship has developed over the years between this leadership group and white economic and political leaders (Jackson, 1981:212). These groups gave leadership to school desegregation planning and other official activities.

The city's second consecutive black mayor was an associate of Dr. Martin Luther King, Jr., and assisted in the civil rights campaigns that he led during the 1950s and the 1960s. The grave site of King, located near Atlanta's Ebenezer Baptist Church that he co-pastored with his father, is "visited daily by hundreds of people from all over the world" (*Afro-American,* July 17, 1982:12).

Boston, the state capital of Massachusetts, is the largest city in New England. Established in 1630, Boston was first recognized as a shipbuilding, textile, and shoe-manufacturing center. Over the years, it has become a major financial, publishing, and cultural center and a hub city surrounded by high technology industries in suburban communities. Boston is recognized nationally for its vigorous cultural and intellectual life nurtured by several colleges, universities, museums, libraries, and centers for the performing arts.

The Boston Latin School, opened in 1635, was the first public high school in the nation. Nearby Cambridge across the Charles River from Boston is the home of Harvard University, one of the oldest and most prestigious higher education institutions in the world. Other schools in Boston with national reputations are the Massachusetts Institute of Technology, Boston University, Boston College (a Jesuit institution), and Northeastern University (a pioneer in cooperative education). The Harvard Medical School, the New England Medical Center, and the Massachusetts General Hospital contribute significantly to medical teaching and learning opportunities in the Boston metropolitan area.

Among other institutions that nurture the intellectual and cultural life are the Boston Public Library, fourth ranked in the nation in terms of number of volumes (National Center for Educational Statistics, 1980:220), the Boston Symphony Orchestra, and the Museum of Fine Arts.

Political life in Boston is significantly influenced by mixed ideology as it has been since its beginning as a colony. A center of American Puritanism, the city also attracted agents of the Church of England who were loyal to the crown. Despite its conservatism in beliefs and leanings toward aristocratic leadership, Boston was home for many abolitionists. The immigrant groups that came to Boston, particularly the Irish, gained prestige and authority by participating in and eventually controlling political power. But the immigrant-dominated power structure denied such opportunity to Italian Americans, black Americans, Hispanics, and other newcomers as long as it could. In effect, Irish power brokers limited the participation in public affairs by other racial and ethnic groups as they had been limited in the past by Bostonians of English heritage.

Thus, Boston political power has been the prize over which the racial and ethnic groups, fragmented into neighborhoods, have fought. The various groups have made expedient coalitions from time to time to further their own group's self-interest but seldom have genuinely cooperated toward a mutually beneficial solution. The absence of a substantial multiracial presence in public offices and repeated fights over racial and ethnic neighborhood turf ownership have been the basis for strife and estrangement in the pluralistic Boston population. To the victor belong the spoils has been the operating principle in the hub city of the Bay State.

From a fur-trading post established in 1795, several communities at the point where the Milwaukee, Menomenee, and Kinnickinnic rivers enter Lake Michigan merged in 1838 to form Milwaukee City, which was officially incorporated in 1848. Although located in the heartland of the nation, Milwaukee is a port and has access to worldwide shipping by way of the St. Lawrence Seaway. Because of its favorable location, Milwaukee has become Wisconsin's largest city.

Milwaukee is basically a manufacturing city. A major producer of heavy machinery and electrical equipment, it is one of the world's leading manufacturers of diesel and gasoline engines and tractors. Its plentiful supply of water also has enabled it to become a leading manufacturer of beer. One brand of this beverage marketed nationally asserts that it made Milwaukee famous.

Because of extensive manufacturing industries and unionized labor, Milwaukee has been described as a working-class city. However, service and other nonmanufacturing employment are making rapid gains. The present labor force is almost equally divided between manufacturing and nonmanufacturing jobs.

To staff the plants during an earlier age, immigrants from Germany and Poland were encouraged to settle in Milwaukee. These two groups have had a significant impact on the city's way of life—German people concentrated on the north side and Polish on the south side.

Germans have been in Milwaukee for more than a hundred years and have become deeply involved in Wisconsin politics. They and the Poles have dominated the city so extensively that racial minority groups such as blacks feel left out and ignored. Black claims of racial segregation in the public schools during the 1960s, for example, were ignored or squelched.

One minority school board member who tried to get the educational establishment to acknowledge some black complaints and urged action on behalf of a modest proposal designed to redress minority grievances was defeated when he sought reelection. Milwaukee refused to place concerns of the black minority on the agenda for community deliberation and action until after a school desegregation lawsuit was filed, a successful school boycott was started, and organized demonstrations and spontaneous rioting occurred.

The Milwaukee community has had good leadership in several sectors, and players follow the leader very well. The labor movement is strong and has effective leadership. A tradition of efficient public administration has existed. A Roman Catholic priest gained national attention for mobilizing racial minorities and leading them in demonstrations against discrimination. Lee R. McMurrin, the chief city school officer, and another resident who is a former federal official (once ambassador to Poland) helped to mobilize Milwaukee in favor of peacefully responding to the court order to desegregate the public schools, despite the initial footdragging of a reluctant school board (Barndt, Janka, and Rose, 1981:237-259).

Seattle, located on seven hills between Elliot Bay of Puget Sound and Lake Washington, is the largest city in the Pacific Northwest. It is the transportation, commercial, and industrial hub for the region and the location of the University of Washington. Seattle is described as a livable city "blessed with a magnificent natural beauty" (Hart-Nibbrig, 1979:30). It is a place where "people just plain *like* the city and feel it their responsibility to do what they can for it" (Hart-Nibbrig, 1979: 33). Settled in 1851-52, Seattle incorporated in 1869.

For many decades after the first settlement until the railroad connected it with the rest of the nation just fifteen years before the end of the nineteenth century, Seattle was a small lumber town. It grew rapidly thereafter, boosted by a number of unique events such as the Alaska gold rush—Seattle being the chief link between the lower forty-eight states and that distant land. In addition to its strategic location, Seattle's other natural resources, for example, coal, contributed to its growth and development. Lumber, of course, continues to be one of its main industries. It also has major food-processing plants. Since World War II, Seattle has become a center for aircraft manufacturing and shipbuilding. The early linkage with Alaska for trading is now expanded to include the Far East.

Before the turn of the century, Seattle had all the qualities of a rough frontier town: radical labor organizers, hard-nosed industrialists, several violent strikes, and widespread prejudice against the Chinese. Almost as if attempting to compensate for these excesses, Seattle has settled down to a "pragmatic reformism" that eschews extremist politics but does not turn its back on the complaints of minorities.

One would hardly characterize the political efforts of minorities as self-determined nor those of the majority as fully altruistic. Through coalition politics, blacks and other minorities have been able to get their agenda for social reform expressed through the white majority leadership and have not had to be self-reliant. Some observers have attributed the responsiveness of authorities to the fact that "Seattle is still primarily a middle-class city with a white middle-class majority" that has the wisdom to seek advice from others and to take corrective action to "avoid turmoil in the city" such as may have occurred if Seattle had waited for the court to order school desegregation. School desegregation in Seattle came about peacefully not so much because of commitment to desegregation but because of commitment to avoid court intervention, if possible. This is the pragmatism of the city power structure. As the white majority continues to dwindle and is further challenged to be more equitable and fair in the distribution of community resources, it remains to be seen whether Seattle's "solid middle road reform community leaders" will continue to be responsive to fulfilling the interests of black Americans, Asian Americans, Hispanics, and Native Americans as well as those of their own group. The future is difficult to predict, but there is evidence that Seattle has learned the value of coalition politics and recognizes the need to expand participants beyond "blue chip," downtown business greats to many more citizens and organized groups. Such an expansion cannot be accomplished without a readiness to compromise (Hart-Nibbrig, 1979:30-35).

The pragmatic orientation of Seattle enables it to act when it should. One of the few cities to develop and implement a school desegregation plan without a court order, Seattle also operated the first public monorail system. Once Seattle determines what action is appropriate, it tends to gain united support from dominant and subdominant sectors of the power structures.

Despite the many differences among Atlanta, Boston, Milwaukee, and Seattle, they have in common their relatively large size, their common status as leading cities in their states or regions, their diversity in racial and ethnic characteristics of populations, and their successful school desegregation plans.

Unlike the plans in many communities that were fashioned by politicians or agents accountable to them, the school desegregation plans in these four communities were designed by professional educators and social scientists with advice from citizens in the community. They therefore merit review as model plans.

To answer what, how, and why questions about these model plans, field consultants with direct responsibility for their development and/or implementation in each of the cities in the study were commissioned to prepare detailed evaluative statements about plan-designs, according to an outline prepared by this author. Specific questions asked may be found in the outline in the Appendix. Information was requested in six basic areas:

1. A description of the educational and desegregational goals and assumptions, if any, of the plan for a unitary public school system.
2. A description of the community and its characteristics, for which this plan is applicable.
3. A description of the scope of the plan in terms of geographic area, population groups, and grade levels included.
4. A description of how the plan will achieve equity for racial and ethnic groups in the availability of educational programs, extracurricular programs, school building facilities, student assignment, and transportation.
5. A description of the policy-making and the policy-implementing associations, and the procedure for recruiting and maintaining a diversified faculty and professional staff in the plan.
6. A description of school-community relations aspects of the plan for a unitary public school system.

Finally, the field consultants were asked to discuss changes, if any, that would enhance their plans.

References

Barndt, Michael, Rick Janka, and Harold Rose
  1981   "Milwaukee, Wisconsin: Mobilization for School and Community Cooperation," in C. V. Willie and S. L. Greenblatt (eds.), *Community Politics and Educational Change*. New York: Longman, pp. 237-259.
Columbia Encyclopedia, The New
  1975   New York: Columbia University Press, pp. 177, 340, 1781, 2464.
Hart-Nibbrig, Nand
  1979   "Policies of School Desegregation in Seattle," *Integrated Education* 17 (Jan.-April): 27-36.
Jackson, Barbara L.
  1981   "Urban School Desegregation from a Black Perspective," in Adam Yarmolinsky, Lance Liebman, and Corinne S. Schelling (eds.), *Race and Schooling in the City*. Cambridge, Mass.: Harvard University Press, pp. 204-216.
National Center for Educational Statistics
  1980   *Digest of Educational Statistics, 1980*. Washington, D.C.: U.S. Government Printing Office.
U.S. Commission on Civil Rights
  1977   *Reviewing a Decade of School Desegregation*. Washington, D.C.: U.S. Government Printing Office.

Part II

STATE AND LOCAL PLANNING

Chapter 4

State Responsibility in School Desegregation Planning: Achieving Equality of Access and Participation

The role of state government in school desegregation has been described by the superintendent of schools in Atlanta as isolated and remote. A lack of strong direction on desegregation policy is the characterization of the state role by the St. Louis superintendent. Detroit's chief school officer found a vacuum at the state level regarding school desegregation assistance. The modest guidelines promulgated, he said, are without clout in overcoming racial isolation in the public schools. A consensus among administrators in many school districts across the nation is, "state government . . . abandoned local leaders in their struggle with desegregation" (Willie, 1982:86).

There are, of course, exceptions to this general finding. Shortly after the *Brown* decision, for example, Alabama, Arkansas, and Virginia gave leadership in opposing school desegregation in executive and legislative branches at the state level. Massachusetts, New York, and Pennsylvania were examples of state governments that gave limited leadership in the enforcement of school desegregation law through state education departments and human rights and human relations commissions. Wisconsin, Connecticut, and Massachusetts have provided state aid for interdistrict student transfers when such movement has a racial-balancing effect. Nevertheless, a recent study of ten communities under court order to desegregate their school systems revealed this finding: "seven of the nine state governments . . . played either a negative role in the implementation of desegregation or a negligible role" (Willie and Greenblatt, 1981:339-340). These states that gave little if any positive desegregation leadership were located in all regions of the United States—North and South, East and West.

With the merging of funding for programs such as the Emergency School Aid Act and civil rights training authorized under Title IV of the Civil

Rights Act of 1964 into state block grants, state governments now must decide what proportion, if any, of their federal grants will be allocated toward achieving school desegregation. Before the new block-grant method of funding, local school districts in forty-three states received approximately $144 million in federal funds under the Emergency School Aid Act. These funds "paid the salaries of state and local desegregation coordinators, enabled local officials to set up magnet schools, supported plans to redraw school boundaries and to pair or cluster groups of schools, and [underwrote the preparation of] special curricula and activities for students in integrated schools" (White, 1982:14). Funds could be used to prepare and implement a variety of desegregative strategies, except mandatory busing. Whether most state governments whose past participation in local school desegregation has been minimal will substantially finance desegregation planning that was formerly supported by the federal government is uncertain.

Increasingly, state government has been cited as a party in local school desegregation cases, since it is the ultimate education authority. The court ordered Missouri to pay a share of the costs of implementing the St. Louis desegregation plan. Court decisions that found Columbus and Cleveland guilty of maintaining a dual system of racially segregated schools found the state of Ohio also liable and ordered it to help pay for the remedy (White, 1982:14).

In view of this trend of assessing liability against the states, the Massachusetts Bureau of Educational Opportunity in the State Education Department stepped up its efforts to prod Cambridge and other communities to comply with the constitutional requirement for a unitary school system. Such efforts at the state level could prevent expensive litigation.

An attorney for the Cambridge school committee advised it to develop a desegregation plan as the state had urged. His opinion was that a desegregation plan voluntarily developed by the local community would be welcomed by the state and probably would gain its cooperation including some financial assistance, since "the State Board of Education . . . may be vulnerable to a court claim that it . . . unconstitutionally overlooked federal law violations and failed to enforce upon [local districts] the long-standing school desegregation requirements" (*Equal Education in Massachusetts: A Chronicle,* 1980:2).

All of this suggests that state governments may find it more beneficial to become involved in, rather than to remain remote from, local school desegregation planning. Such efforts in the long run may be less expensive than court-ordered participation in a remedy of redress as a guilty party or accomplice to illegal local desegregation intransigence. As stated in a conference report of state equal opportunity directors, "the historical reasons for the limited role of the states in desegregation have become less and less valid" (National Project and Task Force, 1978b:9). According to the United States Commission on Civil Rights, "the courts have indicated [in *Taylor v. Board of Education of New Rochelle* (1961)] that . . . purposeful segregation [resulting from actions of state or local public officials even where such segregation is not dictated or sanctioned by state or local law] is unconstitutional," and that "such segregation is unconstitutional [as held in *Webb v. Board of Education of Chicago* (1963)] even when it is accomplished by *inaction* rather than by action" (emphasis added) (U.S. Commission on Civil Rights, 1967:185). Thus, in the future, states may be cited as contributing to the harm unlawfully visited upon individuals in segregated educational institutions not so much for what they did but for what they did not do to control and eliminate the harmful action. State exposure to claims of illegal action is, therefore, increased through deliberate inaction that permits known violations to continue uncorrected in civil districts accountable to the state.

As pointed out by the Center for Education and Human Development Policy at Vanderbilt University, "only a very limited effort appears to have been made to conduct research on the efficacy of state action [in school desegregation]" (Center for Education and Human Development Policy, 1981:2). Yet the National Project and Task Force on Desegregation Strategies believes that "as the 1980s begin, the single most promising strategy for progress in school desegregation may well be that of state initiative" (National Project and Task Force, 1980:5), since the delegation of educational tasks to a local school agency does not relieve the state of its overriding educational responsibilities.

Rather than develop a laundry list of what the state *could* do in school desegregation, probably it is better to approach the issue of state responsibility conceptually and consider what it *should* do and why. Conceptually, state responsibility should differ from that of localities.

Of government, Robert Axelrod states that "each level is able to absorb no more than a certain amount of conflict of interest before the disputes at that level become too severe for the democratic process to handle." Furthermore, he states that "an appropriate allocation of the conflict of interest between . . . levels may help sustain democracy by allowing it to withstand a greater amount of total conflict of interest within the society" (Axelrod, 1970:155). At issue is a determination of the kinds of decisions that more appropriately can be handled at one level or the other. Creative solutions are promoted when appropriate issues and decisions in desegregated education are handled at the appropriate governmental level so that the two levels mutually assist each other in a complementary way. The fundamental issues and decisions in school desegregation have to do with *equality of access to and participation in educational opportunities, and equity in distribution and use of educational resources.*

Equality of opportunity has to do with access to and participation in social organizations such as schools and other institutions. The principles and practices of access and participation delineate rights and responsibilities of individuals. These rights and responsibilities indicate the relationship of each individual to the total society and have to do with *contributive justice,* or one-to-many relationships (Fletcher, 1966:90). If a heterogeneous society is better able to adapt to and manage a social environment and its exegencies because of the varied knowledge, experience, and skills contained therein, then policies and practices that guarantee each person access to and participation in social organization enhance the probability of a society's survival by contributing to its diversity. In a diversified population, it is probable that one or more persons will be present and able to do for another what the other person cannot do for himself or herself. Because no one is self-sufficient and self-reliant for all seasons and all occasions, the total social organization has to use the contributions of all available people. An assumption in contributive justice is that the talents and experiences of each individual can benefit the whole, if available. It is in the public interest, therefore, to facilitate access to and participation in the society by all sorts and conditions of people so that their varied knowledge, experience, and skills are available when needed.

In schooling, equality of access and participation issues have to do with who shall be educated and who shall do the educating. If formal education is for the purpose of equipping people with the knowledge and virtue to manage society as Thomas Jefferson asserted (Jefferson, 1813:114), then a range of people should be educated because society needs a range of talents and problem-solving knowledge for the sake of survival. The question of who educates and is educated pertains to the attributes of individuals needed by the whole and therefore is an issue of contributive justice. Shall students and teachers, for example, of varying race, sex, age, mental capacity, physical ability, and social class have access to and opportunity to participate in learning environments such as public schools for the unique contribution that each person with experience in such a category might make? A pluralistic population means that a variety of people are present and available to teach and be taught by each other that which one cannot learn or teach oneself.

It is in the public interest to educate all of society's people. Justification is required for excluding any category of people from formal education. The justification must demonstrate why permitting some members to remain uneducated in a democratic society is unharmful to the total population. If a case for the absence of societal harm cannot be made, then none can be justifiably excluded from school.

The self-interest of each person to obtain an education is a public good, therefore, since cultivated talents and knowledge benefit others as well as oneself. Although they are rights and responsibilities of individuals, equality of access and participation in a society are universals. That which is universal applies to all because its presence or absence has to do with the survival of all and cannot be accommodated according to the inclinations of individuals. Thus, education is compulsory in a democracy. Universals have to do with principles and practices pertaining to the public good that transcend particular situations. (It is, of course, inappropriate to identify particular principles and practices as universal when they have no effect on social survival and community continuity.) Access to and participation in formal learning environments are ways of developing informed citizens, capable of making appropriate decisions to promote common welfare. For this reason, access to and participation in public schooling is a universal right and a universal responsibility that has to do with the relationship of one to many.

Universal rights and responsibilities of individuals should be guaranteed at an authoritative level, such as that of state government, that is sufficiently removed from the daily activities of the people to avoid yielding to pressure from individuals who may disagree with them. Universal principles and practices are necessary in the implementation of contributive justice that facilitates the balancing of rights and responsibilities by individuals so that "no one gains or loses from his arbitrary place . . . in society without giving or receiving compensating advantages in return" (Rawls, 1971:101). The concept of giving and gaining compensating advantages that John Rawls advances recognizes that a society is more capable of surviving when it is polymorphic or diversified, consisting of people of a variety of talents, temperaments, and interests.

In effect, principles and practices of equality of access and participation guarantee the presence of unlike kind who can accommodate each others' interests, both giving and receiving compensating advantages. Thus, universal rights and responsibilities concerning who shall teach and be taught in school protect the society against the natural inclination for individuals to prefer their own kind and to exclude dissimilar others for whom there would be an obligation to render assistance from time to time. Obviously, a society that progressively excluded dissimilar others in the end could exclude all except those who had the power to exclude. This process eventually would destroy the society, for it would lack the variety of skills and interests necessary to sustain a vital social organization. Since the tendency to exclude most frequently is manifested among intimates and usually is a local phenomenon, the requirement to include is best guaranteed at a higher decision-making level that is less intimate and more impersonal such as that of the state. The essential difference between state and local efforts in school desegregation planning is that state effort should guarantee the rights and responsibilities of all sorts and conditions of people for equal access to and participation in formal schooling.

Based on this conceptual analysis, three functions in school desegregation that are appropriate to undertake at the state level are:

- The formulation and promulgation of principles and the monitoring of practices to achieve diversity among the participants in local learning environments

- The provision of incentives and sanctions that encourage and induce localities to abide by such principles and practices
- The offering of technical assistance for the purpose of (a) identifying alternative ways of achieving diversity, and (b) resolving issues of conflict among contending parties in diversified populations regarding the purpose and practice of public school education at the local level

The National Task Force on Desegregation Strategies recommends that states should undertake these principles and practices to achieve diversity in local learning environments.

- The state legislature should establish a state policy of equal educational opportunity
- The state board should formulate rules and regulations establishing compliance and enforcement procedures for implementing the state legislation (National Project and Task Force, 1978a:4)

The conference report of state equal educational opportunity directors adds that states should:

- Review school construction, renovations, closings, and redistricting decisions for impact upon racial isolation
- Set standards for affirmative action programs in employment for local school districts
- Require multicultural educational experience as a condition for state certification of teachers (National Project and Task Force, 1978b:1, 5)

With reference to diversifying local school boards, states could:

- Require that appointed school boards be diversified so that minority and majority interests are represented among policy makers
- Require single-member districts rather than at-large elections for elected school boards as a way of guaranteeing the inclusion of representatives of a range of populations in local decision-making authorities for public education

There is evidence that state policy requiring diversity in faculty and students of local schools is effective in many but not all communities. Such policy may induce local leaders to act affirmatively despite the resistance of some to conform to the requirement of inclusion (LaPorte, Beker, and Willie, 1967:150-162).

State sanctions as a way of inducing local school districts to abide by principles and practices of diversity are complicated to implement. Sometimes state sanctions require court action for enforcement. While desegregation experts such as Gary Orfield advocate administrative enforcement on the grounds that "courts lack the capacity to effectively monitor compliance with their desegregation orders" (Orfield, 1978:324), the evidence is not convincing that state administrative agency-enforced desegregation is effective when not backed by the court.

The Boston experience is instructive:

After years of defeat in its attempt to enforce the Racial Imbalance Act, the Massachusetts Board of Education moved against the Boston School Committee and its dilatory tactics and began to withdraw state funds. The State Board also demanded that Boston develop a plan to eliminate racially imbalanced schools. Winning on some fine procedural points, the Boston School Committee managed to get state action impounding city school funds overturned, although it never developed a comprehensive school desegregation plan. Frustrated by the flagrant violation of state law, both the State Board of Education and the NAACP charged the Boston School Committee with violation of the United States Constitution. Formal proceedings were brought by black parents and their children against the Boston School Committee in federal court in 1972 (Willie, 1978:81).

It was the court, not a state administrative agency, that finally overcame Boston's resistance to school desegregation.

Leon Mayhew's study reports that the Massachusetts Commission Against Discrimination was established to protect the rights of minorities but "assumed a compromise stance" in coming to terms with the social power of the interests it sought to regulate. Consequently, Mayhew found, "most cases brought to the Commission did not produce substantial and long-run changes" (Mayhew, 1968:271).

State administrative agencies are susceptible to pressure from subdominants as well as dominants. Mayhew discovered that they do work effectively on behalf of the interests of minorities sometimes, but only when the minority community is vocal, demanding, and organized (Mayhew, 1968:271). On balance, however, the outcome of litigation seems to be more comprehensive and of more enduring effect than the remedies of administrative agencies. The litigation, however, usually is for the purpose of enforcing principles and practices required by state or federal governments.

Another example of the difficulty of applying state sanctions against a locality is the experience of the Pennsylvania Human Relations Commission. In 1968 the commission directed Erie to submit a desegregation plan and timetable that would eliminate racial imbalance in all schools and integrate all levels of the school-system staff. The Erie school board proposed several plans, but they were in part unacceptable. In 1971 the commission determined that the Erie schools were still in violation of the law and ordered the school board to adopt a plan within thirty days. The school board refused. Thus, the state administrative agency had to petition the commonwealth court to enforce its order. The court ordered the desegregation of Erie schools in 1975 (Iutcovich and Clyburn, 1981:64-72). While state sanctions are significant in inducing some communities to act affirmatively on matters of diversity, states must be willing to seek court enforcement of such sanctions for recalcitrant localities.

This illustrative review of the inability of some state agencies to apply sanctions against local school boards and make them stick does not mean that sanctions are useless. The threat of sanctions is sufficient to induce some localities to take affirmative desegregation action on their own. In some communities state sanctions have been particularly effective in getting local districts to build new schools on sites that contribute to racial balance and enhance the school desegregation effort. Gregory Anrig insists that "there needs to be some sanction which can be imposed [by the state] after appropriate due process has established a violation" (Anrig, 1979:2). It is fair to classify state sanctions as one of several formal forms of enforcement, including the courts. The latter may be required to implement sanctions of the state.

States have been more effective in the use of financial incentives to encourage desegregation in local communities. Wisconsin, for example, provides state aid for transfer students within a school system when movement from one school to another will improve racial balance. The state also provides special aid to city minority students who transfer to suburban school systems. An administrator of the Milwaukee schools praised the state of Wisconsin for its support of local school systems that must deal with desegregation and said that "these funds had been helpful in achieving desegregation goals" (Willie, 1982:88). Probably one of the largest interdistrict transfer programs in the nation for the purpose of effecting school desegregation is supported by the commonwealth of Massachusetts. The state underwrites the costs for approximately 3,000 black children from Boston and Springfield who commute to suburban districts and attend their schools as full-time students. Massachusetts also "provides for desegregation assistance in the form of 100 percent reimbursement of related transportation costs and 75 percent of the cost of constructing new schools as part of a racial balance plan approved by the State Board of Education." The state provided funds for magnet education programs and other educational improvement projects in schools receiving students as part of a desegregation plan. Massachusetts has provided these incentives, according to the former state commissioner of education, because "the process of desegregation is but the beginning of what should be a process of educational improvement for black and white children alike" (Anrig, 1979:2-4).

Recent developments in Connecticut indicate how the commitment to diversity in local school systems may erode without state incentives. Connecticut had an interdistrict transfer program in which black students participated. These students were transported from central cities to suburban communities. Because the state of Connecticut paid only about one-fifth of the costs of this program, the Hartford school board proposed a substantial reduction in interdistrict transfer to approximately one-sixth of the program's original size, when ordered by the city council to reduce its total budget by several million dollars (*Boston Globe,* July 5, 1982). However, the interdistrict transfer program in Massachusetts has remained constant over the years despite reductions in school spending in some cities because full state funding has continued as an incentive.

Another area in which technical assistance rendered by the state can be most helpful is in conflict resolution. Controversy and conflict associated with school desegregation are not necessarily bad. As Axelrod points out, conflict of interest and the resulting conflictful behavior "can help all the parties to a dispute recognize and begin to solve real problems they have" (Axelrod, 1970:202). Mayhew reminds us, "it may be that the most pioneering change will come as . . . polarized groups bargain for their share" (Mayhew, 1968:294). When contending parties at one level of social organization reach an impasse, the good offices of a third party at a higher level are often beneficial in helping them find a solution that is fair.

State government is uniquely situated in the hierarchy of social organization to perform this function. Staff appropriately trained in ways to encourage good-faith negotiation between local disparate interest groups should be retained and made available to localities in need of mediating assistance. Disputes that could have been negotiated to a just end are sometimes transformed into extensive litigation merely because there is no agency to encourage mediation toward arriving at a workable plan.

Technical assistance by the state in school desegregation can be most helpful in the analysis and identification of assets and liabilities in plans designed by localities to achieve desegregated, unitary educational systems, and the development of model school desegregation plans that, with modification, can be adapted to a range of local settings. The state is uniquely capable of doing these tasks because from a higher and more disinterested level it can see alternatives unknown or unrecognized by localities.

If state government will assume the appropriate functions regarding equality of access and participation, then local government can better perform its planning function pertaining to equity. The planning functions of localities will be discussed more extensively in the next chapter. Presented here is a brief concept of equity so that it may be contrasted with the notion of equality.

A unitary school system is one in which resources are distributed equitably. Equity decisions in education are based on the needs of individuals in the community and the resources available to fulfill those needs. Because students in different localities have different needs and also because resources vary by community settings, it is essential that equity decisions be rendered at the local level. Matters of equity are situational, not universal. What is equitable in one set of circumstances may not be equitable in another. Equity has to do with the most fair decision that can be reached at a particular point in time on the basis of what is needed and what is known to be available.

Decisions of equity are concerned, not with principles and practices that promote the public good, but with those that minimize personal harm. Obviously promoting the public good and minimizing personal harm are linked, but they are different processes.

Equity decisions have to do with the distribution and use of common resources for each person, according to his or her needs. If these resources are distributed and used in ways that are fair, then equity decisions implement *distributive justice* that denotes the relationship of many to one (Fletcher, 1966:90). A community that distributes whatever educational resources are available in a way that meets the priority needs of each student to the extent that it can has a unitary school system. Note that different individuals have different needs; thus, a school system where equity prevails may have schools with varying resources. But resources will vary in accordance with the needs of individuals in equitable arrangements.

While equality of access and participation decisions identify needs of the group or society that individuals with unique experiences may provide, equity decisions are concerned with needs of the individual that depend on the common resources of a community for fulfillment. Equality issues are group-centered, and equity issues are person-centered. In this respect, equity and equality issues are linked. A local community has a better chance of distributing common resources to meet the needs of individuals fairly if representatives of all groups in the community participate in the decision-making process. Who participates in that process is an issue of equality. In this and other ways equality and equity are related. But it should be reemphasized that they are not the same. Equality is more appropriately a function of state government and equity a function of local government.

Specifically, equity decisions should deal with issues pertaining to educational quality such as input, process, and outcome issues that help and do not harm individuals. Planning considerations to achieve these at the local level will be discussed in the next chapter.

References

Anrig, Gregory R.
    1979   "State Leadership in School Desegregation," in National Project and Task Force on Desegregation Strategies (ed.), *School Desegregation and the State Government*. Denver, Colo.: Education Commission of the States.
Axelrod, Robert
    1970   *Conflict of Interest*. Chicago: Markham.
Boston Globe
    1982   "Aim of W. Hartford Is to Bus Students In" (July 5).

Center for Education and Human Development Policy
1981   *State Strategies for Reducing Racial Isolation.* Nashville, Tenn.: Vanderbilt University.
Equal Education in Massachusetts: A Chronicle
1980   "Cambridge Adopts a Desegregation Plan," 2, no. 1 (Sept.): 1-3.
Fletcher, Joseph
1966   *Situation Ethics.* Philadelphia: Westminster Press.
Iutcovich, Joyce Miller, and Elaine Clyburn
1981   "Erie, Pennsylvania: The Effect of State Initiative," in Charles V. Willie and Susan L. Greenblatt (eds.), *Community Politics and Educational Change.* New York: Longman, pp. 64-81.
Jefferson, Thomas
1813   Letter to John Adams on "Natural Aristocracy," in Stuart Gerry Brown (ed.), *We Hold These Truths.* New York: Harper, pp. 114-118.
LaPorte, Robert, Jerome Beker, and Charles V. Willie
1966   "The Evolution of Public Educational Policy: School Desegregation in a Northern City,"*Urban Education* 2 (Nov.): 150-162.
Lubell, Samuel
1966   *Black and White.* New York: Harper.
Mayhew, Leon
1968   *Law and Equal Opportunity.* Cambridge, Mass.: Harvard University Press.
National Project and Task Force on Desegregation Strategies
1978a   *Position Statement on Desegregation.* Denver, Colo.: Education Commission of the States.
1978b   *State Planning to Achieve Successful Desegregation.* Denver, Colo.: Education Commission of the States.
1980   *State Leadership Toward Desegregating Education: A Positive Future.* Denver, Colo.: Education Commission of the States.
Orfield, Gary
1978   *Must We Bus?* Washington, D.C.: Brookings Institution.
Rawls, John
1971   *A Theory of Justice.* Cambridge, Mass.: Harvard University Press.
U.S. Commission on Civil Rights
1967   *Racial Isolation in the Public Schools.* Washington, D.C.: U.S. Government Printing Office.
White, Eileen
1982   "$144-Million Desegregation Effort Imperiled," *Education Week,* 1 (March 24), pp. 14, 16.
Willie, Charles V.
1978   *The Sociology of Urban Education.* Lexington, Mass.: Lexington Books.
1982   "Desegregation in Big-City School Systems: A Comparative Analysis," *Educational Forum* 47 (Fall 1982), pp. 83-96.
Willie, Charles V. and Susan L. Greenblatt
1981   *Community Politics and Educational Change.* New York: Longman.

Chapter 5

Desegregation Planning at the Local Level: Maintaining Equity in the Distribution and Use of Resources

School desegregation is an innovation that began around the second half of the twentieth century in American education. Although authorized by the Supreme Court's decision in *Brown v. Board of Education* in 1954, the desegregation process was accelerated by the Civil Rights Act of 1964. Thus, school desegregation as an accomplished fact in a limited number of communities in the United States is of recent origin—actually a phenomenon of the final trimester of this century. The process recently initiated in several communities has hardly persisted long enough for a full determination of its effect.

By court order and legislative mandate, public schools in the United States are obligated to change from dual to unitary systems. This requirement is a radical rearrangement. Despite propaganda statements by opponents of the process that desegregation has failed, the evidence indicates that the United States has nearly achieved universal education with 95 percent of all school-aged young people in schools, that median years of school completed by minority and by majority populations are similar now, and that the school dropout rate for racial minorities has substantially declined since the initiation of school desegregation. A 1977 publication by the United States Commission on Civil Rights concludes that "desegregation actions taken over the last 10 years were effective in achieving sweeping reductions in the isolation of racial and ethnic minorities within numerous school districts" (U.S. Commission on Civil Rights, 1977:3).

Neal Gross states:

Individuals who manage educational innovations generally receive little or no preparation for their challenging assignment. . . . They attempt to carry out their responsibilities and cope with their managerial tasks as best they can, leaning heavily on intuition, previous work experiences, and "common sense." Their decisions tend to be ad hoc in nature, uninformed by systematic analysis of problems, and made without reference to an overall change strategy.

Moreover, their assumptions about educational change sometimes are "simplistic, misleading, and dysfunctional" and "their conceptualization of the change process and identification of internal and external forces that affect it often are inadequate" (Gross, 1979:20).

At the midpoint of the twentieth century and for a decade or two thereafter, few chief administrators of public school systems had been trained in ways of handling educational innovations such as school desegregation. Neil Sullivan said several superintendents were forced into retirement during the 1960s after passage of the Civil Rights Act and the increased agitation for desegregation because they "could not solve the multidimensioned problem of school integration" (Sullivan, 1976:286). Many more left office during the 1970s due to desegregation-connected events. Boston, for example, had a half dozen superintendents during a single decade.

And, of course, the new officers appointed to lead school districts confronted with racial imbalance and desegregation problems were not always "fully aware of earlier decisions, policies, and information-gathering efforts of their predecessors." Indeed, the flow of information within large organizations like school systems is selective; and threatening information tends to be distorted to serve purposes of the institution, according to Mark Yudoff (1981:247). Thus, school leaders with limited understanding of planning, little training and experience in ways of handling desegregation, and inadequate information of previous policies and practices that discriminated against racial minorities had few guidelines about how to achieve the court-mandated innovation of a unitary public school system.

The minimum guidelines provided by the Supreme Court in *Brown v. Board of Education II* (1955) were confusing for educational planners. For example, the Court clearly stated that "the personal interest of the plaintiffs in admission to public schools as soon as practicable on a nondiscriminatory basis" is the issue "at stake." But then the Supreme Court permitted district courts to which the cases were remanded for the purpose of entering orders and decrees consistent with its opinion to "take into account the public interest," which could be different from that of the "personal interest of the plaintiffs."

Moreover, the Supreme Court in *Brown II* directed the district courts merely to require "a prompt and reasonable start toward full compliance with [the school desegregation] ruling." Explaining this phrase, the Court implied that a school board could delay prompt action in protecting the rights of racial minorities if it could demonstrate additional time "is necessary in the public interest," as long as the defendant acted in good faith. The Court stated that disagreement with the desegregation ruling, however, could not be used as a public interest issue; but it permitted the accommodation of other unspecified public interests in planning for the elimination of obstacles to the admission of racial minorities to public schools on a nondiscriminatory basis. The Court also suggested that the defendant school board was an appropriate planning agency for the development of proposals "to effectuate a transition to a racially nondiscriminatory school system." Left undefined in the Court's ruling was a definition of "public interest"; it also gave no guidance regarding how to "take into account the public interest in the elimination of [discriminatory] obstacles in a systematic and effective manner." To summarize, "the implementation of the *Brown* (1954) decision was left largely to the discretion of lower court federal judges. Initiation of desegregation plans was to come in the first instance from school boards, and they were to take account of local concerns and problems in the desegregation process. This, in essence, was the message of *Brown II* (1955)" (Yudoff, 1981:249).

Ralph McGill believed that the "phrasing of the [Supreme Court] decision, rationally anticipated that the knowledge and skill of educators, of school psychologists, and of the social sciences, would assume direction of the process of desegregation" (McGill, 1964:249). This, however, did not happen. He observed that many school desegregation plans were created "not by educators but by political office holders and lawyers." McGill said some of these plans "hardly met the test of equal protection of the law" (McGill, 1964:249). When school boards in some communities refused to do any more than they were ordered to do, the district court under the supervision of a judge had to fashion plans for the achievement of a unitary public school system. Robert Dentler, a social scientist who has participated in many school desegregation cases as a court-appointed expert, states that "judges . . . are generally ill-equipped by training or by staff limitations to undertake this task." While lawyers have had professional experience with school desegregation, Dentler reports that "few of them are knowledgeable urbanists or students of public education." Finally, he indicates why school systems seldom develop effective desegregation plans: "Agents of the system are themselves products and defenders of the status quo. They often plan against their will and from a base of ignorance about objectives" (Dentler, 1976:127), as Gross (1979) and Yudoff (1981) indicated.

The outcome of school desegregation with respect to equal protection of the law and educational benefits, according to Dentler, is largely a result of "the quality of planning" (Dentler, 1976:126). Among barriers to good planning are not only the lack of enthusiasm and experience of some planners but also their inaccessibility to and lack of knowledge of the racial-minority plaintiffs for whom the plan should yield educational benefits. The "personal interest" of the plaintiffs, said the Supreme Court, is the constitutional issue at stake. As observed by Derrick Bell, "black children need top-quality schools now" (Bell, 1981:177). Yet, most desegregation plans for the redress of the educational grievances of black plaintiffs have been developed by middle-aged, middle-class, white male educational planners. Rachael Tompkins reminds us that "whether plans simply mix students or incorporate other elements is in the hands of those who write the plan" (Tompkins, 1978:109).

If the outcome of school desegregation is largely a result of planning, Barbara Sizemore raises a crucial question: "How can black educators assume a position of leadership in desegregation when [they] formulate none of the theory, . . . construct none of the definitions, design none of the models, and negotiate none of the decisions?" (Sizemore, 1978:63). Nancy Arnez of Howard University is more direct. In an article entitled "Implementation of Desegregation as a Discriminatory Process," she declares that "black parents and the black community have been reactors to actions by whites rather than participants in the planning of those actions" (Arnez, 1978:29). Both Arnez and Sizemore complain that minorities have been excluded from the planning and policy-making process and that this exclusion has resulted in plans that have had "deleterious results for black children" (Arnez, 1978:28). Among the more deleterious or unfair outcomes of desegregation planning mentioned by these educators are relegation of a disproportionate number of blacks to special education classes, the dismissal and demotion of many black teachers and administrators, and the assignment to blacks of longer travel time to and from school for a larger number of grades, compared with whites (Arnez, 1978:28, 33).

Beyond these disadvantages, Sizemore states that the planning priorities appear to be wrong. She sees desegregation as concerned with "education, equality and equity" and in that order. She believes that desegregation should fulfill the needs of black people "for recognition and respect" and that educational policy to achieve these ends should focus specifically on grouping practices, testing procedures, curriculum development, multilingual-multicultural models, disciplinary practices, in-service training, promotion standards, extracurricular activities, and counseling services (Sizemore, 1978:66-67). To Sizemore and other blacks, these are first-generation desegregation problems that should have been but were not addressed in desegregation plans. They are not second- and third-generation problems as claimed by some desegregation planners who consider the initial or first-generation problem to be "the physical reassignment of students" (Chesler, Crowfoot, and Bryant, 1978:213). The priorities indicated by minority education planners focus primarily on educational benefits and secondarily on desegregative or student-assignment strategies. For example, Sizemore acknowledges that "an integrated society is desirable" (Sizemore, 1978:68); but she is more concerned with addressing the problems of black students in desegregated schools, which, according to her, fall into three general categories—discipline, learning, and self-concept (Sizemore, 1978:65).

Reports prepared by Gordon Foster (1973), John Finger (1976), Larry Hughes, William Gordon, and Larry Hillman (1980), and the Vanderbilt University Center for Education and Human Development Policy (Hawley et al., 1981) indicate the prevailing interests of school desegregation planners who are associated with the majority group. Listed first among desegregation strategies by the Vanderbilt University Center is pupil assignment. Its scholars state that the reduction or elimination of racial isolation is the primary objective of such an assignment plan (Hawley et al., 1981:17). Hughes, Gordon, and Hillman, in their handbook for the development of a good desegregation plan, begin with pupil assignment. They begin with the race-mixing strategy because of their interpretation of court decisions which, according to them, declare that desegregation is the issue. Thus "any technique that can . . . be employed to eliminate racially identifiable schools" should be used (Hughes, Gordon, and Hillman, 1980:53-54). Gordon Foster (mentor of these three education planners), while acknowledging that many factors contribute to a unitary school system, places pupil assignment at the head of his list (Foster, 1973:15). John Finger focuses on housing and sees the major function of desegregation plans as the preventing of white flight and the providing of stability in housing. He states that a successful plan has "built-in safeguards . . . to assure residential stability" (Finger, 1976:60-61). In summary, most white education planners are primarily concerned with "the practicalities of assigning pupils so that schools are desegregated" (Foster, 1973:15), and residential areas remain stable without massive change in the racial composition of the population.

This analysis suggests that social location in society as dominant or subdominant in the power structure, member of the majority or minority group, may be associated with the planning strategies emphasized and the priorities given to different components of a desegregation plan. If increased racial diversity with enhanced educational opportunities is the twofold goal of the Supreme Court *Brown* decision, then a diversified planning group is essential in achieving this goal. Otherwise only one aspect of the goal may be emphasized at the expense of the other.

A review of planning strategies by educators who identify with different racial populations reveals that minority-group planners tend to be more concerned with educational outcomes and majority-group planners tend to focus more on the racial balance of student bodies.

Since the fulfillment of self-interest is the basic motive for social participation, the complaint by black educators about their exclusion from the desegregation planning process should be taken seriously. White educators who serve as masters, experts, or planning consultants are more likely to recommend desegregation strategies that fulfill the interest of the majority primarily and that of the minority secondarily. Tilting of planning outcomes toward the interest of one or another group may be done with malice aforethought or unknowingly. Despite the intent, the interest of the out-group is seldom planned for adequately by professionals who identify with the in-group, and vice versa.

Because of the prevailing practice of focusing on race mixing in the public school, some minority students have not experienced the "equal educational opportunity" promised by the *Brown* decision, in the opinion of Derrick Bell (Bell, 1981:197). For this reason, he and other black planners are beginning to express doubt about the efficacy of pupil-assignment plans. Bell states that "the real evil . . . is the persistent pattern of giving priority to the needs and interest of whites in a school system without regard to whether this policy disadvantages blacks" (Bell, 1981:200). Such a policy, according to Bell, is particularly damaging to minority children within the structure of a desegregated school. Bell believes that "school remedies . . . should be addressed to all aspects of racism, not just separation" or racial isolation, and that "those *remedies should focus specifically on techniques intended to improve the educational effectiveness of schools attended by nonwhite children,* whether or not those schools are predominantly white" (Bell, 1981:201, emphasis added). Despite doubts by Bell and black educators about the efficacy of desegregation as a way for minorities to achieve improved education, a majority of blacks, as revealed by opinion polls, favor sending their children to integrated schools. In Boston, for example, 71 percent favored that option (Willie, 1982:6).

As evidence that white school desegregation planners are concerned primarily with student assignment plans that will enable their group to continue as the majority, Sizemore cites the increasing call for metropolitan desegregation (Pettigrew, 1981:163-181). She labels such plans a popular tactic for dispersing blacks and diminishing their power and control of cities. Thomas Pettigrew provides fuel to spark Sizemore's suspicion in his justification of metropolitan proposals: "No metropolitan program of public-school desegregation has experienced an extensive loss of white students" (Pettigrew, 1981:168), he said. Based on this and other facts, Sizemore concludes that the design of desegregation plans is "structured around the need for a white majority" (Sizemore, 1978:59). Sizemore's concern was confirmed in Jacksonville, Florida. Lee Sloan and Robert French report that "as affluent whites fled to suburban Duval County, low-income blacks crowded Jacksonville's central city. . . . A group of reformers proposed a solution to the city's problems—to consolidate the government of Jacksonville with that of Duval County." Sloan and French state that, although the case for consolidation is presented as good government reform, whites recognize they are forfeiting power and control of the city to blacks. Thus, consolidating a predominantly black city with a larger predominantly white county is one way of "holding the line against black power" (Sloan and French, 1977:210-202).

Certainly the interests of whites would appear to be given more consideration by the desegregation planners of the Charlotte-Mecklenburg schools and of city and county schools in Louisville, with reference to the number of whites bused, their age, and the number of years they had to ride great distances to and from school, compared with blacks. "Louisville implemented the desegregation plan by clustering schools that were previously predominantly white or black and transporting students within each cluster according to the first letter of their last name. The plan calls for 84 percent of white students to be transported for two of their 12 school years. . . . Sixty-six percent of black students are to be transported for eight years" (Arnez, 1978:33). In "the Charlotte [-Mecklenburg] plan . . . equal numbers of black and white elementary children were bused, although each black child was bused four years while his white counterpart only two, and the primary school-age black children were bused while the white children bused were older" (Finger, 1976:61). Finger, a strong supporter of busing to achieve integrated education, notes that plans such as these and other variations of them may be inequitable, but he speculates that "complete equity may be less important than feelings of satisfaction and acceptability by children and parents" (Finger, 1976:61). It is not clear whether he is talking about white children and their parents only, black children and their parents only, or children and parents of both races. Regardless, "feelings of satisfaction and acceptability" hardly could be classified as dimensions of the public interest that the Supreme Court said could be taken into consideration. In fact, the Court explicitly said (as mentioned earlier) that the constitutional requirement to desegregate the public schools could not be allowed to yield simply because of dissatisfaction or disagreement with it. Moreover, such inequity intentionally planned is a form of discrimination which desegregation plans supposedly are designed to overcome. Inequitable desegregation plans that discriminate against blacks and other minorities and ignore their personal interest in educational improvement, which the Court identified as the primary issue at stake, are examples of deficient planning. In the words of McGill, such plans "took a decision delineating the rights of children and giving . . . a God-sent opportunity to revise and elevate [a] . . . long-inadequate school system, and dishonestly distorted it" (McGill, 1964:246). "Court-ordered desegregation is usually the greatest opportunity for reform that occurs in urban school districts," according to Ronald Edmonds, Charles Cheng, and Robert Newby (1978:12). Deficient planning may let this moment pass and forfeit the opportunity to change "our social order's most dramatic example of inequity" (Edmonds, Cheng, and Newby, 1978:12), largely because of concern with protecting the interests of the majority rather than redressing the grievances of the minority.

It is probable that school desegregation planning has been deficient and has failed to accommodate the twofold goal of student body diversity and educational improvement in public schools not only because of the homogeneous characteristics of the planners and their social location largely in the dominant white majority group, but also because of the planning model used. Sociologist Mark Chesler and his associates describe the consensus model and the conflict model as two legitimate ways of planning for school desegregation in the local community. They state that planners and "practitioners proceeding from these two models may well pursue desegregation in different ways" (Chesler, Crowfoot, and Bryant, 1978:178).

According to Chesler and associates the consensus model of desegregation "should increase the possibility of order and stability in the society, primarily by altering minorities' feelings of exclusion and injustice." They state that these alterations "may be accomplished best through assimilative processes" which include "subtle pressures . . . to accommodate . . . to white norms and standards" (Chesler, Crowfoot, and Bryant, 1978:178).

The conflict model of desegregation "should increase the possibility of justice in the society by increasing the status and power of minorities" by enhancing their capacity "to negotiate with more powerful white groups for a fair share of resources." Using the perspective of the conflict model, minorities sometimes view desegregation and the dispersal of their children throughout the larger white community as a way of diluting the power that results from their concentration. With the conflict model in mind, minorities may resist desegregation if it will contribute not only to a loss of power associated with the absence of a critical mass, which facilitates the advancement of their interests, but also to a loss of a sense of cultural uniqueness (Chesler, Crowfoot, and Bryant, 1978:178).

Most school desegregation planners opt for the consensus model of planning. It facilitates the protecting of the majority's interest in that the minority is urged to imitate and emulate whites. A major limitation of this model is that it excludes the creative contribution of subdominant dissent. Often dissent introduces into the system correctives for the excesses of the more powerful majority. Richard Korn states the case for the conflict model. There is a tendency for the inheritors of greatness and the passive beneficiaries of liberty to become oppressive as they strive for excellence and preeminence. When this happens, he asks: "Who, then, is left to keep the flame alive—whence comes the regeneration" (Korn, 1968:196), the reform? Korn's answer: "From the oppressed, of course" (Korn, 1968:196).

As reported in an article on "Community Development and Social Change, " "policies and plans that promote the public interest are likely to be those . . . that are forged on the anvil of controversy." Policies that are in the public interest, including those pertaining to school desegregation, have a better chance of emerging from decision-making groups that "have a fine mixture of members with local loyalties and members who represent special-interest groups as well as unaffiliated members at large." While groups so composed may experience tension, "that . . . tension usually is creative with deliberations among representatives of different special-interest groups serving as a self-corrective device for the organization." Moreover, "it is more appropriate to encounter controversy around the conference table where it can be dealt with in a controlled way, where bargaining, trade-offs, and compromises can be worked out" (Willie, 1977:156).

Indeed, some planners have characterized the planning process as that of creating a structure or model within which confrontation can take place continually. As stated elsewhere, "the opening up of the structure to dissident groups is one role of the planner. . . . The planner must bring into the discussion people both dominant and subdominant in the community power structure." Planners who focus only on the dominant people of power may have their plans upset by subdominants who do not have implementation power but who do have veto power (Willie, 1978:91). Thus it is better to have a diversified planning staff of dominant and subdominant representatives. Such a staff is better able to develop plans that are "sufficiently flexible to adapt their operating procedures to changing circumstances." A school board will diversify its planning staff as a way of incorporating the interests of all in desegregation proposals if it recognizes planning, and especially planning for a unitary school system, as "the redistribution of power within a system" (Willie, 1978:93).

With reference to the future, the successful attainment of school desegregation that has been noted by the United States Civil Rights Commission is likely to occur at a diminishing rate unless planning strategies are significantly changed. Minority as well as majority interests must be accommodated in future school desegregation plans. This means that such plans will not be effective unless they are designed to enhance educational opportunities as well as diversify school student bodies.

In the past, planners assumed that "the social and educational policy strands . . . are woven together around the method of assigning students" (Dentler and Scott, 1981:52). Experience has proven this assumption to be false. In fact, most student-assignment plans made desegregation rather than the education needs of children the center of concern and controversy (Sizemore, 1978:62-63). Moreover, they ignored or treated as less important the Supreme Court's requirement that the personal interest of minority children of the plaintiff class be addressed and fulfilled as the central issue at stake.

Future planning for public school desegregation will accommodate the multicultural interests of this nation's pluralistic population as school boards and other public decision-making bodies more appropriately reflect the range of racial, ethnic, and other groups in the local community. As diversity in these decision-making bodies increases due to a changeover to single-member district from at-large elections, power and influence in the local community will be redistributed. Minorities are expected to increase their pressure for local elections by single-member district following the 1982 ruling of the Supreme Court that condemned the at-large system used by Burke County, Georgia. Although that locality is predominantly black, Burke County has not had any blacks as members of the County Commission since the days of Reconstruction, shortly after the Civil War of the nineteenth century (*The Boston Globe,* 1982:3). According to Albert Karnig and Susan Welch, "at-large elections are obstacles" for minority populations. They further state that district elections which "facilitate the representation of geographically defined groups" tend to provide "more proportional black representation" than the at-large system. In summary, "pure district races provide the greatest black representation . . . and . . . pure at-large elections produce the lowest black representation" (Karnig and Welch, 1982:104, 112-113). Because of the existence of residential segregation in most local communities, voting by single-member district almost guarantees that minority interests will be represented among the official power brokers elected to governmental commissions, councils, and committees.

New education policy makers may insist that the planning units that recommend alternative desegregation strategies to school boards diversify their staffs. Such units that reflect the knowledge and wisdom of a heterogeneous staff are more likely to deal with the concerns of the community's minority and majority groups. If this, indeed, is the scenario of the future, school desegregation plans will place emphasis on educational components as well as pupil-assignment strategies.

With as much emphasis on education and a reduction of overconcern about whether or not whites are the majority in a particular school, racial balance will fade as the major concept in school desegregation planning, and the concept of critical mass will gain more prominence. Under this condition of planning, student-assignment strategies will insure that any majority racial or cultural group will receive an education in the presence of dissimilar others. The only concern then will be that the group of dissimilar others is sufficiently large to have an educative impact upon the total learning environment. According to this planning guideline, any group—blacks, browns, or whites—may be the majority or the dissimilar others. The minority, whoever it is, should attain a critical mass by way of a single group or a combination of groups that ideally is one-third of a student body and not less than one-fifth (Willie, 1978:68).

With white planners being less concerned about controlling the definition of desegregation to guarantee white majority control, their attention obviously can be redirected to matters of educational substance. And, of course, they will be induced to do this if other planning colleagues and school board authorities are affiliated with population groups that are different from the white majority. A good omen for the future is the priority that scholars of the Vanderbilt University Center for Educational and Human Development Policy gave to the interests of "the plaintiffs in school desegregation and their lawyers" in the report, *An Agenda for Further Research on Desegregation Strategies*. Individuals in these groups head their list of "audiences . . . who can either create or influence desegregation policy" and to whom research findings in the future should be directed (Crain and Hawley, 1981:2).

It would appear that the real second-generation problem in school desegregation is the rediscovery and recognition of the interest of the plaintiffs' class that won the court case against racial segregation and discrimination. For nearly a quarter of a century following the 1954 *Brown* decision, the interest of plaintiffs was ignored or denied as educators struggled to fashion desegregation plans that would least offend whites who are among the class of people who lost the court case.

It was not until 1967, however, that a chief school officer, Neil Sullivan, would insist that "desegregation must be combined with a general program of education improvement" (Sullivan, 1967:287). A decade later, School of Education Dean Robert Dentler repeated this theme in his observation that a desegregation plan should fulfill the essential objective of equal protection and reverse decades of inferior education (Dentler, 1976:128). By 1981, the agenda for future desegregation research of the Vanderbilt University Center indicated that a critical mass of scholars is now beginning to embrace these twin ideas of the goal of school desegregation offered by the plaintiffs earlier.

In effect, this discussion suggests that the preoccupation and near obsession with racial balance in student bodies that has consumed the attention of many desegregation planners in the past has been too narrow. It also probably focused first on the wrong aggregation. The priority for achieving diversity or racial balance should have been given to the official centers of power where educational decisions are made. When the authoritative groups such as school boards are diversified, other units of the system tend to be fashioned in their image.

One issue that remains unclear and about which outcome projections for the future cannot be made is whether or not school desegregation plans will continue to be systemwide. Expert opinion on the issue varies. One school superintendent said the " 'solution' to *de facto* segregation must involve the *total* community. No area of the city must be made to feel that it is being picked on or sacrificed to solve a total community problem." He said, "*de facto* segregation is a community-wide problem and must be solved on a community-wide basis" (Sullivan, 1967:287). Attorneys representing the Boston Home and School Association contend that "the remedy of desegregation should be applied only to those schools which were segregated because of illegal 'state action' and that schools segregated because of residential population patterns should not be covered by the court order" (Willie, 1978:60-61).

Social scientists Robert Williams and Margaret Ryan warned that "partial desegregation that affects only . . . a few schools in a community opens the door to charges of [favoritism]" (Williams and Ryan, 1954). In other words, those who are required to participate in the desegregation process feel put upon while those exempted boast of special treatment for one reason or another. The Boston experience followed this pattern. "South Boston, Roxbury, and other inner-city Boston neighborhoods included in the first-year partial desegregation plan that was limited to about eighty of 200 schools largely in working-class areas" erupted in violent confrontation (Willie, 1978:61). Long-term desegregation watcher Robert Coles called the partial plan an imposition on the poor. He said that social change cannot occur in just one area while everyone else is let off the hook (Willie, 1978:82).

Gary Orfield believes that plans, and especially computer plans, "that integrate segregated neighborhoods by transferring children from nearly integrated neighborhoods" are absurd (Orfield, 1981:22). He endorses the exemption of integrated neighborhood schools from busing (Orfield, 1981:20). While acknowledging that one of the reasons desegregation plans fail "is because some children are bused but others are not," Finger would accept less equity in a plan "if it gives the promise of creating residential stability and preventing white flight" (Finger, 1976:64, 61).

Dallas desegregation planners had attitudes about residential stability that were similar to those that Orfield and Finger expressed. "Where possible, the plan recommends that students who live in naturally integrated areas should not be reassigned to achieve desegregation elsewhere" (Alpert, White, and Geisel, 1981:164). Because so many whites were exempted from participation in the plan because their home sites were in so-called naturally integrated residential areas, too few were available to reassign to the predominantly black schools. Although the pupil-assignment plan was supposed to redress the grievances of blacks who claimed that they had suffered educationally because of their segregation and racial isolation, it permitted more than half of the black school-age children of Dallas to remain in one-race schools but effectively desegregated whites. The National Association for the Advancement of Colored People (NAACP) contended that this arrangement was unfair and appealed the court order that put into place such a plan. The United States Court of Appeals found the student-assignment section of the Dallas school desegregation plan not acceptable (Alpert, White, and Geisel, 1981:172).

Believing that a system must be viewed as a whole, David Entin states that schools should be rezoned according to "an overall strategy" (Entin,

1973:44). And the United States Commission on Civil Rights reports that involvement of all schools in the whole community is an important factor in successful school desegregation (U.S. Civil Rights Commission, 1977:156).

Another decision that remains unresolved to date is the influence that housing and changing residential patterns should have on school desegregation planning and plans. Orfield believes that if more attention were given to housing patterns and the coordination of school desegregation programs with them, the outcome would be better. He states that "the record is full of missed opportunities" (Orfield, 1981:18). He supports court orders that "impose on school authorities a continuing obligation to deal with the results of spreading residential segregation" (Orfield, 1981:22). Dentler also believes that court-ordered attendance zones should be adjusted yearly, if necessary, to bring student bodies that are tending toward violation of the racial/ethnic ratio guidelines back into conformity. He notes, however, that school systems tend to resist doing this under the guise of maintaining stability (Dentler, 1981:70). Foster rejects the stability defense for not modifying school attendance zones regularly to accommodate shifts in the residential characteristics of the population. He states that all along, school boards were modifying attendance zones regularly "to maintain segregated schools." Thus, there is nothing extraordinary about making periodic adjustments "to maintain desegregation" (Foster, 1973:17).

Some school desegregation planners declare that housing is beyond the control of school desegregation planners and that it would be "dilatory . . . for desegregation . . . to wait for open housing and let the problem take care of itself," although open housing is identified as a logical long-range solution (Foster, 1973:25-26). Williams and Ryan acknowledge that "segregation in the school system is powerfully supported by the larger patterns of segregation" (Williams and Ryan, 1954:240); nevertheless, they state that "successful public school desegregation has been carried out in places where supposedly the prevailing attitudes favored segregation and where other institutions continued to be segregated" (Williams and Ryan, 1954:241). It would appear that school desegregation is associated with what happens elsewhere in the community but is not wholly determined by these other happenings. It is entirely possible that desegregative efforts in schools may stimulate such efforts in other community institutions such as housing arrangements just as activities in other systems influence the schools. Thus, planning for school desegregation need not wait upon the fulfillment of other community plans such as those pertaining to housing.

Clifton Wharton, Jr., is unequivocal in his statement that "in recent years, investment to develop the mind of the black community has paid off . . . for blacks." While income differentials remain between the races, Wharton said incomes for blacks rose rapidly for persons with college educations. He declared that education—especially higher education—

continues to be a major factor in the progress of black society (Wharton, 1972:281-282). Land may be expropriated, property destroyed, other possessions seized and stolen away, but knowledge and wisdom endure. Thus, education probably is the most significant defense that the meek or minority have against the possibility of oppression by the mighty or the majority. In the light of this analysis, it is appropriate to press forward in the design of unitary school system plans that give priority to enhancing the education of minorities. Emphasis on enhancing the education of minorities is based on the principle that what enhances the minority also enhances the majority, but not vice versa. The enhancement of education and the reassignment of students must embrace each other and function as complementary components in unitary school system planning rather than as competing and contradictory components, each excluding the other.

References

Alpert, Geoffrey P., H. Ron White, and Paul Geisel
    1981   "Dallas, Texas: The Intervention of Business Leaders," in Charles V. Willie and Susan L. Greenblatt (eds.), *Community Politics and Educational Change.* New York: Longman, pp. 155-173.
Arnez, Nancy L.
    1978   "Implementation of Desegregation as a Discriminatory Process," *Journal of Negro Education* 47 (Winter): pp. 28-45.
Bell, Derrick A.
    1980   "A Reassessment of Racial Balance Remedies—I," *Phi Delta Kappan* 62 (Nov.): 177-179.
    1981   "Civil Rights Commitment and the Challenge of Changing Conditions in Urban School Cases," in Adam Yarmolinsky, Lance Liebman, and Corinne S. Schelling (eds.), *Race and Schooling in the City.* Cambridge, Mass.: Harvard University Press, pp. 194-203.
Boston Globe, The
    1982   "High Court Eases Test for Bias in Voting Laws" (July 2).
Chesler, Mark A., James E. Crowfoot, and Bunyan I. Bryant
    1978   "Institutional Changes to Support School Desegregation: Alternative Models Underlying Research and Implementation," *Law and Contemporary Problems* 42 (Autumn): 174-212.
Crain, Robert L., and Willis D. Hawley
    1981   *An Agenda for Further Research on Desegregation Strategies.* Nashville, Tenn.: Center for Education and Human Development Policy, Vanderbilt University.
Dentler, Robert A.
    1976   "Urban School Desegregation," in Marvin B. Scott (ed), *The Essential Profession.* Stamford, Conn.: Greylock Publishers, pp. 119-134.
Dentler, Robert A., and Marvin B. Scott
    1981   *Schools on Trial.* Cambridge, Mass.: Abt Books.

Edmonds, Ronald R., Charles W. Cheng, and Robert G. Newby
   1978   "Desegregation Planning and Educational Equity," *Theory into Practice* 17 (Feb.): 12-16.
Entin, David
   1973   "Standard Planning Techniques for Desegregation," *Integrated Education* (March-April): 43-53.
Finger, John A., Jr.
   1976   "Why Busing Plans Work," in Florence Hamlish Levinsohn and Benjamin Drake Wright (eds.), *School Desegregation.* Chicago: University of Chicago Press, pp. 58-66.
Foster, Gordon
   1973   "Desegregating Urban Schools: A Review of Techniques," *Harvard Educational Review* 43 (Feb.): 5-35.
Gross, Neal
   1979   "Basic Issues in the Management of Educational Change Effort," in Robert E. Herriott and Neal Gross (eds.), *The Dynamics of Planned Educational Change.* Berkeley, Calif.: McCutchan, pp. 2-46.
Hawley, Willis D., et al.
   1981   *Strategies for Effective Desegregation: A Synthesis of Findings.* Nashville, Tenn.: Center for Education and Human Development Policy, Vanderbilt University.
Hughes, Larry W., William M. Gordon, and Larry W. Hillman
   1980   *Desegregating America's Schools.* New York: Longman.
Karnig, Albert K., and Susan Welch
   1982   "Electoral Structure and Black Representation on City Councils," *Social Science Quarterly* 63 (March): 99-114.
Korn, Richard R.
   1968   *Juvenile Delinquency.* New York: Crowell.
McGill, Ralph
   1964   *The South and the Southerner.* Boston: Little, Brown.
Orfield, Gary
   1981   *Toward a Strategy for Urban Integration.* New York: Ford Foundation.
Pettigrew, Thomas F.
   1981   "The Case for Metropolitan Approaches to Public-School Desegregation," in Adam Yarmolinsky, Lance Liebman, and Corinne S. Schelling (eds.), *Race and Schooling in the City.* Cambridge, Mass.: Harvard University Press, pp. 163-181.
Sizemore, Barbara A.
   1978   "Educational Research and Desegregation: Significance for the Black Community," *Journal of Negro Education* 47 (Winter): 58-68.
Sloan, Lee, and Robert M. French
   1977   "Black Rule in the Urban South?" in Charles V. Willie (ed.), *Black/Brown/White Relations.* New Brunswick, N.J.: Transaction Books.
Sullivan, Neil V.
   1967   "Desegregation Techniques," in *Appendices, Racial Isolation in the Public Schools.* U.S. Commission on Civil Rights. Washington, D.C.: U.S. Government Printing Office, pp. 285-293.

Tompkins, Rachael B.
    1978   "Preparing Communities for School Desegregation," *Theory Into Practice,* 17 (April): 107-114.
U.S. Commission on Civil Rights
    1977   *Reviewing a Decade of School Desegregation, 1966-1975.* Washington, D.C.: U.S. Government Printing Office.
Wharton, Clifton R., Jr.
    1972   "Reflections on Black Intellectual Power," *Educational Record* 53 (Fall): 281-286.
Williams, Robin, and Margaret Ryan
    1954   *Schools in Transition.* Chapel Hill, N.C.: University of North Carolina Press.
Willie, Charles V.
    1977   "Community Development and Social Change," in Charles V. Willie (ed.), *Black/Brown/White Relations.* New Brunswick, N.J.: Transaction Books, pp. 151-158.
    1978   *The Sociology of Urban Education.* Lexington, Mass.: Lexington Books, D. C. Heath.
    1982   "Busing Defended," *Boston Observer* 1 (April): 5-7.
Yudoff, Mark G.
    1981   "Implementing Desegregation Decrees," in Willis D. Hawley (ed.), *Effective School Desegregation.* Beverly Hills, Calif.: Sage, pp. 245-264.

Part III

MODEL PLANS FOR UNITARY SCHOOL SYSTEMS

Chapter 6

The Boston School Desegregation Plan

Robert A. Dentler

1. Goals and Assumptions

The Boston Plan (BP) was designed as a permanent, workable remedy for constitutionally violative wrongs found in the June 1974 liability opinion of United States District Court Judge W. Arthur Garrity, Jr., in *Morgan v. Hennigan* (CIV. A-No. 92-911-G). A plan prepared by the Massachusetts State Education Department had been adopted as a temporary remedy for one year because it met state legal standards and was the only remedy at hand. It affected only 80 of 208 schools, however, and was thus not systemwide, as was the finding of harm.

When the Boston School Committee voted three to two to reject its mandated plan in December 1974, Judge Garrity formed a Panel of Masters and appointed two court experts to review all proposals and to fashion a federally acceptable alternative. The masters included two attorneys, retired Massachusetts Supreme Court Justice Jacob L. Spiegel, and former State Attorney General Edward J. McCormack, Jr., and two educators, former United States Commissioner of Education Francis Keppel, and Harvard Professor Charles V. Willie. Courts often appoint one master or one expert in desegregation cases. In this case, Judge Garrity innovated and created a four-member panel that not only diversified the professional mix but which combined a Boston Irish leader, McCormack, with a black urban sociologist of national standing, Willie. All four men had ample previous experience with desegregation issues as well. This chapter concerns the 1975 BP adopted by the court based on the report of the masters and amended over the years from 1975 to 1982.[1]

The BP is grounded upon several basic assumptions, as follows:

1. Racial and ethnic segregation in itself harms the hearts and minds of students and deprives them of their right to equal treatment under law.

2. The plan is necessarily preoccupied with ending gross injustices done to black students because the case is a class action suit brought by fifty black parents of Boston school children.

3. Other minorities are affected by segregation and discrimination, however, and therefore the BP assumes a multiethnic rather than a biracial set of remedies, still giving much greater weight to black plaintiffs, however.

4. The BP assumes that the major policy actions the plan should induce are the provision of equal access to schools and programs of study; the replacement of racially identifiable schools with "just schools" (a Supreme Court term referring to the standard of public schools which host all groups and are identified with no one race);[2] and elimination of the continuing ravages of discrimination. Equal access extended to opportunity but not to the equalization of all facilities and programs.

5. The BP assumes that a good plan must take education concerns into deep account and seek to upgrade the quality of teaching and learning in this domain. Thus, the plan reforms and impinges deeply upon education without dictating curriculum or instructional design features.

6. It assumes that special needs programs and bilingual programs are pertinent to multiethnic desegregation but must also enjoy some independence from the constraints placed on regular programs. In other words, students in these programs are assigned by program location, not by racial/ethnic designation.

When these assumptions guided the planning effort, they also generated several pragmatic secondary assumptions. For example, the six principles cannot be realized without *redistributing students*. Bell,[3] Edmonds,[4] Colton,[5] and others have argued that the aims of the *Brown* decision can be met by redistributing resources rather than students or staff. This was not regarded as a workable possibility by parties or the court in Boston, where students and staff had been intentionally separated by race as part of a board policy of racial preference.

In devising a student redistribution policy, the masters and experts therefore concentrated on defining student composition ratios that reflected the subgroup proportions currently enrolled, and on developing means for annual adjustment of the ratios to correspond with demographic changes in residence and in school enrollments over time. Not only the ratios may change: the BP also provides for periodic changes in residence-based assignments. These can be phased in for incoming new students in grades 1, 6, and 9. Other changes to preserve ratios come up as schools are closed or converted to other uses, and as programs relocate. (A fixed attendance-zone plan can be modified without disrupting school continuities for children simply because the system copes every year with many other correlative changes.) Because a multiethnic remedy was sought, and because the system in 1975 was 52 percent white, 36 percent black, and 12 percent other minorities—with 90 percent of the latter being Hispanic—the ratios used were defined as white/black/other minority.

We did not think of the ratios as being governed by *citywide* composition, however, except where a school drew its students from a citywide pool of applicants. Instead, we thought of racial/ethnic ratios as varying to reflect subcommunities of the city such that some subdistricts would be whiter, some blacker, and some more Hispanic than others. Thus, we eschewed any notion of "racial balance," preferring representativeness instead and believing that desegregation *does not* equal majority white schools but rather refers to the absence of racial/ethnic barriers to access and group composition.

The BP assumed that integration, however desirable educationally, refers to coequality in interpersonal relations within a school and does not figure in a structural plan but rather comes up out of system policy and practice. (Implications of this assumption for implementation are examined in the Conclusion.) When a school board initiates a remedy, it may include status effects and other educationally pertinent features. When it defies the constitution and makes no acceptable plan, a court must limit *its* remedy more narrowly to stay within the bounds of the liability findings. So, too, socioeconomic status effects, while vital to the teaching and learning environment,[6] were regarded as lying outside the jurisdictional scope of the remedy.

Inasmuch as four of the six chief planners were research-informed educators, the question before the team was not one of using knowledge about optimal conditions for learning. It was instead one of locating the jurisdictional boundaries governing federal court intervention and then, working within those boundaries, attempting to preserve those optima which could be included. In other words, the connections between desegregation and learning are deep and extensive, but in a "race case" as the court and parties deemed it, only some of those connections could be built in the plan, while others remained the province of the Boston School Committee (board). This is one of the limitations characteristic of litigation as contrasted with board-initiated reform.

The BP was, for all of these limitations, exceptionally comprehensive. Its overarching goals were to achieve equal access to educational opportunities for all students; to eliminate the existing racially dual nature of the system; to eliminate racial identifiability in schools and programs; to require continuing affirmative action toward eliminating all vestiges of racial/ethnic discrimination; and to *upgrade* the structure, operations, and facilities so that as equal access took effect, educational benefits worth obtaining would be in place. These goals did not grow up out of local history, although the means for pursuing them were deeply affected thereby. The goals grew up out of the *Brown* decision, two decades of case law derived from that landmark, and the law of the Boston case formed during the two years preceding design of the BP itself. In this respect, the principles and the design features of the BP were neither novel nor unique to one situation but rather embody the *universal* remedial approaches hammered out nationwide since *Brown*. What was distinctive about the BP was its inclusive comprehensiveness, not its novelty.

2. Description of Boston

Boston is a 47.8-square-mile central city, one of the oldest in North America. A state capital and world class seaport, it lacks the heavy manufacturing base of cities such as Chicago, Cleveland, and Philadelphia, and its land mass is separated at several points by the harbor and the Charles River. Its population approached 700,000 in 1960, but it has been in decline since then and hosts fewer than 650,000 today. If its college-going youth population—greater Boston contains 60 institutions of postsecondary education—were set aside, its permanent resident population in 1980 would have been about 580,000. In 1970, the total city population was 75 percent white; by 1980 it was 66 percent white.

Public school development mirrored the historic changes of this relatively old city. The system is the oldest in the nation. It took its modern form in the 1840s. One of its schools, the Quincy, was built downtown in 1847 as the country's first multiclassroom structure designed specifically for public school use. It was closed, along with over thirty other facilities, most of them built before 1900, by the BP. The public system reached its apex of development between 1910 and 1929, paralleling the era when Irish-American political control over all parts of the public sector supplanted English-American or Yankee control. During the Great Depression, the city and its public schools suffered extreme economic setbacks. No new high schools were built, for example, from 1934 to 1971. At the same time the school staff became extremely inbred. Boston Teachers College, which later became Boston State College, supplied about 90 percent of the teacher force from among city-raised students, and senior administrators were drawn either from those ranks or from a small elite of graduate students supplied by Boston College, a Jesuit institution. Between 1920 and 1970, the traditions of patronage, cronyism, nepotism, and discrimination against ethnic minorities became the hallmarks of both the city government and the schools. These traditions owed much to the Yankees, whose banks, brokerage houses, law firms, and colleges had perfected the arts of inbreeding, discrimination, and exclusion across three centuries. Save for a brief period before the Great Depression, moreover, public schools in Boston did not receive the children of the rich and the professional elites. Protestant and Catholic children of the wealthy were enrolled in nonpublic schools.

Boston's schools were not only aged, dilapidated, and corrupt by 1975; they were also distributed across the face of the city in ways that corresponded to real estate development from 1840 to 1920. An estimated 50 out of 208 schools were so-called neighborhood schools.[7] In 1972, some

30,000 out of 90,000 students traveled two or more miles to get to school each day. The neighborhood schools were of great political salience, however, for Boston is composed of adjacent yet very separate *ethnic enclaves,* and some of these, such as Charlestown and East Boston, are separated from the mainland area of the city. In the tightest-knit of these enclaves, youth did not cross their turf boundaries for any reason other than travel to athletic events, and some adults never left their "islands."

Births in Boston began to decline in 1964. Households were aging; child-rearing families were migrating from New England to the Sunbelt as economic opportunities shifted nationally; and family planning reduced the size of the families who remained. For these reasons the public schools, which had endured overcrowding and double shifts in the 1960 to 1968 era, began to decline in enrollments thereafter. The system claimed it enrolled 96,516 students in November 1970, although later research suggests that the rolls were badly kept and probably reflected 5,000 or more "phantom students" in any one year.[8] By 1973, enrollment had dropped officially to 93,647.

Some 30 percent of the students in 1970 were black Americans, and some 64 percent were white. The black percentage had doubled during the 1960s, as out-migration by white households had doubled. Black immigration peaked and stabilized during that decade: there were 28,822 black students officially enrolled in 1970, and 26,630 enrolled in 1982. Hispanics and Asian Americans increased during the 1970s, doubling their student numbers as white numbers declined by half. The nonpublic schools, meanwhile, hosted over 40 percent of all children and youth and with the exception of two parish schools in the inner city, were 95 percent white from 1960 through 1982.

The BP tried to take all of these historical, geographic, ethnic, and demographic factors into deliberate account. *All parties had already agreed that students could not be desegregatively redistributed without the use of busing.*[9] There were not more than eight small neighborhoods with biracial residential settlements, nor were facilities deployed in accord with housing patterns. The only policy issue around busing was how much? How many white ethnic turfs would be crossed, and how many buses would come and go from Roxbury, the black subcommunity?

The planning team had one other unique challenge to address: The public schools had operated with up to thirteen different grade structures since 1955. There were K to 8 schools, grades 1 to 2 schools, grades 4 and 7 schools, and so forth. This had grown up to cope with overcrowding and to reinforce racial separation. Planning was so poor, moreover, that court records were filled with disputes over the student capacities of facilities. Grade structure uniformities were obviously essential, if the system was to be racially unified.

Dilapidated, fire-unsafe, jerry-built, racially split, and destructured as the Boston system was, some schools were still far superior to others educationally. It was the sense of this and the fact that the nearly all-white schools were, with few exceptions, the superior ones, that had triggered the class action suit itself. Thus, the planning team had to devise ways to equalize access, conserve good programs, stimulate the advent of more of them, and require fully multilingual orientation of all parents to all existing program options, all at the same time.

Some magnet schools were already in place. The masters were particularly impressed with Boston Technical High School, located in the heart of Roxbury, which was already desegregated because the quality of its pre-engineering program drew whites into an otherwise all-black neighborhood. There were other similar schools at all levels. There were also some authentically comprehensive high schools, including the newly constructed, seven-story English High School adjacent to the downtown business district. There were also six new facilities just becoming available through state funding.

For these reasons, the team imposed a uniform grade structure of grades 1 to 5, 6 to 8, and 9 to 12. Kindergartens should have been included, but not all facilities were equipped and state law defined preschool as optional, thus setting up a condition that set kindergartens outside the scope of the plan. Hindsight suggests this was a serious mistake, for it not only left many kindergartens racially segregated; it also created a disjuncture in student assignments between grades K and 1, which prepared kindergartners for life in one school and then assigned them to another school a year later. The uniform grade structure adopted enabled the masters to require four-year comprehensive high schools in every community district (bounded subcommunities built up along voting ward lines but including parts of Roxbury in each). These high schools became the organizing points for the plan.

Examination schools, alternative schools created in the 1960s, and schools with already established reputations for being magnetic educationally, were placed in a Citywide Magnet District. Some others were added and assigned magnet program themes because of their geographic locations and in order to make this *voluntary* desegregation of the plan as large as possible. The BP designated twenty-two schools as citywide magnets, with space for 22 percent of the system's students. These were dotted throughout the city, and entrance to all save three examination schools was to be by computerized lottery of parent applications.

The Boston School Committee (BSC) proposed that fifty-five magnet schools hosting over half of all students be created. The masters rejected this, noting the impossibility of developing their magnetism on this scale and noting the importance of preserving a balance and coequality between the voluntary magnet sector and the community districts. They also selected schools for their location at points where cross-race movement would be vigorously demonstrated. Residents of community districts where magnets were based were given a preference in the lottery for up to 25 percent of the seats.

3. Scope of the Plan

The BP was limited to the public schools of Boston. An interdistrict metropolitan remedy that included twenty-two surrounding suburbs would have been preferable for desegregative workability and for educational quality alike. The masters considered this but rejected it because of the absence of a factual showing that "racially discriminatory acts of the state or local school districts . . . have been a substantial cause of interdistrict segregation," as in *Milliken v. Bradley* (1974, 418 U.S.). Greater Boston would be ideally suited to a metropolitan plan. The suburbs lie within a twenty-mile radius; transport is feasible; they host about 75,000 students, 96 percent of them white; and the METCO Program has carried on one-way busing of urban blacks to suburban schools with state funding since 1968.[10] The BP was also restricted to public schools only in a setting where over 40 percent of all students were nonpublic.

The BP treats all of Boston's districts in the same manner except for East Boston. This is an island subcommunity in the harbor, located next to Logan International Airport, and attached to the mainland of the city by a bridge and one long underwater tunnel running in each direction. East Boston schools were 95 percent white in 1975, but the population of the island was in decline. Public school students there had dropped from 7,000 in 1960 to 5,700 in 1975 and were projected to drop to 4,000 by 1980. With five exceptions, moreover, the fourteen usable facilities in East Boston were in very poor condition.

In order to avoid busing 2,500 children in and 2,500 others out of East Boston during the tunnel rush hour each morning, the court took other desegregative steps there. It designated two of the best elementary facilities as citywide magnet schools, one with a science and mathematics theme and one with a language arts emphasis. It converted a splendid new building just being erected into a city-wide magnet science high school, and it accepted a proposal from the School Committee to desegregate East Boston High School by use of a citywide business magnet. By 1977 black and other minority students were volunteering to enroll in these East Boston-based schools in large numbers, and East Boston whites moved voluntarily toward other magnets outside their neighborhood. Hence, the BP affected East Boston profoundly; yet, it left six old neighborhood elementaries intact as white schools.

The racial/ethnic ratios in the BP were based upon the proportions of white, black, and other minority students residing in each community district, as shown in Table 6-1.

Table 6-1 Public School Students in Community Districts of Boston by Race, 1975

| District | Percent | | | N |
	White	Black	Other Minority	Total
1. Mission Hill-Brighton	44	33	23	9,034
2. Jamaica Plain	45	40	15	9,930
3. West Roxbury	56	39	5	12,710
4. Hyde Park	61	35	4	8,972
5. Dorchester	45	48	7	17,214
6. South Boston	53	33	14	11,514
7. Madison Park	40	35	25	9,772
8. East Boston	95	3	2	5,767
Citywide	52	36	12	84,913

Four of the eight community districts were thus less than 50 percent white from the onset of the plan. Setting East Boston aside, seven varied from the citywide ratio by no more than 25 percent of the average. Therefore, the BP gave a guideline for *each school* within a community district of variance by not more than 25 percent from the district ratios. Each citywide magnet school was allowed to vary from the average by no more than plus or minus 5 percent. Thus, in district 1 in 1975, the ideal percent white (44 percent) could vary in any one school from a high of 55 percent to a low of 33 percent to allow for errors in planning data, sudden facility changes, or short-term demographic shifts. In magnet schools, the error term was smaller because assignments could be made from applications citywide. Most crucially, the ratios were for K to 13 resident students and were to be recomputed each April, prior to planning new assignments.[11]

The BP permits racially isolated schools only in East Boston. It does not presume to "balance" schools in the rest of Boston, however, any more than it leaves any others unaffected. The planning team was explicit in enabling diverse ratios as an antidote to the specious assumption made by some planners that majority white schools are a precondition for desegregation.[12] Initially, in fact, the masters had recommended one community district be 70 percent black, not only to be representative of that subcommunity but in order to demonstrate that racial/ethnic desegregation can succeed whether whites are dominant or subdominant. Following objections from the State Board and plaintiffs' counsel, this feature was dropped from the plan. Even so, the plan continues to rest on the premise that the desired mix should fall within a 70 to 30 range at best and an 80 to 20 range, at least, if each group is to have some social influence over its setting.[13]

The citywide voluntary segment of the BP has succeeded in nearly every school in every year from 1975 through 1982. When too few parents from one group applied in the first three years, some magnets were composed with fewer than maximum student numbers. As the orientation plan took hold and as word of mouth spread that these schools were safe, less tense, and educationally desirable, however, all racial/ethnic groups began to oversubscribe. And, as enrollments declined citywide, the numbers stayed high in the voluntary magnets, rising from 22 percent of all students in 1975 to 29 percent in 1982.

Some community districts have fared less well. For example, West Roxbury was set as 56 percent white in 1975. Resistance to desegregation was so extensive among white parents in that subcommunity, and access to nonpublic schools was so facilitated by higher income levels, that this district was 36 percent white by 1982. Dorchester Community District went from 48 percent to 19 percent white over the same period, as that subcommunity was becoming a residential extension of Roxbury for minority families as early as 1965.[14]

The overall drop in white students from about 50,000 in 1973 to 18,000 in 1982 has had ramifications throughout the community district schools. Given the annually revised guidelines, most facilities are in compliance, but the white proportion has fallen from 52 percent to 32 percent, and some elementary schools are therefore less than 20 percent white, the minimum implied as acceptable by the masters.

Contrary to many journalistic accounts, the BP itself did *not* cause the change from a majority white to minority white condition. Somewhere between 7,000 and 8,000 whites withdrew from the Boston public schools in 1974 and 1975 in reaction against desegregation. After 1976, this flight pattern ended, and from 1976 through 1982 the system has retained its full share of white students. The double effects of birth declines which began in 1964 and accelerated each year through 1980, combined with household out-migrations to the Sunbelt, created the remaining declines. Had Boston not been obliged to desegregate in 1974 and again in 1975, I would estimate that the proportion of white students would have fallen from about 55 percent in 1973 to about 39 percent in 1982.

By 1981 school closings had reduced the number of schools from 208 in 1974 to 123, first in order to upgrade facilities by terminating use of those deemed fire unsafe and structurally unsound, and then to reduce excess capacity. Of the remaining facilities, twenty-seven or one in five were out of full compliance with plan guidelines for students in November 1981, but all except five were within 3 percent of goal. Among the five, two community district high schools, both in Dorchester, were glaringly black segregated. Assigned whites had withdrawn and the School Department had deprived the schools of adequate staff, leadership, and repairs. Upon challenges from plaintiffs, the School Committee pledged to remedy these two schools by 1982.[15]

The score card after eight years of implementing the BP shows that, including the nine districts, 74 percent of all students are currently enrolled in fully desegregated schools. Another 16 percent are enrolled in fully mixed schools which are a few percentage points short of white ratios. The remaining 10 percent are in racially identifiable, black or Hispanic schools—but they are not there for lack of alternatives open to them nor have they been intentionally isolated. On this record, Boston very likely has achieved more complete student desegregation than any other northern city system hosting over 25,000 students.

4. How Equity Was Achieved

Equity has two primary conceptual elements when applied to public school systems: (a) Are resources matched with needs and interests in a *fair*, that is, evenhanded way? (b) Where deprivation has occurred for minorities to the relative advantage of the majority, are these inequities that have accumulated deliberately offset or countervailed? In Boston two other elements which are arguably relevant were *not* included. These are equalization of all facilities and equalization of learning outcomes.

The two primary elements are fulfilled in several ways:

A) The system was unified organizationally so that its chain of authority was made to operate in the same way for all constituencies.

B) The system was rather evenly divided into eight community districts so that each had one or at most two four-year comprehensive high schools linked in feeder patterns with neighboring middle and elementary schools. Resident students were guaranteed seats in these schools, could not transfer among them, and could not cross district boundaries to enroll except for vocational, bilingual, and special education programs.

C) A ninth citywide magnet district offered alternatives on a universalistic, computer-randomized basis to interested applicants. Desegregatively controlled transfers between community district schools and citywide magnets allowed for reasonable freedom of movement.

D) Students were assigned to community district schools on the basis of geocode units from a map of each district. These are like census tracts and were taken from a map in use by the school department, which broke Boston into about 830 small areal units, some comprising only two blocks where population densities are high and some twenty blocks or more. Thus, a student went with his neighborhood group to a nearby walk-in facility at one level and was bused with his group to a more distant facility at another level. Average within-district distances average 2.5 miles and none exceeds 5 miles. Students assigned to magnet schools are bused to elementaries if more than 1 mile distant, to middle schools if more than 1.5 miles, and to high schools if more than 2 miles. The geocode units attached to each community district school ensured white as well as minority busing.

E) All high school students, with the exception of the examination schools, were guaranteed a comprehensive program of academic, vocational, business, and general instruction. Occupational skills training was made available to all but exam students by the court-ordered erection of the Hubert Humphrey Occupational Resource Center, a $40 million facility located in Roxbury but near the business district and open to all for part-time enrollment.[16]

F) Competitive examination and school grade averages were made the sole means for admission to the examination schools (where patronage-based admissions were once commonplace), and 35 percent of entering seventh and ninth grade seats were reserved for black and Hispanic examinees who placed above the median on the annual test.[17] Before court intervention, two of the three examination schools (Boston Latin School and the Latin Academy) enrolled less than 15 percent black and Hispanic students. The remedy is permanently continuous year after year. The goal of 35 percent was attained for entering classes by 1978, and in 1982 Latin Academy was 38 percent and Latin School 27 percent black and Hispanic overall.

G) Bilingual programs were offered to six lingual minorities, including Cape Verdeans and French Haitians; this number was later expanded to nine. These students were assigned before regular students and could cross district boundaries. The numbers of bilingual students grew from 2,200 in 1975 to 7,000 in 1982. Programs are located in schools relatively near residential concentrations of each language group, although only one small elementary facility, the Hernandez, was permitted to be over half bilingual; and state standards were used to set the size of program "clusters." For instance, a high school cluster should contain one hundred or more and a staff of five or more.

H) Students with special needs were mainstreamed wherever possible. Where they required substantially separate classes, they were assigned *before* regular students, and boundaries and geocodes were ignored. Resource rooms and special educators were mandated by the BP for every school, and several special schools for the severely handicapped, visually and speech impaired, and severely disturbed were provided. The system served only 1,481 severely handicapped students in 1975. By 1982 it was geared to serve 2,900, while enrollments overall declined from 85,000 to 56,584. And, by 1982, only one special needs facility was segregated racially—this because of a lack of enough residential schools in the private sector willing to host black children. (Under state law, if an educational plan for a handicapped student calls for residential treatment, the state pays the expense.)

I) The BP did not redesign or redistribute extracurricular programs, but it did require affirmative action of all staff to ensure equal participation. When black students were denied opportunity to join in varsity football tryouts and practice at South Boston High School in 1975, for example, student and parent complaints led the court to place this school in receivership, to transfer the coach, and replace the headmaster.[18] The court also required the formation of Racial-Ethnic Student Councils.

J) Buildings were *relatively* equalized in several ways. The most unsafe and unfit structures were closed for school use. Repairs and renovations were ordered on other plants. New buildings being built were reviewed and put to new, more equitable uses than planned. With all of these efforts, the results remain uneven. Boston is filled with schools lacking playgrounds, gymnasiums, cafeterias, real libraries, and auditoriums. Heating and ventilation are ragged, and some buildings are severely vandalized. Some schools built since 1968 are superb structures, while most built between 1880 and 1929 are falling apart. Many of them were cheaply built a century ago.

The court attempted repeatedly to require ten-year facility planning to improve and equalize these conditions. The city and School Department avoided action repeatedly in an effort to save money and to escape the agony of closing schools. Minority parents joined with attorneys for plaintiffs and the teachers' union to forestall changes in the status quo, preferring their own dilapidated buildings to uncertain changes. In 1981 fiscal cutbacks became so severe, however, that the School Committee closed twenty-seven of its worst facilities in one planning proposal approved by the court.

K) The basic transportation plan has already been described. By 1982 transportation was being provided for 31,371 students out of 58,540, compared with 30,000 out of about 90,000 in 1972. The proportions are currently about half the white, black, and other minority groups.

Equity has been achieved through transportation services in several ways. Two-way busing is universal; proportions are roughly equal across racial/ethnic groups; and carriage is much more widely available than it was before desegregation, while average distances traveled are shorter. After initial waves of white neighborhood hostility, requests for bus service multiplied everywhere for reasons of traffic and weather safety, crossing of rail and thruway barriers, and special, bilingual, and vocational education program access. Boston still lacks a fleet of its own buses, and charter contracting has been freighted with scandals, litigation over charges, and ragged delivery. There are also still many difficulties associated with the use of mass transit buses and subways for some high school students.[19] Overall, however, busing was a code word for the anti-desegregation movement; yet, the BP has installed the city's first complete system of student transportation, with distances comparable to those traveled for twenty-five years in surrounding suburban districts.

Some 41 percent of those bused are citywide magnet students who are transported up to 4.5 miles each way, or an average of 3 miles. As 29 percent of all students are thus enrolled, this network absorbs a larger share of transportation resources. Some 59 percent of those bused are community district students, and 71 percent of all students enroll in these schools.

5. Policy Making and Staffing

The Boston School Committee of five members elected at large for two-year terms makes policy for the system.* Within the confines of State Board of Education mandates and legislative statutes, BSC is in theory autonomous. While it makes its own annual budget, however, the mayor controls the actual revenues and may cut off expenditures in case of overruns. Under a recent referendum, BSC will be elected from thirteen districts as of November 1983, and the boundaries do not coincide with the community districts drawn by the court.

No racial or ethnic minority person was elected to the BSC between 1880 and 1977, when John O'Bryant, a black educator, was elected citywide. In 1980 O'Bryant was reelected and Jean Maguire, black director of METCO, took a seat. Both events are causally connected with the advent of school desegregation. The BP did not touch upon the method of election or any aspect of the laws and customs governing board composition or scope of authority. A separate federal suit litigated in 1976 failed to increase the representativeness of the BSC.

The 1983 BSC is not only different in racial composition from those in the 1950-74 era; it also contains three women; it is no longer a stepping stone to higher office; and the members are no longer professional politicians. One member is from a very wealthy family and is a former teacher. Among the others, three are salaried professionals and one is a housewife. Perhaps the greatest change other than the absence of a disposition to campaign against desegregation is the absence of graft and patronage kickbacks. Pre-desegregation boards were notorious for their profiteering ventures. Two members were tried for bribery and extortion in 1980. One confessed and was convicted. Another had been convicted in 1976. By creating a chain of administrative command; requiring permanent, full-time principals in all buildings; creating a merit and equity-based screening and rating procedure for administrative appointments; removing student assignments from the political marketplace; and installing monitoring operations, the BP cut the lines of patronage and thus changed the very reasons for seeking election to the BSC.

The superintendent is the chief officer hired to manage the system under policies made by the BSC. The system has retained six superintendents since 1972. Some were not renewed after three-year contracts; one was fired after two years; one died of a heart attack; a fifth was made acting; and the sixth, the first journeyman administrator brought in from out of state in over fifty years, survived a one-year contract and gained a four-year term in 1982. Until 1979, the position was so unempowered that it lacked control over finances, personnel, facilities, maintenance, and most aspects of curriculum.

The court plan did not modify this condition, but it did introduce a chain

*An enlarged Committee now includes members elected at large and by districts.

of command. It required the appointment of a deputy superintendent, community district superintendents, and permanent principals and headmasters for every facility. In 1974 about 60 percent of the schools lacked permanent, full-time administrators.

The BP assumed that the best available teaching and learning environment is a facility that hosts full-time staff and students and enjoys some self-determination of its small community of activity. Thus, the masters also rejected proposals for *part-time* sites for "desegregative experiences" as less than optimal. The BP also required the screening and rating of all but the superintendent, deputy, and their immediate assistants. Screening committees composed of parents, teachers, and administrators as specified in a court order introduced not only a merit-based but a desegregative procedure, so that one black appointment was made for every white until at least 20 percent of the administrative positions at all levels were black. In 1971, 4 percent of all administrators were black. By 1980 the proportion reached 20 percent.

In addition, the court established a Department of Implementation (DI), headed by an associate superintendent. It initially contained sixty full-time staff, managed by a black director, and it became the headquarters unit charged with implementing student assignments and managing student records, transportation, facilities, and public information. It also carried the tasks of monitoring compliance, arranging parent council elections, and planning for modifications. Staff of the DI have been "frozen" in place and protected, through court vigilance, against undue manipulation by the superintendent and the BSC.

Apart from the DI, desegregatively appointed administrators serve for three years and have renewable contracts. The units of headquarters and the staffs of district offices have been reorganized so often by the passing parade of superintendents that the court and its officers cannot readily keep track of the players, let alone changes in titles. Under the aegis of the BP, however, the DI, district superintendents, and building principals and headmasters have become *the* line officers of the system.

Nothing has equaled the importance for administrative reform of the introduction of *computerization*. The system's only computer was lodged in a school three miles from headquarters until the court ordered that new, better machines be placed in the DI. In 1978 under the leadership of a former bilingual teacher with a genius for computer applications and the integrity of granite, the computer brought student records under control for the first time. "Phantoms"—no-shows, withdrawals, and duplicate names—were cleaned out. Soon after, transportation plans and school applications were computerized. By 1982 financial accounting became a real operation, and personnel records were on the verge of electronic integration. Lacking this development, the BP could never have been implemented. The advent of the computer, incidentally, was made feasible by a relocation of school system headquarters from shabby, cramped quarters into a renovated, ten-story structure near the federal courthouse.

All administrative ranks have been fully desegregated except for assistant principals. There, turnover has been slow, and all but 8 percent are white. To date, very few Hispanic or Asian-American appointments have been made, as these are encouraged but not mandated by the court. The court order requires eventual attainment of a 25 percent black administrative presence. This standard was not pegged to student ratios but rather to the residential population overall.

Until 1978, the court took a formal affirmative action approach to faculty desegregation. In 1972, 8 percent of the 4,500 teachers were black, and 74 percent of them taught in majority black schools. The court set a 20 percent black teacher minimum in 1975 and an eventual goal of 25 percent, but the approach ordered did not work and, on complaint by plaintiffs, the court revised its order and required a 1.5 percent increase in black teachers annually, from a 1978 base of 14 percent. The 20 percent minimum was attained in 1981, coincident with the first wave of teacher layoffs. The staff had been expanded to 5,443 in 1975, up from 4,500 in 1972, and it was maintained at above 5,000 by the BSC until 1981, while the number of students declined by nearly 30,000.

In 1981 the court upheld the principle of desegregation of faculty, thus overriding the strict seniority clause in the union contract, in spite of a vote to the contrary by the BSC. This order was upheld on appeal. About 700 teachers were laid off in 1981, and another 400 or more in 1982. Had the 20 percent standard been relinquished, hundreds of recently recruited black teachers would have been the first to be fired. Again, the standard was not pegged to enrollments but to the city's population and the teacher labor force estimates made in 1974.

The BP also required a reasonable dispersion of black teachers across all schools. While this was necessary at the outset in order to redistribute the black teachers segregated in black schools, it gradually generated serious hardships in schools where only six out of sixty teachers were black.[20] In addition, as "riffing" (reductions in force) and bumping began in 1981, the problems of distribution became exacerbated, especially where too few or too many black teachers got relocated. Personnel data are only now becoming reliable enough to allow effective monitoring, however. The records were so chaotic even by 1981 that nearly a hundred teachers were incorrectly terminated and had to be restored. For all of this, the teacher force has been successfully desegregated in Boston.

The BP made no provision for staff development, although the teachers' union pleaded for in-service training. The court and other parties regarded this—in spite of advice from the court experts—as the province of the BSC, and it did as little as possible in this regard. When it did provide a few workshops, training was often given by administrators whose schools had suffered from racial violence because of their own ignorance.

The lack of staff development services in general and intergroup relations training in particular has been a source of costly setbacks in progress toward educational improvement. Until 1978 excessive numbers of black students, out of all proportion to their ratios, were failed academically, suspended, or classified as retarded.

6. School-Community Relations

Boston's parent organization before desegregation was the Home and School Association. It had three noteworthy characteristics. Unlike PTAs (Parent Teacher Associations), it was financed and controlled politically by the BSC; some members helped raise funds for BSC members' election campaigns and enjoyed patronage in return; and its membership was 90 percent white parents. The court allowed it to serve as an intervenor in the remedial phase of the BP, where it vigorously opposed the plan from 1975 through 1978.

As a countervailing force, the BP ordered into existence four types of structures: (1) Elective Racial-Ethnic Parent Councils (REPCs) for all schools, to improve race relations, monitor compliance, and advise on programs, (2) District Advisory Councils composed of parent representatives from the REPCs, teachers, and a few other agency members such as professors from paired colleges, (3) a Citywide Parents Advisory Council (CPAC) to give umbrella oversight and spokesmanship for parents, with a city-funded budget of about $500,000 per year, and (4) a Citywide Coordinating Committee of about twenty members appointed by the court, intended to serve as a desegregation policy guidance body, with powers to research, evaluate, publish, and confer regularly with the BSC. The first two units have half-time secretary/coordinators on pay.

Two kinds of assumptions impelled this plan. One was the court's belief that, through these organizations, intergroup bonds would develop, along with a base of support for the equity aims of the BP. Boston was "special" in that extremely few elected officials, business leaders, religious leaders, or civic associations ever voiced any support for court-ordered school desegregation. The court expected that these newly created units would come to play that role over time. The second assumption embraced by the court came from the masters, the experts, and above all from the community relations service director, Martin Walsh: these advisors had a view of public education which assumed that parent inputs are necessary for the achievement of quality desegregated education. They saw parents as a force for the improvement of school practices as well as an antidote to the traditionalism of the BSC and its central office bureaucracy.

The Citywide Coordinating Committee never fulfilled its mission. It was deeply divided from within because opponents to the BP conflicted with supporters, and it was ignored and rebuffed by the BSC. The court dissolved it in 1978 and gave its powers to CPAC. By then, CPAC and the Bilingual Master Parents Advisory Committee (MPAC), mandated by state law, had become substantial forces in school politics. They played a big part in electing the first moderate BSC in decades. They became avenues for the development and emergence of citywide civic leaders from the minority committees, and they helped to stave off disintegration of the system (see Conclusion).

Increasingly, however, they aligned with the teachers' union to resist school closings. They resisted policy movement to adapt to the exigencies of enrollment and resource declines, and they seldom emerged as advocates for the BP itself. Paradoxically, in short, parent inputs did not intensify the base of support for desegregation or for adaptive change; yet, without the presence of leadership and service generated by these organizations, it is probable that the turning point toward BSC moderation and a new rapprochement between white BSC members and black and Hispanic constituents would never have been reached.[21] Their contribution to *structural* revision in the degree of minority inclusion in school affairs cannot be overstated.

In 1982, CPAC began a self-evaluation and replanning effort of its own. It is now mature and capable of charting its future course. If the court approves its recommendations (or many of them), progress toward much fuller parent participation will be made. Prior to this, much of the electoral and committee functioning of the REPCs has been fragmentary.

The BP also designed an elaborate network of college, business, and cultural agency pairings. Some twenty-three colleges and universities, twenty business firms, and innumerable museums and arts institutions and companies are paired with specific schools or with whole community districts in order to provide support and technical assistance, schoolwork explorations, and performing arts activities. Most of the college and cultural pairings have been funded each year by the State Board of Education. Businesses and industries contribute their resources.

School partnership and adopt-a-school innovations have become widespread nationally since the BP in 1975, and some pairing experiments went on in New York City, Kansas City, and elsewhere in the late 1960s. Nothing before or since, from Dallas to Chicago, has equaled the scale, variety, and imaginativeness of the pairings in Boston. The positive impacts of the pairing effort have yet to be researched, but when they are, they will prove to be substantial.

Because of the hostile and indifferent disposition of the BSC toward the pairings from 1975 through 1977, and because of the very cautious approaches taken by the leadership of most of the paired institutions, the vast potential of the linkages was permanently blunted.[22] In addition, in this early period, few principals, teachers, and parent leaders were at all ready to make optimal use of their partners. If the pairings can survive federal, state, and local resource cutbacks, however, and if the voluntary commitments do not disappear when the court withdraws from the case, the potential will continue to ramify and grow.

A serious administrative flaw in the pairings has been the absence of senior officers and staff charged with coordinating and adjusting the activities. This grew out of early BSC defiance, and the coordinating procedures never took adequate root in the shifting sands of headquarters. Several college and university presidents worked hard to coordinate their pairing activities, taking up the slack induced by the BSC; but the long-term successes of pairing have come from faculty-to-faculty collaboration at particular schools where principals and parents have also encouraged co-development. Some outstanding achievements have resulted at the school site level.

Conclusion

The BP was forged during six weeks of intense planning by the masters and experts, followed by six more weeks of hearings and revisions by Judge W. Arthur Garrity, Jr., and his advisors. It has been augmented and amended on at least 300 occasions by the court during a period of seven years.

It differed from many court plans from the pre-*Keyes* decision era in several vital respects. It conceived of racial equity in a more comprehensive and detailed way, prescribing student and staff redistribution in all schools at all levels. It intruded deeply into organizational prescriptions because the system was so divided, chaotic, and corrupt that anything less would have meant that the plan would have remained unimplemented. And, following Judge Garrity's directive, the BP "expressed a deep educational concern."

None of the plan's elements was novel. Each had been designed and tested somewhere else. But the number of these elements and their patterning were unequivocally grander than any equivalent remedial plans in other large urban districts. Perhaps more vital is the fact that the *court did not compromise* on any of the constitutional issues. It came closest to doing so in East Boston and in not including kindergartners, but on the big questions of unifying the system, eliminating racial identifiability, and ensuring equal access, the court went the full distance.

Going the distance means that temporizing or partial remedial design elements were nowhere substituted for the real resolution of equity issues. For example, magnet schools were used as a tool for student desegregation but only within the framework of a comprehensive mandatory plan.[23] So, too, a series of black schools were not left in isolation and then offered open enrollment options or freedom of choice palliatives. When opponents of desegregation heard the plan outlined on television and radio, they knew at once that the BP was a "root and branch" remedy that would prove transformative. *More* disturbing to these interest groups was the fact that the student assignment procedures not only relocated whites into formerly black schools; they also ended the long-standing arrangements through which patronized parents gained special access to the best opportunities the dual system had to offer. Similarly, thousands of veteran white teachers lost their hold on relatively favored niches in the system and found themselves reassigned.

On matters of student redistribution, equalized access, staff desegregation, administrative appointments and desegregation, safety and security procedures, transportation, and the expansion of bilingual and special education services, the BP was powerfully transformative following implementation. By 1979, moreover, the newly unified system had a biracial board of policy makers; it had begun to behave inclusively toward minorities; and the means for controlling one's fate as a black parent or child had improved tremendously.

As these transformations took place, however, Boston's leaders infused the mass media nationwide with reports of their school system as besieged and ruined by court intervention. Mayor Kevin White traveled to other northern cities to present his version of how costly and damaging the BP was. Other city officials followed suit, and school administrators never missed a chance to present their programs to journalists as devastated by the court and its plan. Black and white moderates alike even campaigned citywide for elections in 1977, 1978, and 1979 on the basis of opposition to elements of the BP. By 1977 educational decision makers nationwide had become imbued with the slogan, "Let's not have another Boston."

To this day, as the court completes its withdrawal of direct supervision and mediation, the notion that the basic features of the BP are "rigid" and should be revised continues to haunt the city. The actual rigidities are the very tools—subdistrict boundaries, grade structure uniformities, mandatory assignments, and staff desegregation even in the face of layoffs—which made the plan a monument to the principles set forth in *Brown*. Where they appear to some critics to be rigid, the masters and the judge answered that the injustices were so deep, long-standing, and massive—and the BSC defiance was so unremitting—that nothing less stringent would work. Besides, weakly structured plans and remedies that make capricious trade-offs among interests often generate short-term public acceptance at the price of longer-term inequities that get neglected or even enlarged in the process.

The serious deficiencies of the BP do not reside in these tools. They are, in this writer's opinion, of three kinds. First, the plan lacked adequate foresight. Its designers lacked the vision to foresee the rate of enrollment declines, resource cutbacks, the demise of both federal and local funds for certain crucial programs, and the widespread turning away from concern with racial justice. Worst-case scenarios fashioned by the planners fell short of real trends.

Second, the BP is too complicated. The vacuum created by BSC defiance of the court was so great that it pulled the court too far into administrative rule making. Only when the teacher desegregation order was revised toward a single crude standard of annual gains in percentage of black teachers, for example, was progress achieved. Moreover, the more elaborate the court planning became as others refused to take initiatives, the more the complexities could be exploited for both loopholes and the cultivation of excuses for failures to comply.

Third, and in this analyst's view, most crucially, the BP—for all of its noteworthy educational elements—did not deal squarely with effecting reforms in school practices. Staff development, race relations, support services for students, curriculum change toward multicultural concerns, methods for safeguarding the academic welfare of learners, and procedures for evaluating school outcomes were left to the purview of the BSC and the superintendent. Attorneys for the plaintiffs were the first to take this legal tack. They avoided the educational domain assiduously (except for a special subsuit on student suspensions brought by the Children's Defense Fund) and argued that this was a "race case." When the plaintiffs' attorneys changed tack in 1980 and began to argue educational issues, it was too late. In a litigative situation where plaintiffs remained silent on matters of educational equity and defendants challenged the scope of the court's jurisdiction at every turn, the absence of square confrontation of these urgent issues was to be expected. As the Boston schools staggered under declines in students and then funds, however, the delivery of defective services to students—below standard in every respect in 1970 and in 1975—could not be prevented by reference to the court plan.

The BP achieved its racial equity goals. It also upgraded facilities, reformed the integrity of the board and administration, and brought excluded minorities into the circle of system concerns. But the BP, having gone this far, failed by circumstance to go far enough in reforming the provision of public education itself. As the clouds of indifference toward civil rights and of economic depression gather over the nation, there is the possibility that the great gains made under *Morgan v. Kerrigan, et al.*, in Boston will continue to be eroded. The court is currently engaged in the final, closing task of attempting to consolidate those precious gains for the future.

Notes

1. Because the remedial phase of this case is eight years old, this chapter is necessarily based on implementation events and outcomes, not solely on planning. For a more detailed study of both, see Robert A. Dentler and Marvin B. Scott, *Schools on Trial: An Inside Account of the Boston Desegregation Case* (Cambridge, Mass.: Abt Books, 1981).

2. *Green v. County School Board,* 1968, 391 U.S. 430, 442.

3. Derrick A. Bell, Jr., *Race, Racism, and American Law* (Boston: Little Brown, 1980); and "Integration: A No Win Policy for Blacks?" *Integrated Education* (Sept. 1972): 32-45.

4. Ronald R. Edmonds, "You Can Get Hurt Waiting for the Bus," *Journal of Intergroup Relations* 2 (Oct. 1972): 13-23; and "Desegregation Planning and Educational Equity," *Theory into Practice* 17 (Fall 1978): 12-16.

5. David Colton, *The Feasibility of a Metropolitan School Desegregation Plan for the City and County of St. Louis* (U.S. District Court for Eastern Missouri, 1981).

6. Robert L. Crain and Rita Mahard, *Desegregation and Black Achievement* (Santa Monica, Calif.: Rand, 1977). For an example of how a school board can factor socioeconomic status (SES) into its own desegregation planning, see William T. Donoho, Jr., and Robert A. Dentler, "Busing Toward Excellence: The Quest for Quality Desegregated Education in Harrisburg," *The Urban Review* 6, no. 1 (Sept.-Oct., 1972); 31-34.

7. Louise Day Hicks of the Boston School Committee rose to a seat in Congress on the popularity of the myth of the neighborhood school, which she helped to invent and enshrine. In Boston a few public schools enrolled very nearby resident children, including those in South Boston, Hicks's constituency. Most schools were built on the cheapest available vacant land, however, and residential attendance zones were a bewildering and provisional patchwork of political expedience before 1974. For an early sketch of the myth, see Rosemary Gunning, "Busing Versus the Neighborhood School," *The Urban Review* 6, no. 1 (Sept.-Oct. 1972): 2-10.

8. Dentler and Scott, *Schools on Trial,* pp. 25-27.

9. *Morgan v. Kerrigan,* "Memorandum of Decision," June 5, 1975, pp. 56-58.

10. James E. Teele, *Evaluating School Busing: Case of Boston's Operation Exodus* (New York: Praeger, 1973). Also, Phyllis Myers, "Boston's METCO: What to Do Until the Solution Arrives," *City* 5 (Jan. 1974): 80-82.

11. In 1982 the court allowed a motion by the BSC to set the ratios each April based on K to 5, 6 to 8, 9 to 12 grade levels in an effort to accommodate the differential effects of lower grade level enrollment declines.

12. See George R. Meadows, "Open Enrollment and Fiscal Incentives," *School Review* 84, no. 3 (May 1976): 449-462, for the updated version of the "tipping point" argument.

13. Charles V. Willie, *The Sociology of Urban Education* (Lexington, Mass.: Lexington Books, D. C. Heath, 1978), pp. 67-68.

14. While West Roxbury typifies localities where white middle- and upper middle-class parents transfer their children from public to nonpublic schools with the advent of desegregation, and while Dorchester typifies a locality in transition from a white to a black residential area (with or without school desegregation), both were also being affected profoundly by severe declines in annual births from 1964 to 1978.

15. This pledge expressed an important change in BSC policies from neglect and defiance to concern and moderation vis-à-vis court orders. Still, the ability to plan and really implement desegregative changes lags behind policy: the two high schools remain generally unchanged as of August 25, 1982.

16. The center represents the court's deep concern to equalize treatment in public education, for the state board had erected many superb vocational schools throughout the state between 1965 and 1975, while the BSC and City Hall in Boston did not seek an equivalent facility.

17. Contrary to local popular thinking, desegregation neither demolished nor diluted these "elite schools," as the United States Court of Appeals described them; rather, it boosted their sagging enrollments and beefed up their staffs.

18. Dentler and Scott, *Schools on Trial,* pp. 170-186.

19. The BP permitted continued partial reliance on mass transit for high school students, as requested by the BSC. This was a planning error inasmuch as mass transit has staggered under inflation, cut its services, and been ungovernable (not surprisingly) by agreements with the BSC and City Hall.

20. Dentler and Scott, *Schools on Trial,* pp. 196-201.

21. For a different viewpoint, see Marilyn Gittell, Bruce Hoffocker, Eleanor Rollins, and Samuel Foster, *Citizen Organizations: Citizen Participation in Educational Decision-Making,* final research report, National Institute of Education Contract 400-76-0115 (Boston: Institute for Responsive Education, July 1979).

22. Dentler and Scott, *Schools on Trial,* pp. 121-143.

23. Eugene C. Royster, D. Catherine Baltzell, and Fran C. Simmons, *Study of the Emergency School Aid Magnet School Program,* Contract OE-300-77-0393 (Cambridge, Mass.: ABT Associates, 1979). For more complete data on magnets, see *Interim Report on the Magnet Schools Survey,* Contract No. SB5308(a)82-C018 (Washington, D.C.: J. H. Lowry and Associates, 1982).

Chapter 7

A Plan for Increasing Educational Opportunities and Improving Racial Balance in Milwaukee

David A. Bennett

Section I—A Brief History of the Milwaukee Desegregation Case

The Milwaukee desegregation case began in December 1965, when Lloyd Barbee, president of the local National Association for the Advancement of Colored People (NAACP) and lawyer for the plaintiffs, brought suit against the Milwaukee Board of School Directors, the superintendent, and the secretary-business manager, on behalf of forty-one named black and nonblack children. The case was finally brought to trial in 1973.

On January 19, 1976, the United States District Court for the Eastern District of Wisconsin handed down a decision that found that the entire Milwaukee school system was unconstitutionally segregated. At the same time, the court handed down a partial judgment that directed the Milwaukee Public Schools to begin immediately to formulate plans to eliminate every form of segregation in the public schools of Milwaukee, including all consequences and vestiges of segregation previously practiced by the defendants. The court appointed a special master, John Gronouski (former postmaster general of the United States) to work with the school system to formulate a plan to meet compliance.

The court gave its approval to the plan that the school administration submitted on July 9, 1976. Exactly fifty-nine days remained before the start of school on September 7, when the court ordered that at least fifty-three schools—one-third of the total—had to be within a racial balance range of 25 to 45 percent black. Only fourteen schools met this standard as the school system approached the beginning of the 1976-77 school year.

The traditional third-Friday-in-September enrollment report to the State Department of Public Instruction provided the baseline for all student data for the 1976-77 school year. On the basis of this report, the superintendent reported to the special master that the official 1976-77 enrollment was 109,565. More significant, sixty-seven schools had now met the 25 to 45 percent black enrollment goal, a figure that was 126 percent of the court-required number of fifty-three schools. Beginning in September 1976, the school system embarked on a major desegregation planning effort that involved thousands of Milwaukee citizens.

On March 16, 1977, the district court entered a student desegregation remedy order based to a considerable degree upon the recommendations made by the superintendent (and advanced by the community), which first appeared in draft copy on December 8, 1976. The implementation of the order resulted in 101 racially balanced schools (now defined as having a student population between 25 and 50 percent black) in September 1977. The 101 racially balanced schools met exactly the court standard for the second year.

The Supreme Court, on June 29, 1977, vacated the judgment of the circuit court and remanded it back to the circuit court for reconsideration in light of two recent Supreme Court decisions— *Village of Arlington Heights v. Metropolitan Housing Development Corp.* and *Dayton Board of Education v. Brinkman.* These two cases established a clearer burden of proof and specific tests for linking liability with appropriate remedies. On September 1, 1977, the circuit court in turn vacated both the January 19, 1976, and March 17, 1977, orders of the district court and remanded the entire case to the district court.

Based on the evidentiary hearings that the district court held in January and February 1978, the court on June 1, 1978, issued a decision that essentially reconfirmed its previous findings that the defendants had administered the school system with segregative intent since 1950, and in so doing violated the rights of the plaintiffs under the Constitution. On August 2, 1978, the court ordered that an interim desegregation plan be implemented during the 1978-79 school year; this plan maintained the requirement that two-thirds of the schools would have to be racially balanced.

In July and October 1978 the district court held evidentiary hearings on the issue of present effects that resulted from the intentionally segregative acts found by the court. On February 9, 1979, the court issued a decision holding that the present effects were systemwide and directed the parties to submit proposed desegregation plans designed to remedy those present effects.

In lieu of separate remedy plans, the plaintiffs and defendants forged a settlement agreement in February 1979. The court scheduled hearings for members of the affected class. The hearings were concluded on March 29, 1979, and on May 11, 1979. Judge John Reynolds accepted the settlement as negotiated. On June 20, 1979, the district court was informed that its decision would be appealed by the NAACP on behalf of the objectors to the settlement. The appeal of the settlement agreement to the Seventh Circuit Court of Appeals by the NAACP was unsuccessful.

The faculty desegregation issue has followed a developmental process paralleling the student racial balance remedy. The faculty desegregation goals expressed in the settlement agreement required the school system to maintain two-thirds of the schools in the system with faculties within plus or minus 5 percent of the total percentage of black teachers in the system. The remaining one-third of the schools would have faculties within a plus or minus 10 percent of the percentage of black teachers in the total system. The Milwaukee Teachers' Education Association had taken exception to the process for achieving these racial balance goals, and thus the settlement agreement did not contain statements on the faculty desegregation process. The plaintiffs and defendants joined together in proposing a faculty desegregation process with the understanding that the district court would have to settle the dispute. On May 11, 1979, the court adopted the joint plaintiff/defendant faculty desegregation plan.

Goals of the Desegregation Plan

The first and most obvious goal of the Milwaukee desegregation plan (*Recommendations for Increasing Educational Opportunities and Improving Racial Balance*) was to comply with the various orders of the court, particularly the United States District Court's settlement agreement. This agreement, reached by the parties to the suit, was ordered by the court on May 4, 1979.

The settlement agreement calls for 75 percent of the students to be in racially balanced schools over a five-year period, unless the percentage of black students increases beyond 50 percent (in which case the 75 percent standard would be reduced proportionately). A "desegregated" school for purposes of desegregation is defined as: (1) each elementary or junior high school which has a student population composed of not less than 25 percent and not more than 60 percent black students, and (2) each senior high school which has a student population composed of not less than 20 percent and not more than 60 percent black students. Also, the settlement agreement prohibited all-white schools by requiring at least a 25 percent black population in each school. The settlement agreement provided an absolute guarantee to all parents that, if they desired, their children would be provided education in a racially balanced school.

The most controversial aspect of the settlement agreement is that it would allow some all-black schools. Both plaintiff and defendant attorneys argued that the settlement prescribed a minimum standard for desegregation that met the constitutional requirements; the school board could legislate beyond this standard. Also, it was pointed out that black students were guaranteed seats in racially balanced schools if they so desired.

If the court-ordered numbers are not satisfied, then any arguments on behalf of attaining other goals fall on deaf ears. Therefore, primary attention was focused by the school system on at least attaining, and in most cases exceeding, the requirements of the court. Because the school system exceeded the requirements of the court established in various orders beginning in 1976 and culminating in the 1979 settlement agreement, the administration cultivated great credibility with the court. For example, the settlement agreement calls for 75 percent of the students to be in racially balanced schools. At the present time we have reported to the court that 85 percent of the students are in racially balanced schools.

The goals defined by the court-ordered settlement are themselves a result of assumptions about the Milwaukee community and our three-year history with the desegregation process. The court heard and accepted testimony to the effect that not all schools needed to be racially balanced in order to accept the plan as a means to establishing a unitary school system. The court recognized the increasing minority representation in the system and conceded that there could be a few predominantly black schools if all students were guaranteed the right to attend a racially balanced school if they so desired. However, the reverse was not true; that is, all parties agreed that there were no statistical bars preventing the racial balancing of all predominantly white schools.

Special recognition was made of the Hispanic minority in the settlement plan and the need to develop bilingual education programs. In schools that have such programs, the minimum 25 percent black student enrollment required in all schools can be met with a 12.5 percent black student enrollment and a 12.5 percent Hispanic student enrollment.

Another conclusion in the settlement agreement demonstrates the impact of enrollment changes over the period of time a desegregation remedy is being considered by a court. In 1976 a racially balanced school was defined as one 25 to 45 percent black. In the 1979 settlement agreement a racially balanced school was defined as an elementary or junior high school 25 to 60 percent black and a senior high 20 to 60 percent black. In 1976 black students constituted 37 percent of the total school enrollment, but by 1979 they constituted 45 percent. Obviously, this change of definition comports with the change in the relative black percentage in the school system. However, there is another implied understanding that goes with this change in definition; namely, that a school can be majority black (60 percent) and still be considered racially balanced. In other words, the nation's majority in an individual school could find itself as the minority—a positive outcome. Currently, thirty-five schools in our system have between 50 and 60 percent black enrollment. Those who would see a total desegregation plan allow for the possibilities of a racially balanced school being dominated by minorities will find a substantial laboratory for this notion in Milwaukee.

A second overall goal of the Milwaukee desegregation plan, beyond the primary goal to achieve the court-ordered goals, was to improve the learning environment. It was never assumed that the simple mixing of students of various ethnic backgrounds would alone have much consequence for improving learning. The court order spoke only about equal access to whatever quality of education existed in the community and therefore in similar fashion drew no conclusions about the effects of desegregation on achievement. However, the Milwaukee desegregation plan was formulated on the belief that a great amount of student movement in the system would be engendered by diversifying the educational offerings. That is, parents would be apt to choose other than their neighborhood school if there was a compelling motivation to do so. Therefore, in the development of the desegregation plan the use of magnet schools, or what we call in Milwaukee specialty schools, was envisioned. Currently, Milwaukee operates about forty specialty school programs. Children from all over the city have access to these programs, which represent some of the very finest learning opportunities.

Actually, the seminal work in the development of specialty school programs was begun six months prior to the court order. The superintendent, in the fall of 1975, submitted to the board three alternative programs—High Schools Unlimited, Schools for the Transition, and Options for Learning. At meetings on January 6 and February 3, the board endorsed the concepts contained in these alternative programs, with the understanding that specific planning for their implementation would involve broad segments of the community and the teaching staff.

The High Schools Unlimited concept recognized the fact that a single high school could not offer the variety of educational and career education courses required by all its students. High Schools Unlimited can be illustrated by viewing each Milwaukee senior high school as a triangle. At the base of the triangle would be the standard curriculum available at all high schools in the city. In the center section of the triangle would be advanced subject-area programs each high school could offer in common with one, two, and three other geographically scattered high schools. At the top of the triangle would be a Career Specialty Program unique to that school and not available at any other high school in the city.

Currently, the specialty school program at the high school level has developed the following career specialty programs:

- Agribusiness and Natural Resources
- Applied Technology
- Communications and Health
- Community Human Services
- Computer Data Processing
- Earth, Energy, and Environment
- Finance and Commerce
- International Studies
- Law, Law Enforcement, and Protective Services

- Marketing and Word Processing
- Medical, Dental, and Health
- Small Business Management
- Tourism, Food Services, and Recreation
- Transportation
- Visual and Performing Arts

The Schools for the Transition concept proposed that schools for students in the transition years between elementary and senior high school be so diversified in program and organizational structure that they would offer alternatives in education to attract pupils citywide. The schools would not only expand learning options for pupils in elementary schools, but would retain the exploratory nature of traditional junior high schools so that young people would be guided properly into the specialties offered by High Schools Unlimited.

The Options-for-Learning concept envisioned modes of instruction-specialty elementary schools primarily located in the central city. With attractive newer schools in the periphery of the city and magnet programs in the central city, two-way movement of students was predicted.

Essentially, the specialty-school concept led the desegregation enterprise and, in another sense, was the fuel that drove the entire desegregation engine. By concentrating public attention on the specialty-school concept and the broadening of educational opportunities, leaders assumed that some of the negative imagery of desegregation could be ameliorated.

The third goal of the desegregation plan was to maximize the opportunities for choice and minimize the number of mandatory assignments. It was assumed that if an individual made a conscious decision in favor of a particular school after weighing the alternatives available, that the combination of choices made by all students and parents could be largely satisfied within racial-balance requirements. We never envisioned a completely free-choice system. While an attendance-area choice existed for all students, choices other than the attendance-area school would have to be in the direction of improving racial balancing. Rather than projecting the racial-balance goal paramount in the public mind, we chose rather to emphasize the existence of varied educational opportunities and consciously worked to inculcate in the minds of our community the importance of matching available programs with the needs of children. School personnel worked hard to counsel and prepare parents to make this choice. The result was that the numerical goals of the court were satisfied, while at the same time we satisfied 98 percent of the first choices that parents and guardians made. Approximately 88 percent of the eligible students had choice forms returned to them. Most of the students for whom no choice form was returned were assigned to their neighborhood school.

The fourth goal of the desegregation plan was to develop as much stability and predictability as possible. By this we meant giving certain assurances to parents regarding the school choices they made. Once a child was in a particular school, parents were guaranteed the opportunity to have their children complete that school's program. Furthermore, if programs existed one year, it was thought important that they should exist the next. The desegregation plan was designed to create as much stability and predictability as possible within the clear constraints that schools had to be closed in response to a declining enrollment and evaluation decisions had to be made regarding the continuation of certain programs. It was felt that the plan could encourage the continued participation of parents in the choice process when trust, faith, stability, and predictability were thought to exist. In this respect the Milwaukee approach contrasted markedly with most desegregation plans.

Clustering or pairing designs, as well as redistricting designs, are constantly subject to the vicissitudes of population shifts. Therefore, the participation in student exchanges and the redrawing of district lines become the only tools for meeting continuing racial-balance requirements. The choice process, by contrast, is a dynamic one. It ensures movement every year as students and parents make choices available to them. This guaranteed movement, therefore, compensated for population shifts in a much more reasonable and equitable fashion.

A fifth goal of the plan was to accomplish court-imposed goals in a peaceful fashion. There were many elements inherent in the plan that contributed to its peaceful implementation. I have already commented on the notion of highlighting the program opportunities rather than the numerical student-movement goals. The widespread involvement of the community in the planning process contributed toward goal consensus and the building of a school community coalition to integrate the schools peacefully. It was also felt important to develop a strong school-based human relations program. Finally, the incremental implementation of the court order allowed us between 1976 and 1979 to increase the number of racially balanced schools. We started primarily at the elementary level, where we felt we were more likely to have peaceful success. The fact that between 1976 and 1981 we have had only one incident of a racial nature in one high school is, I believe, testimony to our success in meeting this goal.

A sixth goal of the desegregation plan was to develop community acceptance of it, on which the very success of the desegregation plan relied. If parents failed to accept the opportunities to investigate the educational programs in other than their neighborhood schools, then the plan was doomed. Once again, the emphasis on choice was believed to be a major contributor to the achievement of this goal. The Milwaukee community had an opportunity to shape its own desegregation destiny by the school choices that students made. If these choices failed collectively to meet the court-imposed standards, then it was equally clear to the community that a mandatory student-assignment backup provision would immediately be invoked. This straightforward revelation of both a desired plan and a plan to be in effect if the desired plan failed contributed to the support of the choice process.

The final goal of the desegregation plan was to maintain control of the school system in the hands of the board and the administration. Unfortunately, the majority of the board chose to fight the court order with all legal means available to it. This decision had two unfortunate results. First, it cost the taxpayers over $2 million in court costs. Second, the district court judge lacked any faith in the school board's commitment to carry out his order. In fact, in his original order in 1976 he immediately appointed Special Master John Gronouski to work with the school system in compliance. When the school board independently came up with its first plan for compliance, Federal Judge John Reynolds called it "the rankest form of deception."

This is not to say that individual members of the board did not themselves have credibility in this process. But the posture of the majority caused the board to be portrayed in the media as the archetypal villains in the case. Consequently, the actions of the board during the desegregation case were largely ridiculed by the press and rejected by the court.

The administration survived and even flourished while walking this tightrope between the board and court by joining with a formidable ally—the community. By the time the administration submitted a plan to the board and the court, the support of literally thousands of involved citizens was evident in it.

The leadership of the system consciously chose to follow the directions of the court earnestly and work toward meeting its court-ordered obligations, not out of a sense of resignation, but rather from a sense of opportunity. The administration considered the possibilities of program renewal and integration to be a positive opportunity to change the course of the district's two-hundred year history. We felt the principal danger lay in others assuming the mantle of responsibility for the school system. The future of the system depended on the administration's aggressively meeting the requirements of the court in a manner that was designed to succeed rather than prove the failure of desegregation. When a court or special master or some other individual assumes the leadership in desegregation, it can ultimately lead to the responsibility for operating the entire school system. The administration viewed desegregation as the most important event in the history of the Milwaukee system, and it concluded that it wanted to provide leadership in this most important period.

Section II—The City of Milwaukee

Milwaukee is by far the largest city in the state of Wisconsin. Its 1980 federal census population was 636,212. Located in the southeast quadrant of the state, Milwaukee borders Lake Michigan ninety miles north of Chicago. The city was founded by early French fur traders who settled the port of Milwaukee at the junction of three rivers (the Milwaukee, the Menominee, and the Kinnickinnic), an ideal place for commerce with the Indians. The three sections of the city, demarcated by the junction of the three rivers, each grew as independent settlements. Today there are approximately 1.5 million people residing within the Standard Metropolitan Statistical Area. Table 7-1 shows the distribution of the city population.

Table 7-1 Population of Milwaukee by Race, 1980

	Number	*Percent*
White	466,616	73.3
Black	146,940	23.1
Other race	22,654	3.6
Hispanic	22,111	4.1

Source: U.S. Bureau of the Census, *Census of Population, 1980* (Washington, D.C.: U.S. Government Printing Office, 1982).

There were a total of 164,240 children from birth to 19 years in the city of Milwaukee as of June 30, 1981. Of this group 87,346 attended public schools, and 31,238 attended parochial or private schools. The balance of the students were either preschool age or teenagers who had left school.

Between 1970 and 1980, the total population of the city of Milwaukee declined 11.3 percent. During that ten-year period, the black population grew about 40,000, and Hispanic and other racial populations increased about 25,000. The white population during the same period declined about 50,000. Of the total black population of the Standard Metropolitan Statistical Area 98 percent live in the city of Milwaukee, virtually all on the north side of the city, and especially highly concentrated in residential areas bordering the downtown on the near north side. The Spanish-speaking population is concentrated in the near southeast area of the city, although there are smaller concentrations in the northeast section. Milwaukee has remained residentially isolated by ethnic and racial groups. There is a strong Polish identification in the southern area of the city, and the German and other northern European groups are well represented in the northwestern sections.

Heavy industrial manufacturing has dominated the Milwaukee economy since the early 1900s. While beer is what might have made Milwaukee famous, the manufacture of heavy industrial equipment is appropriately thought of as the economic lifeblood of this community.

Politically the city is governed under a weak mayor form; the democratic incumbent, Henry Maier, has served as mayor for the last twenty-three years. Milwaukee has had a unique tradition of socialist mayors beginning in the 1930s and ending in the late 1950s. City government has long enjoyed a reputation of honesty and integrity, and the level and types of city services are extensive. For example, it is not uncommon to expect the city garbage collectors to enter a home's basement in order to remove the garbage cans. The city enjoys a labyrinth of outstanding parks including a well-developed lakefront area. Golf courses and other playgrounds are much in evidence. Professional sports teams in most major sports, a symphony orchestra, an opera, a ballet company, and other cultural groups create the fabric of a rich cultural/recreational heritage. The relatively high property taxes support extensive public services including the school system.

The Milwaukee public school system's boundaries are coterminous with those of the city; however, the governance of the schools is completely independent from that of the city. Current enrollment by ethnic group is shown in Table 7-2.

Table 7-2 Public School Enrollment by Ethnic Group, Milwaukee, 1982

	Number	*Percent*
American Indian	1,090	1.2
Black	42,631	48.7
Asian	1,242	1.4
Spanish-surname	5,709	6.5
White	36,140	41.3
Other	619	0.9
Total	87,431	100.

Source: Official Fall Enrollment Report, Milwaukee Public Schools, Sept. 17, 1982, p.3.

Milwaukee currently operates 15 high schools, 18 middle schools, 103 elementary schools, and 9 other schools, for a total of 145 schools. There are approximately forty magnet schools and programs. (See chapter appendix.)

Section III—The Scope of the Milwaukee Desegregation Plan

The United States District Court's finding of liability in the desegregation case applied only to the city of Milwaukee. Therefore, the court limited its attention in terms of remedy to the school children and staff of the Milwaukee Public Schools. In order to understand the court's finding, a few selected passages are quoted below.

SELECTED PASSAGES OF THE REYNOLDS DECISION

The Board and the Administration, in adhering to and carrying out the neighborhood school policy, acted with the knowledge that the total effect of their actions in furtherance of that policy would be the segregation of black and white students in separate schools. . . .
The Board knew that adherence to the neighborhood school policy would result in a high proportion of racially imbalanced schools but believed, in good faith, that

such a policy would produce the best possible educational opportunities for all students in the system, regardless of race. . . .

During the early 1960s, open enrollment plans were considered by some to be a means of accomplishing desegregation. Time proved them wrong. . . .

The majority of school board members have historically taken the position that the Board is under no obligation to take affirmative steps to effect further integration or racial balance or to lessen the percentage of black pupils in any or all schools within the system. The Board has consistently refused to take any acts that would lessen the degree of racial segregation resulting from residential patterns and the neighborhood school policy as modified by the Free and Open Transfer Program.

The law is not so blind as to only proscribe school segregation which is the result of legislative enactments bearing on the face the mark of governmental action violative of the Equal Protection Clause of the Fourteenth Amendment. The law equally forbids more subtle means of achieving the proscribed end of governmental segregation on the basis of race. The facially neutral actions of state authorities constitute illegal and unconstitutional *de jure* segregation if they are intended to and have the effect of racial separation.

Segregation was the result of the cumulative effect of the various decisions made by school officials, and segregation that results from the actions of school authorities is illegal and unconstitutional when those actions are intended and made for that purpose. . . . The Constitution does not guarantee one a quality education, it guarantees one an equal education, and the law in this country is that a segregated education that is mandated by school authorities is inherently unequal.

The Court concludes that the defendants have knowingly carried out a systematic program of segregation affecting all of the city's students, teachers, and school facilities, and have intentionally brought about and maintained a dual school system. The Court therefore holds that the entire Milwaukee Public School system is unconstitutionally segregated.

Accordingly . . . the Court will file a partial judgment permanently enjoining the defendants from discriminating on the basis of race in the operation of the Milwaukee Public Schools and ordering the defendants . . . to begin the formulation of plans to effectively eliminate racial segregation from the public schools of Milwaukee, including all consequences and vestiges of segregation previously practiced by the defendants.

Despite the narrow focus of the court, the comprehensive desegregation approach takes into consideration metropolitan involvement. In order to understand this apparent paradox, it is necessary to explore a parallel history with regard to racial-balance activity. While the court was concerned about achieving a unitary Milwaukee public school system, the Wisconsin state legislature began to show interest in voluntary metropolitan planning. In 1975 a Milwaukee state legislator proposed the reorganization of certain northern suburban school districts with certain high school attendance areas within the city of Milwaukee. While this particular idea was greeted with a considerable lack of enthusiasm, the Milwaukee legislator continued to pursue other more voluntary strategies with officials of the Milwaukee Public Schools. After countless hours considering the merits of various voluntary approaches, in the spring of 1976 a few Milwaukee legislators presented a financial incentive-based plan for improving racial balance within large city systems and allowing for racial-balance movement between city systems and their suburban counterparts. This bill enjoyed strong bipartisan support and ultimately in April 1976 was signed into law by the governor as Chapter 220.

There were two aspects to Chapter 220. The first aspect of the legislation provided additional state aid (33 percent) for each student whose transfer within the city system resulted in the improvement of racial balance. For purposes of this legislation all schools in the Milwaukee system are classified in two categories--those less than 30 percent minority and those more than 30 percent minority based on the hypothetical enrollment of all students in their attendance-area schools. Actually a computer program was designed to tabulate students by ethnic classification in their original attendance-area school. When, for example, a black student living in an attendance area whose student population would be at least 30 percent minority transfers to a school that is less than 30 percent minority, this transfer would yield the Milwaukee district an additional 33 percent state aid for that student. Currently approximately 23,000 student transfers within the city of Milwaukee qualify the system for this additional 33 percent aid per pupil, earning for the district an additional $19 million yearly from the state.

The second aspect of Chapter 220 provides financial incentives for suburbs to participate with cities in voluntary movement of students between the systems. Chapter 220 requires that each year a planning council—that is, three board members, the superintendent, and one citizen from the suburban community—meet with a similarly constituted group in Milwaukee. The planning council may draw up some type of plan for the exchange of students, which may ultimately be accepted or rejected by either school board. If the suburban district and the city district voluntarily decide to draw up a contract, it will specify the number of students in the exchange and other administrative details. Then the opportunities are advertised in the respective districts. Only minority students can move from Milwaukee into suburban schools, and likewise, only majority students can move from the suburbs into minority schools in Milwaukee. There is in the legislation a strong fiscal incentive for participation in this program. For example, when a minority student enrolls in the suburban school, Milwaukee counts the student for state aid purposes as if the student were still enrolled in the Milwaukee system. Then, in turn, the suburban district receives from the state the full cost of educating that child. The full cost of transportation is also reimbursed by the state. The suburban school districts are able to absorb minority students at various levels within their system without any appreciable increase in total cost. Presently more than a thousand students from Milwaukee are enrolled in seventeen participating suburban districts, and better than 200 students from the suburbs are enrolled in Milwaukee programs, primarily the specialty programs. Milwaukee presently receives approximately $19 million a year in additional state aid for the intradistrict transfers and an additional $450,000 for the interdistrict transfers. So while the federal court-ordered goals in no way apply to the suburban districts, the existence of Chapter 220 has provided an additional avenue for minority students in Milwaukee and majority students in the suburbs to participate in integrated schooling.

The federal court was careful not to specify educational requirements in the court order. It did so in response to a plea from the Milwaukee school district officials that such specification could jeopardize the system's application for federal desegregation money. Moreover, the system felt that it could best determine the educational impact of the plan. The court was satisfied with dealing with the primary issue of access.

The first section dealing with the goals of the desegregation plan explained that the plan attempted to devise a solution to the numerical requirements of the court through heavy reliance on an educational enhancement approach. In order for a choice plan to work effectively, there had to be motivation for choice. We assumed that the primary motivation for most parents and students would be the belief that there stood beyond the available attendance-area school another school where a more appropriate educational opportunity existed. The immediate goal in implementing this plan was to acquaint the public with these available opportunities. The success in achieving desegregation goals was inextricably bound in the educational enhancement of the system.

The Milwaukee desegregation plan was comprehensive, including all grade levels. The court specifically exempted the kindergarten level, although the implementation of the plan includes not only kindergarten students but also four-year-old kindergarten students. The court reasoned that it would be inefficient and unnecessary to transport kindergarten students for half-day sessions. However, in the development of the specialty school concept at the elementary level, it had become apparent that the kindergarten level or in many cases the four-year-old kindergarten level was becoming the entry grade into the highly sought-after schools. Waiting lists at higher grade levels attest to the importance of making early application to these programs.

In 1976 and 1977 the court's accounting method for measuring the level of desegregation attainment was the individual school. In 1976 the school system was required to have one-third of its schools racially balanced; in 1977, two-thirds of its schools. This was fortuitous. Under this arrangement it was certainly easier to balance the smaller elementary schools racially than it was to balance the larger high schools. The racially balanced elementary school counted toward desegregation at the same weight as a racially balanced high school. The school system naturally concentrated on racially balancing the elementary level first. This was also compatible with our belief that it is better to begin desegregation at the lowest grade levels in order to build a foundation of racial and ethnic understanding that will help at higher grade levels. Most of the middle schools and high schools came into compliance during the 1978 school year, although substantial progress at these levels was evident as early as 1976. The Milwaukee plan has equal applicability at all age levels. It is true that it may be preferable to begin at the elementary level, for example, but the notion of choice and specialization is evident at all grade levels.

Presently 85 percent of the students in the system attend racially balanced schools, including 100 percent of the white students and about two-thirds of the minority students. The most controversial aspect of the settlement agreement was that it allowed some all-black schools. The district was successful in racially balancing inner-city schools when they were converted to citywide specialty schools. Inner-city schools that remained attendance-area schools generally remained all black. Both plaintiff and defendant attorneys argued that the settlement prescribed a minimum standard for desegregation that met the constitutional requirements; the school board could legislate beyond this standard. Also, it was pointed out that black students were guaranteed seats in racially balanced schools if they so desired.

An opportunity for all members of the class to be heard on the proposed settlement was given from March 26 to 29, 1979. Approximately fifty individuals testified on their views of the settlement agreement. The court felt it important to have this full and complete hearing in light of the Seventh Circuit Court of Appeals reversal of a settlement agreement involving the infamous Chevrolet engines in Oldsmobile bodies. In that case the circuit court argued that the district court had not given adequate hearings to the objectors in the class action. The hearings were concluded on March 29, 1979, and on May 11, 1979, Judge John Reynolds accepted the settlement as negotiated. The Seventh Circuit Court reviewed the settlement agreement ordered by the district court and concurred in the district court's decision.

While the plan meets the legal requirements for a unitary system, there still remain considerable objections to the notion that approximately twenty all-black schools continue to operate in the system. In 1979 the Milwaukee Board of School Directors directed the administration to develop plans that would give special consideration to these schools. This policy resulted in a school effectiveness pilot project entitled Project RISE. This project was one of the nation's first large-scale experiments with the growing body of school effectiveness literature. The research and writings of Brookover and Lazotte (1977), Brophy (1979), Edmonds (1979), and others were instrumental in focusing the design of Project RISE. Eighteen elementary schools and two middle schools designed their own specific effectiveness plans within the overall school effectiveness philosophy. After three years of full operation the project has resulted in substantial improvement in these minority isolated schools. The system is so encouraged by the results in this pilot project that effectiveness techniques are being extended to the balance of our schools over the next five years.

It is important to note here that the school effectiveness plan is not intended as a substitute for racial balance in the way that compensatory education programs were often used in defense of racially segregated schools. The results of the school effectiveness planning in racially isolated schools has assured minority parents that quality all-minority schools exist in our system and that access to them can be a legitimate choice within the philosophical framework of our choice plan. In other words, one need not make the choice for a specialty school or a school in an all-white neighborhood in order to be secure in the knowledge that a quality program exists. Minority, racially isolated schools were not left as the dumping grounds for those uninformed regarding the benefits of the total school system. In this sense, the school effectiveness movement provided an essential piece to the desegregation puzzle in Milwaukee; namely, insuring that the relatively small number of racially isolated minority schools contributed positively to the choice process. There remains the guarantee that a minority student at any time may enroll in a racially balanced school. Parents receive a letter reminding them of this guarantee on a yearly basis pursuant to the court order.

The level of interaction between minority and majority students differs from school to school. It is safe to generalize that in Milwaukee you will see more interaction at the elementary level than at the secondary level, and secondly that the specialty schools tend to exhibit a greater amount of student interaction and parent involvement than do attendance-area schools. Some extracurricular activities, particularly at the high school level, continue to be racially identifiable despite prodigious efforts to break these molds. Special activity buses are provided in all the elementary schools to assure the opportunity for after-school participation of students who are transported on a daily basis. In turn, these after-school activities are scheduled on the night when the activity bus is available. There is no ready source of statistics regarding the level of racial and ethnic interaction in extracurricular activities.

Section IV—The Equity of the Milwaukee Desegregation Plan

There were certain aspects of the Milwaukee system as it existed in 1976 that had to be changed in order to allow the desegregation plan to work. Certainly, a fundamental requirement was the introduction of a uniform grade-level structure. Prior to 1976 practically every imaginable grade-level structure existed in the system. However, in the plan adopted by the court, grade-level structures were limited to two types, both of which were compatible with one another. The primary structure would be K to 5, 6 to 8, and 9 to 12, and the secondary, compatible structure would be K to 8 and 9 to 12. In implementing this grade-level structure, it has subsequently been determined that the 6 to 8 middle school would not be fully implemented until 1984. Currently we operate with a 7 to 8 middle school. It is particularly critical for a choice system to have a consistent grade-level structure. All students and parents would not have an equal opportunity to enter certain schools were they not in a similar grade-level pattern. For example, a citywide high school might be organized on a 9 to 12 basis, but unless students at the middle level were completing their school at the eighth grade level rather than the ninth grade level, they would not have equal inclination for choosing the ninth grade entry level into high school. Clearly those who make the ninth grade choice have a secure spot for the balance of the high school experience while others must compete for a limited number of tenth grade seats in this example.

Another important feature of the plan was the way it handled "feeder patterns." As with the grade-level structures, the feeder patterns in 1976 were in considerable disarray. For example, feeder patterns split children coming out of a particular elementary school into as many as three junior high schools. Rather than trying to disrupt this pattern, we needed only to set up different decision rules regarding the students who had transferred into a school from another attendance area. For example, if a minority student were attending a racially balanced school that divided three ways for junior high attendance-area purposes, the minority student could choose any one of these three junior high schools, or his/her attendance-area junior high school. By contrast, the majority student attending the same racially balanced school could only attend the junior high that was his/her attendance-area school. Feeder pattern problems, which can be difficult technical challenges under some desegregation models, were neatly handled in Milwaukee. Majority and minority students tended to follow feeder patterns rather than return to their neighborhood schools. So when a base of racially balanced elementary schools was created, the eventual contribution to racial balance at the middle and high school levels was assured. Finally, it is important to note that specialty schools were in some cases designed to establish natural feeder patterns. We are currently developing a middle school creative arts citywide specialty program to accommodate the desires of parents whose children are being promoted from the elementary specialty creative arts program.

In summary, the Milwaukee desegregation plan offers parents the following choices: (1) to apply for their attendance-area or feeder-pattern school (all students live in a designated attendance area); (2) to apply for a specialty school (specialty schools are nonattendance-area, citywide schools and are available primarily in central city locations); (3) to attend another attendance-area school where a student would enhance racial balance. (The assignment system relies on the definition of two types of attendance-area schools—white attendance-area schools and black attendance-area schools. Black attendance-area schools are those with more than 30 percent black students in the residential area. White attendance-area schools have fewer than 30 percent black in the residential area.) Finally, a special opportunity exists for minority students: (4) to enroll in programs in cooperating suburban districts under Chapter 220.

Each year the student-assignment process with these various choices is organized in a three-stage process. The first stage is the citywide enrollment stage, which is completely voluntary, and participation in no way precludes or unnecessarily limits the choices in subsequent stages. Parents and guardians are informed of the citywide schools, program designs, grade levels, and locations through various media. They then make their choice. All choices are received by the system and compared to the openings available and the racial-balance requirements.

We attempt to have a racial-balance representation in each of our specialty schools closely approximating the citywide racial representation. In some cases at certain grade levels applications exceed the available spaces or the applications do not distribute themselves in a racially balanced manner. In either case, the same solution is applied. We randomly sample the available applications and put the remaining students who are not chosen for the program on a waiting list, also randomly determined. All of this is done in public every year with invitations sent to the media. Following this processing, the results of the applications are mailed to the parents and guardians. It is crucially important in the design of this program that this stage occur first and that the results of this stage are known to parents. Clearly, parents who need to have a school assignment for their child the next year must know the results of this first stage in order to know whether to participate in subsequent stages of the student-assignment system. Also, we believe it is important to limit the initial choice to one school; otherwise some parents and guardians would "beat the system" by applying for more than one school in this initial stage. It is also the case following stage one that there may continue to be openings for certain races at certain grade levels. This information is also published and made known so that parents will have additional opportunities to apply for citywide schools at the subsequent stages.

The second stage of the student assignment process is the mandatory stage in that it requires the participation of parents and guardians in order to assure the student an assignment for the following school year. The participants in stage two of the student assignment system are those students who need an assignment for the following year either because they are new to the school system or because they are moving from elementary to middle school, or from middle school to high school. We process the choices in a similar manner to the processing pattern in stage one except the citywide racial distribution rule is replaced by the racial-balance ranges directed by the federal court. This gives substantially more latitude and allows for the satisfaction of most of these choices. However, in a very few cases, either because of racial balance requirements or school capacity requirements, we have to select a random sample in certain schools at certain grade levels. When a parents' second-stage choice cannot be satisfied, we alert parents to this result and invite them in for individual counseling regarding alternative choices. In our definition these are the only mandatory choices, although it has been our experience that in many cases the parents are perfectly satisfied with the alternative choices available to them. Only about 2 percent of the total school population do not receive their first choice and require counseling at this step.

Following the second stage of the student-assignment process, theoretically all students in the system have an assignment for the coming school year. However, it is our experience that students and parents for various reasons wish to have the opportunity to reconsider their present school assignment; thus we have created the third stage of the student assignment process, the transfer stage.

The transfer stage, like stage one, is totally voluntary. There is no requirement that parents or students participate at this stage. This is the opportunity, however, for parents who are dissatisfied with their present school assignment, or wish to take advantage of moving to an assignment they feel is more advantageous for their child, to indicate this desire by filling out a transfer application. It is also at this stage that we advertise and attempt to fill the balance of our citywide seats that are still available. In order for a transfer to be granted, the transfer must meet the requirement of improving the racial balance that has previously been mentioned.

There are other equity steps in this student-assignment process that are important to point out. At all stages in the student-assignment process the parent or guardian has the right to make a personal appeal when he or she believes that there are special mitigating circumstances that should allow the enrollment of a child in a particular school. Frequently, for example, parents may have special hardship or health reasons that require their child be enrolled in a particular school even though the enrollment does not meet the racial balance requirements. The court, at the urging of the school system, established in its order an appeals board. This appeals board is composed of a multiethnic group of administrators who will hear and rule on these cases. There have literally been thousands of appeal cases since 1976, and a large number of these appeals have been granted. This is an important element in the system in that any system may have general and impersonal rules that are intended to be fair and equitable but simply cannot account for all of the individual cases that need special consideration.

Finally, an appeal step does exist beyond the appeals board. It is called the monitoring board and was established by the court to hear from individuals and groups of individuals who for various reasons have felt that they have been injured in the student-assignment process. Since its establishment in 1979 the monitoring board has heard only two cases. It is a mechanism, however, established by the court to allow for the court's presence in this desegregation process but without unnecessary intrusion. The monitoring board also has the responsibility in the fall and spring of each school year to review the racial-balance statistics of the school system to ensure that they comply with all requirements of the final order.

I previously mentioned two types of schools within the Milwaukee plan. These are attendance-area schools and nonattendance-area, citywide schools. All citywide schools are specialty schools for all of the students attending them. Most of the citywide schools are located in the central area of our city. Also, most of these citywide schools are one-of-a-kind programs. On the other hand the attendance-area schools may be traditional, comprehensive schools or specialty schools. Therefore, in this syllogism while all citywide schools are also specialty schools, not all specialty schools are necessarily citywide schools. The attendance-area specialty programs have developed as a result of entrepreneurial activity on the part of the staff, the principal, or the community. This kind of a special effort is encouraged by the leadership in the system. There is yet a third variation on this configuration. Some schools have within them programs that are treated on a citywide basis. For example, all of our high schools have a career specialty program that enrolls students during the first period of the student-assignment process. Bilingual programs and programs for the academically talented are also enrolled during the first stage of the student assignment process. We attempt to give special attention to the enrollment of handicapped students in appropriate magnet-school programs.

The decision to locate our most desirable citywide schools in the inner city was a very conscious one. It was reasoned that in order to encourage the movement of white population into schools that otherwise would not be viable choices, we had to redesign the program offering. While we never contemplated a large number of white parents choosing these inner-city schools, we felt that if the program were attractive enough, there would be a sufficient number of white and black parents who would willingly enroll their children. This has proven to be the case far beyond our initial expectations. We are now in the process of expanding some of these specialty school offerings in order to accommodate additional majority and minority oversubscription.

The choice of the kinds of programs that would be developed as specialty school offerings was largely made through the community involvement process. We also had citizens who formed technical advisory committees to help us with the choice and development of our high school career specialty programs. Citywide specialty schools hold to a more stringent racial-balance requirement than do the attendance-area schools. In this way we can assure the equity of opportunity proportional to the ethnic representation in the system as a whole.

One of the key philosophical issues in the establishment of a magnet-school plan is the matter of entrance requirements and elitism. Milwaukee elected to establish the vast majority of its magnet programs without entrance requirements. We felt that good counseling would result in wise, appropriate decisions by parents and guardians. Even in the very few programs that have entrance requirements, for example, the gifted and talented specialty schools at the elementary and middle school levels, the requirements are written as broadly as possible to be as inclusive as possible. We believe that there are many more gifted and talented students than could ever be accommodated in a single school. Many of the magnet programs, particularly at the high school level, do maintain performance standards *following* initial enrollment in the program. We believe that standards for maintenance of eligibility in programs are preferred over entrance requirements. Sometimes, however, there are problems when, for example, by the random sampling process, a gifted dancer is denied access to a creative arts magnet school. We believe, however, that it is best to come down on the side of equity rather than attempt to evaluate the talents and desire for the programs on the part of parents. The latter system would lay the schools open to the appearance and reality of favoritism.

There remains a full range of extracurricular activities and programs in our schools through the process of desegregation. Some schools substantially improved their extracurricular offerings, but no schools have a less comprehensive program than they did before 1976. One obvious potential problem with the choice system is the temptation on the part of athletic coaches to recruit for their sports programs. As part of the implementation of this program we established clear rules that coaches could not contact students outside their attendance area. Despite the limits on coaches' proselytizing and their adherence to our rules, there remain strong student peer group communications regarding what schools to go to for certain athletic programs. However, it is encouraging to add that schools' fortunes may shift from year to year based on rumor and reputation. In any event, whatever problems occur in this area are not considered serious.

As mentioned earlier, there continue to be problems in the racial identification of certain extracurricular activities. In some racially balanced high schools cheerleaders are white and drill-team members are black. However, it is encouraging to view the less structured activities at the elementary level and note the almost complete absence of racial identification in the Brownie troops and the Boy Scout groups that meet after school during the activity evening. The high schools have consciously sought to review their practices in the selection of students for certain activities. We make sure, for example, that those who judge cheerleader tryouts are aware of our goals of equal racial representation. These efforts have to date resulted in considerable improvement, although some problems still exist.

Another potential impediment to participation in extracurricular activities is the matter of transportation. The introduction of the late activity bus on one night a week for the elementary schools and the scheduling of these activities on that night have reduced the problem at that level. At the high school level students receive bus passes that allow them to travel by public transportation any time during the day. However, it must be recognized that for some students at the elementary level and at the secondary level the distance and time involved in transportation, no matter how well organized, will be a disincentive for participation.

In 1970 the enrollment in the Milwaukee public schools was 133,000 students. In the 1981-82 school year the enrollment was 87,000 students. Although this decline in enrollment has had some adverse financial impact upon the school system, an important benefit of this decline has been the relief of overcrowded school conditions. Moreover, the choice plan that underlies our desegregation approach allows us to control school enrollments and better assure that no school or program is overcrowded. Schools presently in use in Milwaukee vary from those built in 1880 to three $20 million high schools completed within the last three years. The city school system has long been recognized for the high quality of maintenance of our schools regardless of age. As with most cities the older buildings tend to be in the inner city and newer buildings in the outer city. Construction since 1970, however, has been balanced throughout the city. Most of our attractive citywide specialty-school programs are located in relatively old inner-city structures. The Golda Meir School for the Gifted and Talented, for example, is an elementary building located opposite a brewery and was built in 1890. It has been named an official landmark following its renovation. At Elm School for Creative Arts, another facility built before 1890, the building underwent an artistic redesign that is a bold statement for its educational program. On the exterior a large painted rainbow encircles the entire building. Inside, rooms and spaces are identified with supergraphic headings and colorful paint decor. In our school-closing decisions we have attempted to have areas of the city represented in those closings, while at the same time assuring that when attendance-area or specialty schools are closed, these students are relocated in better facilities than the ones that they left.

Another fundamental building block of the desegregation plan is the reliance on attendance areas. Some school desegregation plans in adopting the concept of choice have felt the need to do away with attendance areas. We believe that attendance areas are important in the successful administration of the plan and in the psychology of the community. In the Milwaukee choice plan, the attendance areas are perceived as just one of a number of potential choices. By relating students back to their attendance areas, definitions of minority and majority schools and other building-block determinations can be made. However, the choice plan has relieved us of one major burden associated with attendance areas, the need to redistrict from time to time. Except for the consequence of school closings that occasion the breakup and assignment of a closed attendance-area school to its nearest neighboring district, we have not required any redistricting since the advent of the court order. Prior to the court order, redistricting was a perennial topic of concern and debate. Since we control enrollment through the student assignment process, there is no need to be overly occupied with the notion of attendance area except as a means of identifying a student with an area and with a potential school choice.

In 1976 for the purposes of organizing the community for desegregation planning, we divided the system into three major geographical zones—the east zone, the west zone, and the north zone. These zones were organized with a population representative of the city as a whole. In the event that the choice system did not satisfy the requirements of the court order, we had intended to use the zone structure and its subunits as a means of pairing and clustering schools for mandatory assignment purposes. However, this backup system was never brought into play and is now largely disregarded in the minds of the public, as well as the school system. In no small measure do we value the relief of the burden of redistricting attendance areas brought about by the adoption of a choice plan. Also, there is the substantial alleviation of the problem associated with changing residence. In our system, students who are enrolled outside their attendance-area school need not concern themselves or the system with their change of domicile (except for change of transportation). Only those students who have chosen the attendance-area school and then move outside that attendance area are involved in a process of determining whether or not they can remain in their former school. They are allowed to remain if they enhance the racial balance of their former attendance-area school, if they are a senior, or if they are part of the citywide program within that school.

One clear disadvantage of this choice plan is the labyrinth of transportation routes occasioned by the exercise of choice. In the first year of the student assignment experience, a single inner-city elementary school attendance area had students enrolled in more than eighty separate elementary schools across the city. We were required to set up transportation routes to accommodate these students. To our knowledge no system had ever attempted to design a transportation system to accommodate this complexity. Not surprisingly in 1976 and again in 1977 we experienced a breakdown in our ability to transport students successfully. In the fall of 1976 we had a substantial number of students not being picked up on time and delivered from school according to schedule. In 1977 our transportation system designed for exceptional education students completely came apart at the seams. We contracted with Ecotran, a private transportation routing service based in Cleveland, for assistance in the design of our transportation policies, as well as the execution of the routing system. Fortunately, this resulted in a completely successful turnaround for our transportation program. The control of the system exercised through the Ecotran contract has allowed us to save better than $3 million in transportation costs since the inception of the order in 1976.

Our transportation eligibility statements are rather complex. Basically, however, elementary students who live a mile or more from their assigned school are provided with transportation. Middle school and high school students who are two miles or more from their school and also a mile or more from a public transportation stop are also provided yellow bus transportation. Most students, however, at the middle school and high school level ride public transportation rather than the yellow bus. The distance that students ride and the difference in the racial proportion of students who are transported are not the issue they would be were the system involved in substantial mandatory assignment of students. Transportation for most parents is treated as a convenience to allow the student to get to his or her school of choice. The fact that nine times as many blacks are transported as whites reflects the difference in their choice patterns, not a difference in burden or responsibility. Nevertheless, the daily visual realization of this difference continually resurrects the issue of "black burden" in desegregating the schools.

Section V—Board and Staff in the Desegregation Plan

The Milwaukee Board of School Directors is currently undergoing a reorganization based on a change made at the state legislative level three years ago. Previously the Milwaukee board consisted of fifteen members elected at large to six-year terms. Under the reorganization the Milwaukee board will ultimately have nine members, eight of whom are elected by combined aldermanic districts and one elected at large to four-year terms. There currently are twelve board members, and in spring 1983 they will achieve their nine-member requirement. The Milwaukee school system is fiscally independent and operates under special state legislation as the only city of the first class. In 1983, only one member of the board is black. Under the at-large arrangement, and during the entire period of desegregation planning, three members were black. Of the twelve members, six are female. When analyzed, the change to district representation from the at-large representation resulted in no obvious benefit in terms of racial representation, but definitely brought an improved geographic representation. It is unlikely in the foreseeable future that the current configuration of the aldermanic districts would result in more than two board members being minority.

Milwaukee is one of the few remaining dual school systems with two chief administrative officers. One is the superintendent of schools, and the other is the secretary-business manager. Both report independently to the board, have independent staff, and are identified positions in the special state legislation establishing the Milwaukee school district. The superintendent is chosen by the board. State statutes require that the first contract must be a three-year term and all subsequent terms are five years. The secretary-business manager serves at the pleasure of the board without a specific time contract. The secretary-business manager can only be dismissed by a two-thirds vote of the board. The superintendent can only be dismissed for cause during the contract term and can only be nonrenewed with one year's notification. Lee McMurrin, the current superintendent, came to the system in the fall of 1975 and was present when the initial federal district court order was given in January 1976. McMurrin assigned the responsibility for the design and the implementation of the desegregation plan to Dr. David Bennett, who at that time was general assistant to the superintendent and now is deputy superintendent of schools. In addition to the superintendent's position and deputy superintendent's position, the chief administrative positions of the school system under the superintendent are the assistant superintendents. Their titles are: assistant superintendent administrative and pupil personnel services, assistant superintendent curriculum and instruction, assistant superintendent exceptional education and supportive services, assistant superintendent human resources, assistant superintendent municipal recreation and community education, and assistant superintendent planning and long-range development. Under the secretary-business manager are the department directors. The assistant superintendents and the directors of these administrative units are recommended by the superintendent or secretary-business manager respectively and appointed by the board, and they serve at the pleasure of the superintendent or the secretary-business manager without contract or term of office. Currently there are one black assistant superintendent and one black business department director. The primary responsibility for implementing the plan to achieve the unitary school systems lies with the deputy superintendent. The individual schools are headed by building principals recommended by the superintendent and appointed by the board. Principals gain tenure after three years and at that point can only be removed for cause.

When the federal court made its findings with regard to a nonunitary system, it pointed out the need for both student and teacher-staff racial balancing. However, in its review of the evidence regarding field-base administrative staff, the court noted that Milwaukee has had a long history of racially balancing its field administrative staff with substantial representation of minority groups and women as well as the existence of minority staff members in majority communities and vice versa. Currently there are 138 principals, and 37 (27 percent) are black and 35 (25 percent) are female.

There are a total of forty-eight administrators in the Milwaukee system above the rank of director, forty-three white and five black. There are a total of 139 principals, 101 of whom are white and 37 of whom are black.

There are two Hispanic principals. Finally, there are a total of 5,228 teachers, 4,174 (80 percent) of whom are white, 933 (18 percent) of whom are black, and 75 (1 percent) of whom are Hispanic. The remaining 1 percent represent other ethnic minorities. Both field administrators and teachers are distributed without reference to the racial composition of the student body. Since 1976 there have been no dismissals of administrators of any kind, and fewer than ten teachers have been dismissed for cause.

Both our professional and clerical/technical staff members have received extensive in-service education in intergroup relations skills. In 1976 a permanent office of special assistant to the superintendent for human rights and staff development was created for the purpose of directing and coordinating all human relations training. Reporting to this office is a human relations staff composed of ten professionals and fifteen community aides who provide direct human relations services to the schools as well as training for central office and other personnel in the system. We also make extensive use of outside consultants and provide in-service credits for course work taken in human relations. Some training has been mandatory; other portions of it are offered on a voluntary basis. There has been excellent participation in the voluntary programs. Since 1976 we have offered thousands of human relations training programs that have involved students and parents as well as members of our staff. Since the beginning of our desegregation implementation in 1976 and 1977, literally every staff member in the school system has had some form of human relations training. The training has also included bus drivers and school crossing guards, who were not employees of our system. In the final court order is a requirement to provide a comprehensive, citywide human relations training program.

Milwaukee is currently operating under an affirmative action plan. Progress with this plan has slowed substantially in the last two years due to declining enrollments and the policy of staff attrition. In other words, when central office administrative positions come open, many are simply not filled. Field-based administrative positions continue to be filled affirmatively.

If the superintendent and his or her immediate staff have a key role to play in the overall response of the challenge of desegregation, then the principal has the key role in dealing with the plan at the local school level. Research on school desegregation is replete with statements that the principal is a most important individual in the process of desegregation. As with the superintendent, the values and beliefs held by the principal are important determinants of how successfully his or her school will meet the desegregation requirements. The school teaching staff takes its cue from the principal. The activist principal has the opportunity to take advantage of the desegregation change process and make other necessary changes in the school. Conversely, the school principal can view desegregation as a burden placed upon the principal by the courts and the central office and direct the staff and school accordingly. During periods of litigation and following a court order, principals are sought out by the press for comment. Their work schedule includes additional evening meetings occasioned by the desegregation process, and they often have a major role to play in the student-assignment process.

The school principal was the key figure in the student-assignment process under the Milwaukee desegregation plan. The principals assumed direct responsibility for counseling students and parents in directions that would serve student program needs and at the same time increase the racial balance in the system. This responsibility required of the Milwaukee principals a substantial reorientation. They no longer served the insular interests of their attendance-area community but now were expected to receive students from outside their community and at the same time counsel students from the neighborhood into other schools. For principals and counselors long used to extolling the virtues of their own school, the responsibility for counseling students out of the school was particularly onerous.

The principals were required to become transportation directors. For most principals having a substantial portion of their student body transported to school each day was a new experience. Because the Milwaukee desegregation plan was based on parent choice, the resulting transportation network is considered to be the most complex in the nation. The transportation problems fell most directly on the school principal, who received transportation complaints and was expected to deal successfully with them.

Not surprisingly these new requirements and, for some, the hiatus between their personal values and the goals of desegregation occasioned an increase in the number of retirements and other resignations from our school system. However, the vast majority of the principal corps gave unstintingly of their time and talent to achieve the desired results.

It is important to comment briefly upon the minority administrators and their special concerns in the litigation and desegregation process. It must be remembered that through the litigation process the school system was officially defending itself against the charges of discrimination. As a group the minority administrators were almost universally opposed to the defense premise and were, therefore, extremely uncomfortable with what they saw as the inherent hypocrisy of the system. While wanting to be part of the team and meet their responsibilities with the administrative structure, they had special problems during those moments when personal views and system views clashed. The minority community looks to the minority administrators for greater input in the desegregation process than they can often deliver. There is also the matter of job security. While northern desegregation approaches have not followed this pattern, it has been common in some southern desegregation remedies for minority administrators to lose their positions to white administrators. By itself the knowledge that this overt pattern has not been the recent practice may not be sufficient to reduce anxiety.

During the desegregation process the "affirmative action" responsibilities of the system come into sharp focus even if the litigation does not precisely touch upon it. When the top leadership of a school system going through desegregation is predominantly white, there cannot help but be some challenge to this circumstance, and the minority administrator wonders if he or she properly ought to be the challenger. Even in situations where minority representation is evident in the leadership of the system in the desegregation process, these individuals will often be singled out by members of their own community as targets of derision for not delivering what the minority community expects. Urban school desegregation is an event played against the backdrop of changing racial representation in the city and a shift in the city's power structure from white to minority. The importance of this larger context cannot be underestimated in understanding the course of litigation and desegregation.

The faculty desegregation issue has followed a developmental process paralleling the student racial balance remedy. The faculty desegregation goals expressed in the settlement agreement would require the school system to maintain two-thirds of the schools in the system with faculties within plus or minus 5 percent of the total percentage of black teachers in the system. The remaining one-third of the schools would have faculties within a plus or minus 10 percent of the percentage of black teachers in the total system. These different criteria for staff desegregation were a result of negotiations between the teachers' union (who wanted all schools to meet the more liberal 10 percent standard) and the plaintiffs and defendants (who wanted all schools to meet the more strict 5 percent standard). The Milwaukee Teachers' Education Association had taken exception to the process for achieving these racial balance goals, and thus the original settlement agreement did not contain statements on the faculty desegregation process. The plaintiffs and defendants joined together in proposing a faculty desegregation process with the understanding that the district court would have to settle the dispute. On May 11, 1979, the court adopted the joint plaintiff/defendant faculty desegregation plan. Since 1979 the staff has been racially balanced in accordance with the requirements of the federal court order. Efforts at increasing the absolute number of minority teachers have been frustrated by the declining enrollment as well as the specialization requirements in hiring. Nevertheless, the percentage of minority teachers (currently, approximately 18 percent) in our system continues to increase.

The court also had a significant impact upon relations between the school system and its employee units. The Milwaukee Teachers' Education Association (META) was recognized as the only intervenor in the desegregation case. The union was effective in parlaying its intervenor status into not only protecting the rights of the employees it represented through fourteen years of collective bargaining, but also improving its current contract with the help of the special master. During spring 1977 the MTEA struck the school system for seventeen days. The strike was resolved when the special master took it upon himself to intervene in the negotiations. Because he had dealt with the issue of staff desegregation in connection with the court order, he had some respect from both sides in the contract dispute. What came to be called the "Gronouski language" in the contract has, through the course of decisions, improved the position of the association vis-à-vis the board with respect to such basic issues as seniority and right of assignment. Therefore, the court in setting up the instrumentality of the special master had impact upon the school system well beyond original intentions and expectations.

The teachers' union (MTEA) leadership found in the court a handy foil in protecting its own position with its membership. Sundry ignominies suffered by the teachers could be blamed by the MTEA leadership on the courts. The MTEA, with its intervenor status, was involved in the attorneys' discussions leading to the settlement agreement. The settlement agreement spoke to all aspects of remedy save a staff desegregation remedy. The matter of staff desegregation was placed before the district court, with the plaintiffs and defendants advocating one procedure for attaining the staff desegregation goals and the MTEA leadership another. The MTEA leadership enjoyed the enviable position of incurring no loss regardless of the outcome. If the judge decided in favor of the MTEA, the leadership could claim victory over the plaintiffs and defendants. If the court imposed the plaintiffs' and defendants' remedy, then the MTEA could conveniently blame the court for modifying the contract and divest themselves of any responsibility. The court became the chess board on which the school system and one of its bargaining units moved their pieces.

Section VI—The School-Community Relations Aspects of the Milwaukee Desegregation Plan

From the outset of our desegregation planning the involvement of community was extensive and was deemed necessary to the ultimate success of the plan. Beginning in 1976 and continuing in each year of the court order, representatives were elected at the local school level to serve on an areawide advisory council. In turn the areawide council level representatives were chosen for what was named the Committee of 100. The Committee of 100, with representation from all over the city, had a major responsibility for detailing the program planning for desegregation. In September 1977 guidelines for involvement were provided through the Committee of 100 structure. These guidelines made it clear that the administration would include in its plan for adoption by the court the program recommendations made by the Committee of 100. In the fall of 1977 the Committee of 100 representatives and curriculum staff members spent countless hours reviewing materials, which they in turn shared at the areawide level and ultimately with the school board. Literally thousands of individuals were involved in the intimate details of desegregation program planning. The administration was able to include better than 90 percent of the recommendations that came from the Committee of 100 in its ultimate plan. The Committee of 100 also served as an open forum, as their monthly meetings allowed parents and concerned citizens from all over the community to come together to voice their desires and concerns. Ultimately the Committee of 100 members and their associates at the school level came to form the cadre of initial volunteers for the specialty school programs. They were the first who truly comprehended the nature of the program and willingly participated in it. They were instrumental in convincing their friends and neighbors to give the expanded educational opportunities serious consideration. The Committee of 100 was geographically, racially, and ethnically representative of the entire city. It also brought together conflicting views and in that sense was a true microcosm of the city's attitude toward desegregation. Committee of 100 meetings were viewed as a friendly, open atmosphere where differing viewpoints could be expressed and debated without fear of adverse consequence. Also very active in planning efforts at this time, in concert with the Committee of 100, were the Milwaukee City Council of PTAs, Coalition for Peaceful Schools, and members of the clergy, business, and union interests. In 1977 the Metropolitan Milwaukee Association of Commerce coordinated the distribution of brochures explaining the desegregation plans to commerce members and employees in the metropolitan area. Individual businesses contributed some of their finest technical personnel to work with the school system in establishing our career specialty programs at the high school level. These individuals were of immeasurable assistance in designing the career specialty programs and in making them relevant to the future economic needs of our society. In addition, all of the radio and television stations joined together in an unprecedented simulcast in August 1977. At this time the various specialty school programs and other details involving the desegregation process were explained. Some forty-five volunteers handled over a thousand phone calls in a one-and-a-half-hour period following the simulcast. Since the adoption of the settlement agreement in 1979, the primary community involvement activity is focused back on the individual school. PTAs and independent PTOs are the bulwark of involvement. Schools have countless numbers of volunteers who work in all aspects of school programming.

Starting in 1979, partnership programs were developed with high schools and major Milwaukee industries largely as a result of Superintendent McMurrin's contacting the heads of corporations directly or through the Association of Commerce. Each one of our high schools had a particular industry partner. The purpose of this partnership was to allow the business partner to advise the school on career opportunities. In many cases the career specialty of the school had a direct relationship with the particular industry chosen. Also, programs at all levels of our system have established linkages with community-based organizations and university personnel. For example, our creative arts programs at the elementary level make special use of the arts groups in our city. In a very special program in the Lincoln Downtown Educational Center individual arts groups have bartered space in a former high school building. For the privilege of using this space, the artist or performing group provides special services to the school system usually in the form of performances or tutoring in their particular talent area.

The overall monitoring of court-ordered desegregation is the responsibility of the monitoring board. As mentioned previously, the desegregation process has gone so smoothly and effectively that the monitoring board has had only a couple of occasions to meet on an issue. The five monitoring board members were appointed by the court, and it is a multiethnic/multiracial group of individuals.

The court has served as a sounding board for diverse community groups and individuals. Some groups take their very existence from either being in support of or being against the decisions of the court. During heightened periods of litigation these groups are most effective in communicating their views and promoting the interests of individuals within their respective groups. When litigation ceases or enters a hiatus, these groups tend to atrophy; the leadership in some cases grows resentful when the spotlight is no longer on them. Whereas most of these groups are ad hoc, a few of them are creatures of the school system itself, and when they suffer decline in interest and participation, the school system bears special concern and responsibility. Since 1973, a number of groups have been formed to support the desegregation effort. Surprisingly, very few "anti-busing" groups have had much staying power in Milwaukee. Chief among the ad hoc supporting groups is the Coalition for Peaceful Schools. This group is an amalgam of many religious and social institutions and has served a dual role of supporting desegregated education and serving as a watchdog over administrative procedures.

The school system created the Committee of 100, which reached its zenith of importance in the desegregation process during the summer of 1977. The Committee of 100 actually developed specific school plans that became part of the administration's submission to the court. However, with the vacating and remanding of the order in the fall of 1977 and the institutionalization of the desegregation process, the practical need for the Committee of 100 underwent classic goal displacement in that it changed its charter (with school board approval) to include the general review of quality education. The Committee of 100 arrived at this point after having been accorded no formal role in the desegregation monitoring process. However, it continued to be recognized by the board until it dissolved of its own accord in 1980.

The litigation process brings into existence certain groups and for a period gives them and certain individuals in the groups unusually high visibility. Although community involvement in such a major issue as desegregation is commendable, such involvement also creates a challenging residual problem for the system when the "thrill is gone" for these groups and the system settles into a new state of dynamic equilibrium. Nolan Estes, former superintendent of the Dallas Public Schools, described community involvement as "Making love to an eight-hundred-pound gorilla—possible to start, but awful tough to stop."

This is in no way to denigrate the community involvement experience in developing the Milwaukee desegregation plan. We believe that one of the most outstanding features of the plan was the grass-roots involvement of literally thousands of Milwaukee citizens in the planning process. They participated at local councils in each school. In turn, these local councils made recommendations to larger aggregate units of high schools, middle schools, and elementary schools, respectively. Finally, atop the entire involvement structure stood the Committee of 100. The Committee of 100 was composed of individuals elected from all areas of the city and, consequently, represented highly divergent viewpoints in the planning process. The Milwaukee public school staff worked with the Committee of 100 and its subcommittees for hundreds of hours during the 1976-77 school year, and their combined efforts resulted in a plan adopted by the court in the spring of 1977. Many of the individuals who served on the Committee of 100, as well as all councils at the local school and regional bases, were among the first to enroll their children in the specialty schools and encourage their friends and neighbors to do the same. Without this kind of nuclear support the efforts to involve the greater community would have been much less successful.

Section VII—Financing the Milwaukee Desegregation Plan

The implementation of the Milwaukee desegregation plan has involved massive effort and considerable expense. It could not possibly have been accomplished without financial help from outside the district, but getting that help involved dealing with a maze of rules and policies.

For example, one of the major and obvious problems with Emergency School Aid Act (ESAA) federal funding is that by design it was intended to diminish over time. It supported only those activities that were a result of the desegregation effort itself and therefore created unfortunate and unnecessary divisions within and among schools. Another inherent problem is the way in which federal priorities shift. In our first year of ESAA funding in our system (1977), the program gave top priority to remedial reading and math programs. We established such programs in accordance with this priority. However, in recent years ESAA program priorities have shifted into areas such as human relations and improving student conduct. When these new program areas are funded, original programs in reading and math are left without federal support and no local or state means to pick up the financial burden. Another inherent problem with ESAA funding was that, generally speaking, it followed Title I design in that it supplemented the regular educational program. That means that Title VI programs were "pullout"; that is, they removed children from the regular program to provide the supplemental program. "Pullout" programs can be destructive to continuity of program. Now, the latest chapter, Chapter II of the Education Consolidation and Improvement Act, 1981, has eliminated the categorical desegregation money altogether and introduced an entirely new set of priorities, distribution assumptions, and administrative processes.

Beginning with the 1982-83 school year the federal funding for desegregation and some twenty-six other separate funding sources were combined under Chapter II funding. Because Milwaukee was so successful in gaining desegregation aid (up to $7.5 million a year), it was inevitable that the school system would suffer substantially under the new Chapter II distribution formula. It appears that the school system will receive only about $3 million under Chapter II funding, causing some considerable program dislocation and reduction. This experience underscores another clear problem of federal funding in education. Rules can dramatically change from one administration to another and result in substantially different funding distributions in accordance with a different philosophy regarding the federal role in education. That the present administration has little sympathy for urban education in general and activities associated with desegregation in particular is evident. This means that school districts will have to rely further on local and state resources to gain the necessary additional funding for desegregation activities.

At the state level, Wisconsin has taken the lead in support for desegregation, with what has come to be called Chapter 220, passed in 1976. While the court and the litigation process had no direct effect in creating Chapter 220, it probably could not have come into existence had not the Milwaukee public schools come under court order to desegregate. The court order generated considerable sympathy on the part of legislators throughout the state and served as an entrée for other types of political pressure to be applied that resulted in the legislation. Chapter 220 provides for additional state aid for urban districts that desegregate students within their system as well as districts that participate in voluntary city-suburban student transfers to enhance racial balance. Not only did the state provide the participating school system additional aid through the state-aid formula, but it also picked up 100 percent of the transportation costs.

What Chapter 220 has meant to Milwaukee is $19 million (1981-82 school year) in general revenue. The supplementary money from the state has made possible the voluntary, educational-program-based desegregation. Even if the money were considerably less, the symbolic importance of a state contributing help to a major district that is trying to help itself on the desegregation issue is considerable. It says something important about priorities and puts the state on the affirmative side of the desegregation issue.

Recent Developments

The Milwaukee desegregation order will expire in June of 1984. In anticipation of this transition date, the Milwaukee School Board, with its newly elected "liberal" majority, has been involved for the last fourteen months in a serious study of desegregation's future. With 58 percent minority students in September 1983 and prospects for an ever increasing minority student population, the Board has reasoned that not only will the system be unable to racially balance the remaining all black schools (20), but it will be impossible to retain the present 120 schools in balance. Consequently, the Board has turned its attention to the possibility of increasing metropolitan integration. In October 1983, the Board invited twenty-nine suburban districts to work cooperatively with the Milwaukee system to exchange additional students and staff under the funding provisions of Chapter 220, so that Milwaukee is maintained with a student population 45 percent white, 45 percent black, and 10 percent other minority. At the same time the Board gave directions to its attorneys (David Tatel from the firm of Hogan and Hartson, Washington, D. C., and Irvin Charne from the firm of Charne, Glassner, Tehan, Clancy and Taitelman, Milwaukee, Wisconsin) to complete preparation for the filing of a metropolitan desegregation law suit.

It is anticipated that either voluntarily or through court direction our future desegregation activity will reach well beyond Milwaukee's borders. Even though the Milwaukee desegregation experience has been innovative, the new challenges of suburban integration will undoubtedly cause the development of new techniques and racial balance definitions. Making this expanded program compatible with the existing Milwaukee desegregation plan will require the extensive participation of city and suburban residents and a commitment of goodwill that characterized the "can do" attitude of desegregation planning in Milwaukee in 1977.

Some Postscript Observations

By our own assessment and also, fortunately, by outside assessment, the Milwaukee Public Schools had one of the most successful experiences in implementing a court-ordered racial balance plan of any school system in the country. This none-too-modest remark is tempered by the observation that the plans developed by other school systems were carefully reviewed and selectively borrowed as Milwaukee put together its own eclectic version.

Therefore, what success we have had is in part attributed to successful components from the experiences of other cities.

At the heart of the plan is the substance of educational renewal; school staffs at all levels approached the task of desegregation with unrelenting enthusiasm and inexhaustible energy. The presence of the desegregation challenge had the effect of pulling staff members together in cooperating patterns that had not existed before in our system. Petty concerns, commonplace in any large organization, were suppressed by the unremitting attention to the desegregation purpose.

As well as spotlighting personalities in the school system and community, the desegregation process in Milwaukee heightened the visibility of many school system practices, including those practices substantially unrelated to desegregation. For example, how successfully a school system communicates with the public and how successfully it lobbies with state and federal sources for additional funds are but two examples of practices that were highlighted even though they had no direct relationship to litigation or the desegregation plan.

However, the Milwaukee school desegregation plan is not for the faint of heart. It requires an enormous amount of work and staff talent to put together effective educational alternatives. In turn, staff at the local school and central office level must become personally committed to making these plans work and communicating their attractiveness to the public as a whole. It must also be clear that this is not the least expensive model that has been developed for school desegregation. The combination of additional program costs and providing an expensive transportation arrangement to accommodate the various program choices causes the bill to skyrocket. However, we have concluded that the result is well worth the cost. Desegregation created in Milwaukee a climate and potential for change. It was clear to those who took leadership responsibility that this opportunity was unprecedented in the school system's history and to miss this opportunity for leadership would be tantamount to missing the biggest educational opportunity of a lifetime. This planning process also sparked the imagination of the involved community. The community took a substantial role in the process, and people of goodwill everywhere in the community had come together in the common cause of this challenge. It was not an outside consultant or a single judge who determined the fate of the Milwaukee system; rather, the people in the system—the parents and students affected by the system—made the crucial determinations of the desegregation design.

In looking back over the desegregation processes since 1976, there simply are no major policies or administrative practices that I would have preferred to have done differently. This is not to suggest that the plan has reached perfection, rather just to say that the practice was thoroughly wholesome and took a very positive attitude toward the challenge of desegregation and program improvement. When minor mistakes in policy and practice were uncovered, they could be quickly corrected in an atmosphere where the court, school system, and community worked cooperatively together. Also, the plan is a dynamic one. We change some substantive aspects of it each year as the community involves itself in the review of our program decisions. We continue to expand educational opportunities in areas of need and under the student-assignment plan continue to exceed the numerical goals of the court. In fact, the three-stage student-assignment process is so ingrained in the tradition of our system that it feels as though the process has always been with us. Were the district to attempt to return abruptly to a strict neighborhood-school system at this point in time, I believe the action would meet with almost universal community resistance.

Appendix 7-1
High School Specialty Programs

HIGH SCHOOL	CAREER SPECIALTY PROGRAM
Bay View	Visual and Performing Arts
Custer	Applied Technology
Hamilton	Word Processing and Marketing
Juneau	Finance and Small Business
Madison	Energy, Environment, and Electronics
Marshall	Communications and Media
North Division	Medical, Dental, and Health
Pulaski	Transportation
Riverside	Community Human Services
South Division	Tourism, Food Service, and Recreation/ Lifetime Sports
Vincent	Agribusiness and Natural Resources International Studies
Washington	Computer Data Processing
West Division	Law, Law Enforcement, and Protective Services

Appendix 7-2
Middle and Elementary School Specialty Programs

Key to abbreviations and numbers

Column A = Grade Level
K = kindergarten; a number refers to a grade
Column B = Method of Instruction or Special Program Emphasis

1–Traditional/Regular; 2–Open Education; 3–Creative Arts; 4–Continuous Progress; 5–Physically/Multiply Handicapped; 6–Teacher/Pupil Learning Center;

7–Environmental Education; **8**–Business Development and Skills Center; **9**–Vocational Evaluation and Programming Center; **10**–Montessori; **11**–Gifted and Talented; **12**–Bilingual Academically Talented; **13**–Multi-Language; **14**–Developmental High School; **15**–College Bound; **16**–Technical; **17**–Bilingual Developmental Center; **18**–Individually Guided Education (IGE); **19**–Multi-Unit Individually Guided Education; **20**–Mathematics and/or Science; **21**–Fundamental; **22**–Health, Physical Education, and Science; **23**–High Intensity Learning Center; **24**–Basic Skills/Academic Enrichment; **25**–Performing Arts Specialty; **26**–Technical Education Specialty; **27**–Humanities and Fine Arts; **28**–Academic Emphasis; **29**–International Education; **30**–Communications Arts Center; **31**–Early Childhood Education; **32**–4-year-old Kindergarten; **33**–Pre-School Program for 3-4 Year Olds; **34**–Head Start; **35**–WE INDIANS Program; **36**–Multicultural Arts; **37**–Career Guidance Specialty; **38**–Deaf and Hard of Hearing; **39**–City-wide Program for the Retarded; **40**–Visually Handicapped; **41**–Autistic Classes; **42**–Alternative Exceptional Education; **43**–Generic Early Childhood; **44**–Emotionally Disturbed; **45**–Programs for the Academically Talented; **46**–Bilingual/Bicultural Center; **47**–Multicultural Education; **48**–Evening High School; **49**–Effectiveness School Plan; **50**–GED Alternate High School; **51**–School Age Parents Program.

Exceptional education classes for the learning disabled, emotionally disturbed, and for the retarded are located at many elementary, middle, and high schools. Call 475-8139 for information. High school career specialty programs, described elsewhere in INFO #32, are not listed here.

MIDDLE SCHOOLS

	A	B
Audubon	7-8	1, 27, 41
Bell	7-8	1, 45
Burroughs	7-8	1, 38, 45
Edison	7-8	18
Eighth	6-8	19
Fritsche	7-8	1, 25, 40
Fulton	7-8	1, 26
Kosciuszko	7-8	18, 35, 46
Morse	7-8	1, 41
Muir	7-8	1, 23, 45
Parkman	7-8	28
Robinson	6-8	2
Roosevelt	6-8	11
Sholes	7-8	8, 21, 38
Steuben	6-8	18, 35
Walker	7-8	21, 35
Webster	7-8	1, 5, 45
Wright	7-8	13, 21, 45

ELEMENTARY SCHOOLS

	A	B
Alcott	K-6	1
Allen-Field	K-6	1, 12, 34, 35, 46
Auer	K-6	6, 34, 45
Barton	4K-6	1
Berger	K-6	1
Blaine	K-6	1
Brown	K-6	1, 34
Browning	K-6	1, 45
Bruce	K-6	1
Bryant	K-6	1
Burbank	4K-6	1
Burdick	4K-8	1
Carleton	K-6	1
Cass	K-8	1, 41
Clarke	K-6	1, 45
Clemens	K-6	1
Clement Ave.	K-6	4
Congress	4K-6	1
Cooper	K-6	1, 38
Curtin	4K-6	1
Doerfler	K-6	1
Dover	K-6	1, 45
Eighty-eighth	K-6	1
Eighty-first	4K-6	1, 45
Eighty-second	4K-5	13
Elm	4K-6	3
Emerson	K-6	1, 5, 41
Engleburg	K-6	1, 40

Fairview	K-6	1, 39	Manitoba	K-6	1, 5, 45
Fernwood	K-8	1	Maple Tree	K-6	1, 22, 41
Fifty-fifth	4K-6	1, 13	Maryland	K-8	1
Fifty-third	K-6	1	Meir	3-5	11
Forest Home	K-6	1, 34, 46	Mitchell	K-6	1, 35
Franklin	K-6	19	Morgandale	4K-6	17, 38, 43, 46
Fratney	4K-8	1			
Gaenslen	K-12	5, 38	Neeskara	K-6	1, 38
Garden Homes	K-6	20	Ninety-fifth	K-6	1, 40
Garfield	K-6	2	Ninth	K-6	1, 34
Garland	K-6	1	Oklahoma	K-6	1, 41
Goodrich	K-6	1, 29	Palmer	K-6	19, 45
Grandview	K-6	19	Parkview	4K-6	1, 43
Grant	K-6	1	Philipp	K-6	21
Grantosa	K-6	1, 43	Pierce	K-6	1, 46
Granville	K-6	19	Riley	K-6	1
Green Bay	K-6	1	Seventy-eighth	4K-6	1, 41
Greenfield	K-6	1	Sherman	4K-6	36
Hampton	K-6	1	Siefert	K-6	1, 34
Happy Hill	K-6	1	Silver Spring	K-6	1
Hartford	K-8	1, 30, 45	Sixty-fifth	K-6	1, 41
Hawley	4K-6	7	Sixty-seventh	K-6	4
Hawthorne	K-6	1	Story	K-8	1, 35
Hayes	K-6	1	Stuart	K-6	1
Hi-Mount	K-6	1	Thirty-eighth	4K-6	2
Holmes	K-6	1, 34, 46	Thirty-fifth	K-6	1
Hopkins	K-6	20, 45	Thirty-first	K-6	21
Humboldt Park	K-6	1, 43	Thirty-seventh	K-6	1, 45
Irving	4K-6	1, 38	Thoreau	K-6	19
Kagel	K-6	1, 46	Tippecanoe	4K-6	1
Keefe	4K-6	1	Townsend	4K-6	4
Kilbourn	K-6	1, 34, 43	Trowbridge	K-6	21
Kluge	4K-6	1	Twentieth	4K-6	1, 34
LaFollette	4K-6	1, 45	Twenty-first	4K-6	6
Lancaster	K-6	1, 43	Twenty-fourth	4K-6	1
Lee	K-6	1, 34	Twenty-seventh	K-6	1, 46
Lincoln Ave.	4K-6	1	Victory	4K-6	19
Lloyd	4K-6	19	Vieau	K-8	1, 46
Longfellow	K-6	1, 46	Whitman	K-6	21, 43
Lowell	K-6	1	Whittier	K-6	1
MacDowell	Ages 3-10	10, 34, 41	Wisconsin Ave.	4K-6	1, 35, 46

Although not all schools have a specialty program, all schools and grade levels are in some ways affected by the comprehensive, full-day desegregation plan.

References

Brookover, W. B., C. Beady, P. Flood, J. Schweitzer, and J. Wisenbaker
    1979   *School Social Systems and Student Achievement: Schools Can Make a
    Difference.* Brooklyn, N.Y.: J. F. Bergin Co.

1980   *School Social Systems and Student Achievement: A Social Systems Approach to Increased Student Learning.* Tallahassee, Fla.: National Teacher Corps, Florida State University Foundation.

Brookover, W. B., et al.
1982   *Creating Effective Schools—An Inservice Program for Enhancing School Learning Climate and Achievement.* Holmes Beach, Fla.: Learning Publications, Inc.

Brookover, W. B., N. M. Brady, and M. Warfield
1981   *Educational Policies and Equitable Education: A Report of Studies of Two Desegregated School Systems.* Procedures and Pilot Research to Develop an Agenda for Desegregation Studies (Final Report), R. L. Green, Project Director. East Lansing, Mich.: College of Urban Development, Center for Urban Affairs, Michigan State University.

Brookover, W. B., G. Ferderbar, G. Gay, M. Middleton, G. Posner, and F. Roebuck
1980   *Measuring and Attaining the Goals of Education.* Alexandria, Va.: Association for Supervision and Curriculum Development.

Brookover, W. B., and L. W. Lazotte
1977   *Changes in School Characteristics Coincident with Changes in Student Achievement* (Executive Summary). East Lansing, Mich.: College of Urban Development, Michigan State University.

Brookover, W. B., and J. Schneider
1975   "Academic Environments and Elementary School Achievement." *Journal of Research and Development in Education* 9: 83-91.

Brophy, J. E.
1979   *Advances in Teacher Effectiveness Research.* Occasional Paper No. 18. East Lansing, Mich.: Institute for Research on Teaching, Michigan State University.

Brophy, J. E., and T. L. Good
1974   *Teacher-Student Relationships: Causes and Consequences.* New York: Holt, Rinehart and Winston.

Brophy, J. E., and J. G. Putnam
1978   *Classroom Management in the Elementary Grades.* Institute for Research on Teacher Research Series No. 32. East Lansing, Mich.: Michigan State University.

Edmonds, R. R.
1979   "Some Schools Work and More Can." *Social Policy* 9: 28-32.

Chapter 8

The Seattle Plan for Eliminating Racial Imbalance

William Maynard

I. Introduction

The integration of the schools of Seattle was mandated by the choice of the people, not by court order.

Background

Since 1963, the Seattle School District has worked to improve racial balance in the schools and has also worked to provide the opportunity for a multiethnic education for all children. The position of the school board is that a quality, integrated education will best serve the needs of the children of Seattle.

The city of Seattle is unique. We have one of the most diverse student populations in the United States and are fortunate to have a culture reflecting the beauty of this multiethnicity.[1]

Largely because of neighborhood housing patterns, minority ethnic groups were concentrated in specific areas of the city. As this trend continued, schools within these areas became increasingly racially imbalanced.

In 1963 the school board initiated efforts to reduce racial imbalance through the implementation of the Voluntary Racial Transfer (V.R.T.) program. This program was established by the superintendent, Forbes Bottomly, and a Community Advisory Committee. In that first year, 247 students transferred to schools outside their neighborhood areas. The program reached a peak in 1969, when 2,600 students enrolled as Voluntary Racial Transfers. (During the year 1976-77 the number of Voluntary Racial Transfers declined to 1,647; approximately 90 percent were minority students.)

In spite of these efforts, racial imbalance continued to increase in the schools. In 1971 the school board made a second major effort to reduce this imbalance through the establishment of middle schools and the mandatory assignment of students to insure racial balance. By 1976, 1,426 students had volunteered to attend another school in the Voluntary Racial Transfer program, and another 560 students had been mandatorily reassigned in the middle school program.

Student enrollment by ethnicity was changing rapidly. In 1967 thirteen schools were identified as racially imbalanced. By 1976 the number had increased to twenty-seven. This number, however, depended upon whether the definition of racially imbalanced schools applied was that of the state of Washington or that of the Emergency School Assistance Act guidelines. The state defined a racially imbalanced school as having an enrollment of 40 percent of a single minority. Under this definition four of the twelve high schools, three of eleven junior high schools, and twenty of eighty-four elementary schools were segregated. Under federal guidelines, one additional high school, one junior high, and seven elementary schools were segregated.

In June 1976 the school board selected David Moberly as the new superintendent. One of his primary goals was desegregation. At the same time, with the help of a grant from the Office of Education, the Desegregation Planning Office was established, and William Maynard was appointed as the director. This office was assigned the task of developing a desegregation plan for the 1977-78 school year.

During the planning process, Superintendent Moberly directed that only voluntary strategies be used, although no definition of "voluntary" was provided at that time. By September 1976, the superintendent directed that magnet schools and magnet programs be the sole means of desegregating the schools.

In January 1977 thirty-one proposals for magnet-school programs were presented in a survey format to all parents of students within the school district. Both parents and students were surveyed to determine which programs were most appealing. Although racial quotas and enrollment limits were established for the various programs, the superintendent directed that a student who selected one program but later changed his mind could withdraw and return to his original school or select another program. The intent of the plan was to place the programs in strategic schools to attract minority students to white schools and white students to minority schools.

The desegregation goals for the magnet program were to (1) maintain 1,600 Voluntary Racial Transfers, (2) maintain 500 mandatory middle school transfers, (3) recruit 1,000 new volunteers to the magnet programs, and (4) recruit an additional 1,000 students to the magnet programs for each of the following years. If the students moved out of schools in which they were of majority race and into schools in which their group was the minority, desegregation could be accomplished. However, the same process would have to be repeated each year.

Selection of the schools for magnet program placement was critical. The criteria for selection were as follows:

1. The results of the parent-student survey.
2. Capacity of the buildings.
3. Ease of transportation, for which the district was to pay the cost.
4. Equity of moving white and minority students.
5. Whether the school currently received Voluntary Racial Transfer students.
6. How the choice of a particular school would affect the district in any court action.

In February 1977 the superintendent recommended the magnet program to the board, and two weeks of community hearings were scheduled. The magnet plan was adopted by the board on March 11, 1977. Twenty magnet programs were placed in thirty-two schools, and some existing special programs were relocated in order to draw minority or white students. An intensive recruiting plan was initiated in April 1977. It was conceivable that the magnet programs could be filled voluntarily without significantly reducing racial isolation.

On April 21, 1977, the National Association for the Advancement of Colored People (NAACP) filed an official complaint with the Department of Health, Education, and Welfare asking the federal government to investigate segregation of the schools in Seattle. The NAACP stated that it did not believe that the desegregation plan would work. Leaders of the American Civil Liberties Union (ACLU) indicated that they had been working with the NAACP, but would wait until mid-May before deciding whether to join in the complaint.

In May the Desegregation Planning Office presented the school board with various strategies that could be adopted as a backup plan should the recruitment of volunteers not reach the established goal. These strategies included pairing two schools from different neighborhoods, clustering schools to provide students with a limited choice, any of which would improve the racial balance of the school chosen, a forced choice of schools not including the student's home school, an enrollment lid which would limit the number of students of a certain race that could attend a given school, grade reconfigurations in which grades K to 3 would attend one school and 4 to 6 attend another, and boundary realignments.

In mid-May the NAACP and ACLU pointed out that the school board had never made an official commitment to end school segregation, nor had it adopted a definition of racial imbalance. Resolutions officially committing the school board to end segregation were necessary in order to develop backup plans should the voluntary means fail, and in order to avoid a lawsuit by these organizations. On June 8, 1977, the Seattle school board, through Resolutions 1977-8 and 1977-9, directed that racial imbalance in the schools be eliminated by the fall of the 1979-80 school year. The resolutions defined racial imbalance as:

The situation that exists when the combined minority student enrollment in a school exceeds the Districtwide combined minority average by 20 percentage points, provided that the single minority enrollment (as defined by current federal categories) of no school will exceed 50 percent of the student body.

The board further directed that at least one-half of the elimination of racial imbalance occur in the 1978-79 school year. This one-half elimination could occur in one of three ways:

1. By eliminating racial imbalance in at least 50 percent of those schools identified as racially imbalanced; or
2. By reducing racial imbalance by one-half in all schools identified as racially imbalanced; or
3. By a combination of these measures.

The Board of Directors, not the courts, mandated the integration of the schools of Seattle.

Board Resolution 1977-8 directed that "racial imbalance be eliminated through the use of 'educationally sound strategies.'" In meeting this directive, the district planners have developed plans essentially designed to meet the educational needs of the children in our schools. These have been identified as:

1. Equal educational opportunities for all children
2. Provisions for the safety needs of all children
3. A choice of educational options
4. A curriculum which includes:
   a. Basic skills emphasis
   b. Multiethnic/multicultural education
   c. Career readiness education
   d. Sex equity education
5. Provisions for the maintenance of ethnic identity for both minority and majority students
6. High expectations of academic achievement
7. Assurance that every child can succeed in school

In developing the planning structure for desegregation, the Desegregation Planning Office made provision for the following major concerns:

- The personnel and financial resources needed to plan educationally sound desegregation strategies
- The personnel of interagency cooperation in planning
- The need for citizen and community involvement in the planning process
- The necessity for an ongoing information process

These resolutions provided the framework for the final planning processes and ultimately the final plan. The board had established the date of December 14, 1977, for the adoption of the final plan.

In July, the District-Wide Advisory Committee for Desegregation, composed of citizens representing community groups, presented to the board criteria for evaluating desegregation proposals.

BOARD-APPROVED CRITERIA (May 1977) for Evaluating Desegregation Plans (Including 1977-78 Contingency Plans)

The Plan:
1. Is consistent with Board's established educational goals.
2. Would place no greater burden on minority than majority students.
3. Recognizes need for ethnic identity of different minority students, and is sensitive to ethnic heritage. (Strong feeling that small minority groups should not be divided and scattered—that we should encourage transfer of minority students in large enough groups to maintain a sense of cohesiveness.)
4. Provides for a system of desegregation within schools as well as between schools. (Plan would not contribute to segregated classrooms or programs.)
5. Results in a reduction of racial isolation in those schools currently defined as racially isolated by School Board definition and ESAA standard.
6. Recognizes need to preserve and enhance already integrated schools.
7. Encourages integrated housing.
8. Is sensitive to special educational needs of students, e.g., bilingual, special education, etc. No movement of such programs will take place without careful analysis of effect on students.
9. Provides for in-service training programs for all school personnel and provides for community participation in those programs.
10. Provides for the screening and placement of school personnel who have demonstrated interest and ability in working with students of diverse backgrounds. Provides for evaluation of school personnel. (Screening, placement and evaluation to be consistent with employee bargaining agreements.)
11. Provides for right of appeal to any student transferred. Process should ensure that hardship transfer or exemption is given on a case-by-case basis and does not favor one group over another.
12. Includes a specific program to develop inter-racial understanding among students. Includes elements to both prevent and deal with possible conflicts.
13. Includes grades K through 12.
14. Is possible to implement on the basis of cost effectiveness and on the basis of time and District resources.
15. Creates and maintains stability and predictability to extent possible—creates consistent feeder patterns and continuity of programs.

16. To the extent educational options are available they will not favor one group over another.
17. Provides for evaluation of success criteria at specific checkpoints.
18. Any desegregation plan will take into consideration each of these criteria at stage of implementation.

Through the voluntary transfer programs, racial imbalance was reduced in only thirteen of the district's twenty-seven racially imbalanced schools. Because of the board's new resolution to eliminate racial isolation by the 1979-80 school year, an estimated 2,400 new students would have to be recruited in each of the following years. The Desegregation Planning Office announced that strictly voluntary desegregation would not work. In addition to the numbers of volunteers that would need to be recruited each year and the cost of magnet programs, many of the magnets had to be placed in overcrowded minority schools in order to attract white students. To accommodate the white students, minority students would have to be mandatorily reassigned. The result would have been voluntary desegregation for white students and mandatory for minority students.

In September the Desegregation Planning Office presented the District-Wide Advisory Committee (DWAC) with four plans for eliminating racial isolation. DWAC's task was to review these and to make recommendations. Three of the plans—expanded magnets, enrollment lidding, and a three-zone plan—were primarily voluntary, and the fourth—boundary realignment—was a mandatory plan. Each was designed to meet the criteria presented by DWAC. After DWAC's review the plans were to be presented at thirty community meetings held during the month of October. During November the Desegregation Planning Office and DWAC together would review public comment and submit a final proposed plan to the school board on December 1, 1977.

Also in September, at the insistence of the Desegregation Planning Office, all school program changes or contemplated administrative actions that might effect desegregation had to be preceded with a "Desegregation Impact Statement." Prior to school opening, for example, two high schools implemented new courses that were similar to magnet courses in other schools. These were brought to our attention by the impact statements. These statements became an effective tool in monitoring the desegregation process throughout the implementation of the plan.

Prior to the October community hearings a fifth plan was submitted to the Desegregation Planning Office by the Urban League. This was a mandatory plan involving triads of schools and was included in the community presentations.

In November at the request of the Desegregation Planning Office, Superintendent Moberly recommended to the board that only one plan be submitted on December 1. It was feared that if two plans were submitted, one would be perceived as a "throwaway." The results of the community input varied and were inconclusive. However, the highest rated plan was one that incorporated magnet schools with mandatory student assignments as a backup.

Although the superintendent, the board, and the majority of the community wanted first a voluntary and second a mandatory student-assignment plan, DWAC and the Church Council for Greater Seattle insisted upon a plan that was mandatory with voluntary backup features. Their concerns were the yearly instability of a voluntary first plan. The church council's criticism also included its view that "magnet schools are elitist and serve families with parents who are sophisticated enough to take advantage of them" and that "magnet schools offer a superior education to some children, but they rob resources from other programs and thus give other children an inferior education."

The final plan with fixed student assignments and voluntary enrollment permitted was submitted to DWAC on November 22, 1977, for review. After revisions, the plan was presented at community hearings during the following week.

On December 14, 1977, the Seattle school board voted for a mandatory desegregation plan. The vote was six in favor and one opposed.

Stated below are assumptions of the Seattle Plan. They have to do with the ultimate purpose of school desegregation and the conditions under which students learn how to get along with each other. Also mentioned is the assistance the teaching staff should receive to facilitate optimum conditions of learning.

With a mandatory student-assignment strategy, every school should have equal access to district resources and considerable freedom for the development of educational programs at each individual school. Seattle school officials clearly indicated that Seattle would not implement a strategy for desegregation that relied simply on student movement. Rather, the plan had to focus on providing a quality education.

For quality education to occur in a multicultural setting, minority students should not bear responsibility for a disproportionate share of movement to achieve desegregation. While the plan emphasized the benefits of multicultural education, it also found value in ethnic identity and attempted to achieve both goals.

Furthermore, it was assumed that the success of each child in school is dependent not only on his or her ability to master academic requirements, but is also dependent upon the kinds of relationships developed in school. Ability to get along with others is critical and is as important in multiethnic classrooms as in job situations. It is a skill that can and must be taught in schools.

Some fifty studies have been made of student interaction under interracial conditions. These studies show strongly that positive interracial interaction usually leads to the development of positive racial attitudes.[2]

The importance of staff development cannot be overemphasized.

Precisely because integrated education is new, it requires personnel capable of doing new things in new ways. Consequently, adequate preparation should include programs to retrain or supplement training of teachers and principals. Nancy St. John states:

The principal and his/her faculty have the responsibility for structuring the interracial climate of the school. Their nonracist attitudes, commitment to equality, justice, and democratic decision making, their optimism as to the potential of the minority group child and determination to raise his achievement and aspiration, set the stage for meaningful integration.[34]

A 1976 report by the United States Commission on Civil Rights summarized the desegregation efforts of twenty-nine separate school districts throughout the United States. Each district was rated on ten separate variables relevant to the desegregation of schools. One of the variables that correlated most highly with a successful desegregation effort was staff training.[4] A question-and-answer format in the *Education Daily* (July 11, 1977) summarizes the position of the Office of Education regarding human relations training. In 1977 this federal agency believed that human relations programs may be the most productive activity in desegregating districts. In addition, such programs may have an even larger impact on improving basic skills than direct skills development.[5]

The Seattle Title VII ESAA Community Advisory Committee indicated that staff training was the first priority in providing an appropriate climate at each magnet school. A subcommittee of Seattle principals of magnet-school programs rated staff development training as the first priority to ensure the success of the magnet schools. The Seattle school administration has indicated that a comprehensive and well-defined staff training program is the first priority. In summary, staff training programs are needed to facilitate integrated education.

Few school districts have made adequate provision for staff development. The investment that most districts make in their personnel is almost negligible, particularly when compared with that of business and industry. If desegregation/integration is to succeed within the framework of providing quality education by using sound educational strategies, it will succeed at the building and classroom levels through the efforts of principals and teachers. Here is where the investment must be made.

II. A Description of the Community

Seattle is an hourglass-shaped city located in Washington State. Its western boundary is Puget Sound and its eastern boundary is Lake Washington. The total population of Seattle is nearly 500,000; suburban communities outside Seattle consist of about 500,000 additional people. When the Seattle Plan was adopted (December 14, 1977), 65.3 percent of the 58,353 public school students were white, 18.3 percent black, 9.7

percent Asian American, 2.9 percent Native American, and 3.8 percent Hispanic. The unique ethnic diversity of the city for a four-year period is shown in Table 8-1. Enrollments and ethnic breakdowns of private schools were not made available to the Desegration Planning Office.

Table 8-1 White-Minority School Enrollment Percentages, Seattle, 1976-80

Year	White	%	Black	%	Asian	%	Hisp.	%	Native Amer.	%	Total
1976-77	41,767	67.6	10,763	17.4	5,625	9.1	1,999	3.2	1,665	2.7	61,819
1978-79	33,629	62.4	10,699	19.9	5,846	10.8	2,131	4.0	1,580	2.9	53,885
Oct. 1980	27,482	56.6	10,338	21.3	7,257	15.0	2,031	4.2	1,406	2.9	48,514

Source: Seattle School District, *Annual Report,* June 1981.

Seattle's blacks live in the narrow middle of the city and have expanded into the southeastern section. The predominantly white sections are in the north and in the southwest. Asian families live primarily in the southeast. Hispanics and Native Americans live throughout the city.

A major factor of concern to the development of the Seattle Plan was a severe decline in enrollment which began in 1964. At that time, 100,000 students attended public schools, but this figure had dropped to less than 53,000 by 1978. The white population has dropped primarily due to declining birth rates and some outward migration. Asian immigration has increased, while the black population has remained relatively constant. These factors resulted in a yearly increase in the percentage of minority students enrolled in the school and a difficulty in accurately predicting individual school enrollments and ethnic breakdown.

In 1977 the Seattle school district was composed of twelve high schools, eleven junior high schools, six middle schools, and eighty-four elementary schools. Students also had the option of five alternative school programs and thirty magnet programs.

In the 1960s, several predominantly black elementary schools were closed by the Board of Directors. Their students were transferred to predominantly white schools. In 1972 a middle schools plan was implemented. This plan moved black students to white schools. Over a ten-year period the district tried voluntary desegregation through a Voluntary Racial Transfer program. It was utilized primarily by black students who volunteered for predominantly white schools, and it involved more than 2,175 students. By 1976 twenty-seven of Seattle's schools had student bodies in which whites were the minority. These schools were classified as segregated.

Pressure to desegregate these schools increased from the ACLU, NAACP, and the Office of Civil Rights. A new superintendent was hired that year and was told by the school board that desegregation was the top priority. Attorneys for the school district also had been warning the board about the potential for litigation. In July 1976 a director of desegregation was appointed, and the Desegregation Planning Office established. The office personnel consisted of the director, an assistant to the director, two planners, one public relations specialist, and two secretaries. During the final nine months of planning, five additional planners joined the team. The director reported to the deputy superintendent and initially was allocated a budget for salaries only. In addition to the responsibility of developing a plan to desegregate the schools, the director became the district liaison to all community groups involved in desegregation and supervised the Human Resource Associates Department (eighty people) and the Human Relations Training Department (ten people). The latter two responsibilities were transferred to other departments during the final ten months of planning.

Initially, the new superintendent proposed to desegregate the city schools by way of voluntary enrollments in thirty magnet programs that were established throughout the school district. After extensive recruiting of student volunteers, it became apparent that the schools could not be desegregated and remain so by voluntary methods alone. The Desegregation Planning Office then presented five optional plans for board and community consideration. The planning office analyzed the advantages, disadvantages, and costs of each plan. From these options was developed the Seattle Plan, a combination of voluntary and mandatory strategies. The plan was adopted by the Board of Directors for the school district on December 14, 1977, and was implemented in the fall of 1978. By 1980 virtually all of Seattle's schools were desegregated peacefully and without court order as seen in Table 8-2.

Table 8-2 Changes in Racial Composition of Schools in Seattle, 1976-80

School Name	Minority % 1976-77	Minority % 1977-78 (Ex. Spec. Ed.)	Minority % Oct. 1980 (62.5 = segregation)	WK+	WOK+
Cleveland*	72.8	72.82	63.2		
Franklin*	78.3	76.61	60.5		
Garfield*	72.5	78.42	55.7		
Rainier Beach*	63.8	58.9	54.5		
Mercer*	79.1	80.14	52.1		
Sharples*	75.3	74.89	51.9		
South Shore*	59.4	69.15	51.4		
Beacon Hill*	87.0	85.71		54.4	52.5
Brighton*	87.4	86.93		64.3	60.4
Coleman*	94.7	96.03		closed	
Columbia*	74.3	78.22		64.8	61.9
Dearborna Park*	82.5	77.41		56.4	51.5

Table 8-2 *(continued)*

School Name	Minority % 1976-77	Minority % 1977-78 (Ex. Spec. Ed.)	Minority % Oct. 1980 (62.5 = segregation)	
Dunlap*	77.0	80.60	62.6	61.0
Emerson	46.4	49.00	61.1	62.3
Gatzert*	89.2	91.55	69.1	62.2
Graham Hill	65.6	63.74	60.5	54.4
Hawthorne*	72.3	72.53	closed	
High Point*	70.0	70.85	62.3	55.3
Kimball*	78.3	87.86 vol.	45.7	46.6
King*	64.4	66.04	49.5	51.4
Leschi*	96.0	90.13	56.3	51.4
Madrona	N.A.	N.A.	58.3	56.0
Maple*	50.7	55.38	57.7	56.6
Minor*	90.8	85.39	54.5	50.6
Muir*	72.9	76.67	57.3	53.6
Rainier View	49.0	49.77	58.5	61.1
Van Asselt*	84.0	84.02	54.5	53.4
Whitworth*	68.4	68.52 vol.	55.2	54.2
Wing Lake*	84.1	86.25	57.1	54.9
Washington	N.A.	N.A.	50.0	50.0

+WK/with kindergarten, WOK/without kindergarten
*Segregated by board definition, June 1977

The Board of Directors was composed of seven individuals—four white women, one black woman, and two white men. Of the seven, one white woman consistently opposed desegregation strategy that was other than totally voluntary. She cast the only opposing vote to the final plan. Two of the women favored some mandatory strategies throughout the entire planning process. The remaining board members initially favored voluntary strategies and throughout the planning process moved more and more toward a "fixed assignment" model.

III. The Seattle Plan for Eliminating Racial Imbalance

Perhaps as important as the plan itself is the process by which the plan is developed. It is through this process that a plan becomes unique to the community.

Because it was determined that the totally voluntary plan would not result in the desegregation of the schools and because of a need for continued community support, five plans were developed by the Desegregation Planning Office for citizen and board consideration. The major question became "voluntary movement first and mandatory backup" versus "mandatory assignment first and voluntary movement secondary." Since the majority of the board and the community were initially committed to voluntary movement first, this theory had to be tested. The five plans represented options based upon both concepts. In the review process it became apparent that in order to accomplish the goals of total desegregation, a "fixed assignment" plan was necessary with voluntary options. This approach became the final plan. It included the Voluntary Racial Transfer program, magnet programs, alternative schools, and schools already integrated as well as mandatory student assignments.

The student data base that was utilized became a key factor in the final planning stages. In fact, the effects of selecting the appropriate data base had to be demonstrated, as this would ultimately determine district attendance, placement, and transfer policies. The other key factor was the placement of alternative schools and special programs. A discussion of the student data bases utilized in desegregation planning follows.

Each year approximately 11,000 students attended schools other than their "neighborhood" school. This movement is made up of students who transfer in special education, Voluntary Racial Transfer program, alternative schools, special programs, disciplinary transfers, hardship cases, and the mandatory middle school program. As the district enters a period of controlled enrollment to achieve desegregation, we must carefully reexamine the effect of this movement upon desegregation, and we must reevaluate policies to assure that they support desegregation wherever possible.

A desegregation plan that redraws attendance boundaries and restructures the grade spans at certain schools should not allow students to transfer out of the assigned attendance areas. Planning for desegregation through boundary changes or grade changes needs to start from the areas where students live, and to proceed to assign areas of the city together in patterns that accomplish the needed desegregation. Therefore, our plan used a "neighborhood" data base. A "neighborhood" data base enables the planner to determine how many students live in a particular school attendance area and the ethnic diversity of school student bodies.

The voluntary aspect of the plan (drawing white students into previously minority isolated schools and drawing minority students into previously predominantly white schools) permitted all student transfers that improve the racial balance of the receiving school. By the same token, student transfers that did not improve racial balance were undesirable. Thus, students could not "shop around" for placements at schools that did not enhance racial balance. Our plan of mandatory assignments with voluntary features seemed to require less movement of students for desegregation than plans which use mandatory assignments by neighborhoods only. In reality, however, the total movement of students is almost the same. The voluntary aspect of the plan simply takes advantage of existing progress toward desegregation and does not require current racial transfer students to return to neighborhood schools for reassignment elsewhere.

The district currently operates several "alternative schools" and special programs, which provide a style of instruction different from that usually encountered in regular district schools. Some of these alternative schools currently contribute to the district's desegregation efforts, but some do not. Particularly, eight popular alternative schools that were neighborhood-based did not contribute to the desegregation goals. Since the parents desired and supported these programs, the Desegregation Planning Office recommended that they remain, subject to relocation or replication. Alternative schools were eliminated from the desegregation plan until a thorough assessment of them could be made, including enrollment policies and locations and their impact upon desegregation. Eventually alternative schools would be analyzed as if they were magnet schools.

The district recognizes both a legal and a moral responsibility to address the special learning needs of its students who have limited command of the English language because they come from non-English-speaking homes. Currently the district operates bilingual programs and English-as-a-second-language (ESL) programs in a number of schools. Bilingual tutoring is often provided where there are only a few students in school who need special assistance, and some bilingual teachers and aides have "itinerant" assignments which move them from school to school on a regular schedule. If students with limited English-speaking abilities are assigned to or select schools which cannot provide a full bilingual program in their native language, the district will adjust the pattern of the bilingual tutoring service to fit these students' needs or allow such students to transfer to schools that provide such services.

The services of the Bilingual Programs Office staff and translators will also be used to translate and interpret information about the desegregation plan and options for parents and students of limited English-speaking ability, and to make personal contacts, as needed.

Title I and Urban, Rural, Racially Disadvantaged (URRD) programs had been established in predominantly white or predominantly minority schools. These programs either will be relocated, or an identical "mirrored" program will be created in another area of the city. The goal is to maintain the programs but on an integrated basis.

Before desegregation, minority schools tended to enroll over capacity, and schools which were under capacity were predominantly white. In a totally voluntary plan that used magnet schools only, such schools in buildings overenrolled by minorities would force the movement of some minority students out of those schools to make space for whites. Placing magnet programs in a predominantly white school was not a problem. Because equity of movement for minority and majority racial populations was a key criterion, the Facilities Utilization Study was critical. Information derived from the study enabled us to avoid assigning students in a way that would violate this criterion—voluntary movement for white students and mandatory for minority students.

The first step in developing the plan was to model each such school's enrollment down to the recommended capacity. This was done by displacing students whose movement out of the home school would enhance (or maintain) racial balance. Portable classroom space that has been common to our overcrowded schools was eliminated, and the actual level of student enrollment was keyed to building capacities.

It was apparent to the Desegregation Planning Office and to the District-Wide Advisory Committee that strictly voluntary strategies would never accomplish the desegregation goals. Many in the community and some members of the school board were not ready to accept a mandatory plan. In order to have the community and the board experience a range of strategies available and alternative outcomes associated with specific strategies, four plans were developed by the Desegregation Planning Office with the direct assistance of the District-Wide Advisory Committee. A fifth plan that originated in the mid-1960s was submitted by the Urban League. It was revised and updated by the Desegregation Planning Office. All five plans were submitted to the board and were presented for community review before a final plan was prepared. The final plan merged the best features of the Urban League's plan with the best features of the fourth plan designed by the Desegregation Planning Office. The final plan was adopted late in 1977 for initial implementation during the 1978-79 school year.

Some of the key factors that influenced the school board to adopt the Seattle Plan with fixed student assignments were the following:

- The District-Wide Advisory Committee and the Desegregation Planning Office worked very closely together toward building a final plan and presented a united proposal
- The mayor consistently supported the district's desegregation planning
- The editorial boards of both major newspapers consistently supported the desegregation efforts
- The minority community supported the plan
- A committee of leading business people, through the Chamber of Commerce, supported the plan
- There was a wide base of community review throughout the planning process
- The board resolutions and criteria for desegregation left few, if any, options other than those presented in the final plan
- For the majority of the community, there was an underlying pride in accomplishing the desegregation task without a court order

The major concern with which the board had to deal was changing from an all-voluntary plan in January 1977, to a mandatory plan in November

1977. The turning point occurred in June when the board adopted the resolution to "eliminate racial isolation" by the fall of 1979. This was perceived as a legally and morally binding decision, and it became obvious to the board and the superintendent that desegregation could not be accomplished through voluntary strategies.

A major reason for the passage of the board resolution took place in May 1977. A letter to the board was jointly drafted by the mayor, the Seattle Urban League, the Municipal League, and the Chamber of Commerce. These civic leaders urged the adoption of the goal. In addition, the mayor personally contacted the superintendent and some individual board members. He made it clear that he did not want the Seattle schools under court-ordered busing.

The superintendent directed the Desegregation Planning Office to develop a plan using fixed assignment as the primary strategy and voluntary options as the secondary strategy. This plan incorporated key components from each of the five preliminary plans which were presented to the community. Thus the plan used zones, pairings, and triads; and allowed for boundary adjustments, ethnic lidding, and a continuation or expansion of the various options available to students. In summary, this plan contained the following characteristics:

- The plan provided for feeder pattern continuity, program stability, and predictability for a student who enters kindergarten through twelfth grade.
- The plan preserved the successful portions of the current VRT, magnet-school, and middle school programs.
- The plan allowed the district, to the extent feasible, to honor a perceived commitment to current magnet-school parents to continue those programs.
- The plan provided for equality of educational opportunity for all students.
- The plan provided for educational options for those who desire them within a framework of ethnic lidding and space availability.
- The plan preserved and enhanced already integrated schools.
- The plan allowed children from the same neighborhood, regardless of race, to go to school together.
- The plan was equitable for both minority and nonminority families.
- The plan provided stability over time.
- The plan allowed for program diversity within schools and throughout the district.
- The plan allowed for parent/student choices both among programs within schools and among programs in different schools.
- The plan allowed for the preservation of ethnic identity as represented by current neighborhood groupings.
- The plan allowed for maximum amount of nonrecoverable costs to be used for program improvement.

- The plan was economically feasible within known and/or reasonably acquirable funds.
- The plan encompassed all high school attendance areas of the school district.
- The plan provided that the number of students who moved included 54 percent nonminority and 46 percent minority.
- The plan provided for classroom desegregation as well as school desegregation.

Figure 8-1 Geographic Attendance Zones

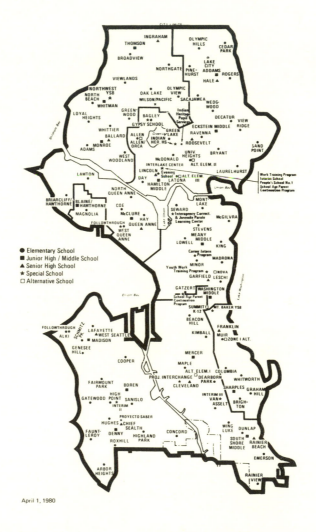

Source: The Seattle Plan for Eliminating Racial Imbalance, revised edition, December 13, 1977.

Overview of the Seattle Plan

The Seattle Plan is a comprehensive desegregation program designed to eliminate racial imbalance in Seattle public schools. Racial imbalance is defined as "the situation that exists when the combined minority student enrollment in a school exceeds the district-wide combined minority average by twenty percentage points, provided that the single minority enrollment (as defined by current federal categories) of no school will exceed fifty percent of the student body."[6]

There are four basic components to the Seattle Plan.

Zone Organization

The Seattle Plan divides the school district into three zones to assist in student movement, to structure program development, and to maintain geographic identity. The zones have been designed to eliminate racial imbalance in all minority-impacted schools and to maintain that status on an ongoing basis within each geographic area.

Zone I includes the Franklin, Ingraham, Ballard, and Queen Anne/McClure geographic attendance areas. Zone II includes the Hale, Roosevelt, Lincoln, and Garfield geographic attendance areas. Zone III includes the Queen Anne/Magnolia, West Seattle, Cleveland, Rainier Beach, and Sealth geographic attendance areas.

Paired or Triaded Elementary Schools

To eliminate racially imbalanced elementary schools, the primary process is the pairing or triading of schools. Most minority-imbalanced elementary schools have been linked with predominantly majority elementary schools in pairs or triads using a change in grade structure as the student movement strategy. Generally, students are divided by grade levels (for example, one school in a pair houses grades 1 to 3 and the other school houses grades 4 to 6). In the 1980-81 year of the plan there will be fifteen such arrangements of pairs or triads involving approximately one-half of the district elementary schools. Kindergarten students remain in their neighborhood schools in 1980-81 as they did in 1978-80.

Assignment Patterns for Secondary Schools

Racial imbalance is eliminated in secondary schools through the use of school assignment patterns. Elementary schools are assigned to middle and junior high schools within their zones, and middle and junior high schools are assigned to high schools within their zones according to established patterns which eliminate racial imbalance in the secondary schools as students progress in grade level.

Education Options

An important feature of the Seattle Plan is the provision for educational options. Student transfers for such options must be consistent with the

Seattle Plan and not contribute to racial imbalance. There are four types of transfers for educational options:

1. The Option Program Transfer is available to students interested in one of the option programs. Students may apply for these programs at grade levels 1 through 12 if their transfers will not tend to cause racial imbalance in the sending or receiving school. A limited number of options for kindergarten are available. Space availability in the receiving school and racial balance of the option programs are additional criteria considered in the processing of these transfers. Option Program Transfers are generally limited to the zone of the applicant's residence except for high school students.

2. The Alternative Program Transfer is available to students interested in one of the alternative education programs. Students may apply for Alternative Program Transfers if their transfers meet specific program requirements and criteria for space availability and racial balance. Such transfers are also subject to the same requirements as listed above for Option Program Transfers.

3. The Individual Opportunity Transfer is available for elementary, middle, and junior high school students who seek educational opportunities not available in their assigned schools. Students may apply for Individual Opportunity Transfers within zone if their transfers will improve racial balance in both the sending and receiving schools and there is space available in the receiving schools.

4. The Voluntary Racial Transfer program is available to senior high school students who seek educational opportunities provided by a specific senior high school setting. Students may apply for Voluntary Racial Transfers throughout the city if their transfers will improve racial balance in both the sending and receiving schools and there is space available in the receiving schools.

Transportation

Students will be provided transportation under the following guidelines:

Elementary Students

1. Students assigned to schools outside their neighborhood in the pair/triad feeder patterns will be provided bus transportation if the students reside over two miles from school.

2. Students transferring to schools outside their neighborhood for option programs and individual opportunity transfer students will be provided transportation if the students reside over two miles from school and bus transportation is feasible.

Secondary Students (includes middle school, junior high, and senior high)

Students whose district assignment, or approved option, Voluntary Racial Transfer, or individual opportunity assignment is to a school that is over two miles from home will be provided with transportation, either by charter bus or Metro bus pass, as determined by the Transportation Office.

Before/After School Activities Transportation

Students eligible for transportation who are involved in activities before or after regular school hours are entitled to transportation. The number of students involved will determine the mode of transportation to be used.

Kindergarten Transportation

Some optional programs are available to kindergarten students. Qualified kindergarten students will receive transportation if it is feasible.

How the Plan Works

The key to a student's school assignment is the elementary school serving the area in which the student lives. This "home school" area determines student assignments at all grade levels. Home school areas and their respective school assignment patterns are identified.

For middle, junior, and senior high schools, the new school assignment patterns apply at all grade levels of three-year schools and at the lowest three grade levels of four-year schools during the 1980-81 year. This permits students at the highest grade level of a four-year school to complete work at the secondary school they were attending prior to the adoption of the Seattle Plan.

The authority and responsibility for the assignment, placement, or transfer of students resides with the Office of Student Placement.

Educational Options

The Seattle Plan includes the opportunity for students to transfer to a school that has a program option that emphasizes certain subjects or skills or an alternative program, or to schools that have educational opportunities not found in their assigned school. Each of the three zones has educational options. Students may apply for transfers within zones if these transfers contribute to racial balance and/or will not tend to cause racial imbalance in the sending or receiving school. In addition, there are some options that are "all-city," and students may transfer out of zone to these options if they qualify and are eligible, and the transfer contributes to racial balance and/or will not cause racial imbalance.

Option programs are open to handicapped and nonhandicapped students alike. If any qualified handicapped students apply and are accepted for an option program, such a program will be made accessible to them.

Parents and students should read the descriptions and/or phone building principals to discuss the programs at their school. Parents are required to fill out an application for a program option whether it is located at their assigned school or at another site. Once a decision is made about an educational option, an application should be filled out. Parents of kindergarten students applying for an option should do so directly with the Student Placement Office.

Applications for transfer to an option program should be sent to the Student Placement Office as soon as possible for the best possible opportunity for the transfer requested. Applications for transfer will be considered on the basis of space available in the option program, school, and/or transportation feasibility.

At the elementary level, program options in all three zones emphasize subject matter such as multiarts, science, and career education; approaches to learning such as early childhood education, open concept, instruction for student with language disabilities, foreign languages, alternative schools, and programs for gifted and talented students. Similar options are available in all three zones at the junior high/middle school level. Option programs at the high school level include advanced placement, the humanities, marine, environmental, and health sciences, multi-arts, business administration, mass media communication, foreign languages, alternative schools, and programs for gifted and talented students.

IMPLEMENTATION TIMELINE   COMPLETION

A. *ADOPTION OF DESEGREGATION PLAN*   December 1977
   Board adopts basic Desegregation Plan

B. *PRE-IMPLEMENTATION PLANNING*   March 1918
   Administrative units develop key procedures and processes necessary to implement Desegregation Plan by September 1978, in areas of transportation, program and curriculum development, staffing, facilities, student selection and transfer, instructional materials and equipment, staff development and training, student, staff, and parent orientation, public information, administrative assignment and management, Special Education programs, Bilingual programs, compensatory programs, budget, assessment and evaluation, school climate, negotiations, legal and data processing.

C. *DELINEATION OF GRADE RECONFIGURATIONS*   January 1978
   Communities, principals, and staff involved in pairs and triads propose alternate grade reconfigurations to administration.

D. *APPROVAL OF BUDGET FOR PHASE I*   March 1978
   Budget for Phase I implementation (March to August 30, 1978) activities is approved.

E. *LOCATION OF AUXILIARY PROGRAMS*   March 1978
   Auxiliary programs and services such as bilingual, special

education, alternative and compensatory programs are determined.

F. *NOTIFICATION OF STUDENT ASSIGNMENT*   April 1978
All students whose assignments are changed by the Desegregation Plan are notified.

G. *APPLICATIONS FOR VOLUNTARY OPTIONS*   April 1978
Students select or reaffirm options such as Magnet Schools, VRT programs, alternative schools, and other program transfers.

H. *APPOINTMENT OF ADMINISTRATORS*   May 1978
Selection and assignment of administrators and program managers for schools directly involved in desegregation announced.

I. *INITIATION OF STAFF DEVELOPMENT, TRAINING, AND ORIENTATION ACTIVITIES*   May 1978
Staffs in schools directly affected by Desegregation Plan are notified of assignment and begin staff development, training, and orientation activities.

J. *NOTIFICATION OF STUDENT PLACEMENT*   May 1978
Students and parents are notified of placement in Magnet Schools, Alternative programs, and program options.

K. *ESTABLISHMENT OF TRANSPORTATION ROUTES*   July 1978
Transportation routes are established and parents and students are notified.

L. *INITIATION OF PRE-SCHOOL ORIENTATION ACTIVITIES*   September 1978
All staffs directly involved in Desegregation Plan receive pre-school orientation.

M. *OPENING OF SCHOOL*   September 1978
Desegregation Plan for 1978-79 is initiated by start of school.

N. *PRELIMINARY ASSESSMENT AND READJUSTMENT*   October 1978
Preliminary assessment is made of student assignments, program implementation, and staffing, and readjustments are made.

O. *PRELIMINARY PLANNING FOR 1979-80*   December 1978
Preliminary planning begins for 1979-80 school year and second year desegregation plan is proposed to Board.

P. *PROGRAM ASSESSMENT AND EVALUATION*   December 1978
Preliminary effectiveness of 1978-79 Desegregation Plan is determined.

BUDGET ESTIMATES

Table 8-3 is a summary of preliminary estimates of the cost of the desegregation plan for 1977-79 as determined in December 1977. The estimates are based on information provided by the Instructional Services Division, the Desegregation Planning Office, and the Transportation Department.

The total additional requests include both 1977-78 fiscal year startup requests as well as 1978-79 budget requests. The Budget Office minimal budget estimates are for the same period. The Budget Office minimal budget estimates require more than $4 million in new revenue over and above current levels of support. Some of this revenue may be available from the state of Washington for transportation costs. Other costs may be offset by additional federal grants or reprogramming of present grant monies.

IV. Community Involvement: The Key to a Successful Plan

The community involvement processes involved in implementing the Seattle Plan used existing citizen committee structures as much as possible.

The following district citizen groups have roles in the implementation of the Seattle Plan:

1. District-Wide Advisory Committee for Desegregation (DWAC)
2. Citizens Advisory Committee for the Budget
3. Special Education Parents Advisory Committee
4. Bilingual Advisory Commission
5. Compensatory Education Parents Advisory Committee
6. Transportation Advisory Committee
7. Title VII Citizens Advisory Committee

(Note: These groups were selected because they were already established and had continuously been involved with the school district. The Urban League and other civic groups were represented on the DWAC.) Additionally, the Seattle Council of PTSA (Parent, Teacher, Student Association) and other community organizations are expected to participate through their regular organizational structure. In addition to outlining briefly the role of the above groups, the community process calls for special involvement of school/community groups in the three following categories:

1. The schools involved in each pair/triad arrangement.
2. The schools not involved in a pair/triad arrangement at the elementary level.
3. Those schools which become part of a new "feeder" pattern at the secondary school level.

Table 8-3 Preliminary Budget Estimates Worksheet, Seattle, 1977-79

Description	1977-78 Fiscal Year				1978-79 Fiscal Year	
	Adopted Budget	"Startup" Requests	Total	Estimated Minimal Budget	Requested Budget	Estimated Minimal Budget
Public information	$ 74,000	$ 40,000	$ 114,000	$ 114,000	$ 106,000	$ 25,000
Student recruitment	71,000	50,000	121,000	71,000	25,000	15,000
Desegregation services (includes federal grants)	1,754,740	5,000	1,759,740	1,754,740	2,895,000	2,695,000
Curriculum writing (includes federal grants)	172,500	270,000	442,500	262,500	160,000	50,000
Staff training	437,096	250,000	687,096	437,096	765,000	260,000
Student placement	128,820	150,000	278,820	228,820	215,000	200,000
Transportation	2,270,687	557,000	2,827,687	2,827,687	7,600,000	6,300,000
Evaluation	47,074	—	47,074	47,074	50,000	—
Data processing	60,800	30,000	90,800	90,800	30,000	50,000
VRT receiving schools	172,935	—	172,935	172,935	200,000	—
Educational improvements	4,298,486	100,000	4,398,486	4,298,486	5,000,000	3,800,000
Facilities modifications (Includes portables)	174,000	949,000	1,123,000	174,000	100,000	100,000
Conflict intervention/prevention	41,585	60,000	101,585	41,585	60,000	60,000
Middle schools	651,950	—	651,950	651,950	—	—
TOTALS	10,355,673	$2,461,000	$12,816,673	$11,172,673	$17,206,000	$13,555,000

Source: Instructional Services Division, Desegregation Planning Office, and Transportation Department Reports, Seattle Public School District, 1979.

District-Wide Advisory Committee for Desegregation

The by-laws for the District-Wide Advisory Committee for Desegregation (DWAC) state that the committee's purposes are:

1. To recommend to the superintendent appropriate contingency plans for Phase I of the desegregation plan
2. To recommend to the superintendent a desegregation plan and suggest corrective action where necessary
3. To monitor the implementation of the desegregation plan and suggest corrective action where necessary
3. To advise the superintendent on other desegregation matters as may be referred to the committee by the superintendent

Citizens Advisory Committee for the Budget

The Citizens Advisory Committee for the Budget has as its stated purpose "To advise and make recommendations to the Superintendent on matters relating to the School District Budget and budgeting process." One of its priority issues is "Evaluation of the costs of Desegregation Programs."

Special Education Parents' Advisory Committee

A special desegregation subcommittee of the Special Education Parents' Advisory Committee has been formed. The subcommittee assists in the planning process for the special education program delivery system within the Seattle Plan.

Bilingual Advisory Commission

The district used the Bilingual Advisory Commission as a primary source of community involvement in providing guidance on implementing the bilingual education portion of the Seattle Plan. The Bilingual Programs Office is establishing a community communication network to receive direct input on desegregation matters and other issues of concern to bilingual education. In addition, there is involvement of the Urban-Rural-Racial-Disadvantaged-funded bilingual program advisory committees.

Compensatory Education Parents Advisory Committee (CEPAC)

The change of school attendance arrangements has an impact on eligibility for Title I, Elementary and Secondary Education Act (Compensatory Education) funds in individual schools. The Compensatory Education Parents Advisory Committee (CEPAC) will help make determinations regarding the distribution of such funds.

Transportation Advisory Committee

The District Transportation Advisory Committee has been inactive for some time. Because of the substantial increase in transportation requirements for desegregation purposes, a citizen group to advise on transportation practices is desirable. The director of business and plant is responsible for restructuring the committee and having it assume its role by March 1, 1978.

Title VII Citizens Advisory Committee

This was a decision making committee which determined school district priorities for Title VII programs. The district applied for federal funds to assist in implementing the Seattle Plan. The Title VII Citizens Advisory Committee was involved in the application process and held a public hearing on the applications before they were submitted to the federal government.

In Seattle, had it not been for key leaders effectively managing community politics, desegregation may well have not become a reality. The key political people included two mayors, leaders of the ACLU, Church Council of Greater Seattle, NAACP, Urban League, Municipal League, Chamber of Commerce, the publishers of the two major newspapers, and one of the three major television stations.

The continuous and visible pressure through lawsuit from the ACLU and the NAACP kept the issue and the school board moving toward what became the final plan. The church council's stand supporting mandatory desegregation influenced the entire community and considerably broadened community support for the final plan. In a bold and highly visible decision, the Catholic archdiocese made it clear that students trying to avoid the desegregation plan would not be accepted in Catholic schools.

One of the most significant political moves occurred in May 1977. A letter from the mayor, endorsed by the Municipal League, the Chamber of Commerce, and the Urban League, was delivered to the school board president. This letter provided public support of the three most influential civic groups for desegregation. This support moved the board president from his previous position of strictly voluntary strategies to the acceptance of mandatory backup strategies.

The importance of the newspapers and television would be difficult to measure. Certainly had they been adamantly opposed to desegregation, the result would have been community polarization and strife. Although the issue was emotional and newsworthy, the editorial writers and reporters of both major newspapers and one television station were exceptionally sensitive to the issue. Editorials were timely and consistently supportive. Although neither of the other two television stations was opposed to desegregation, the one station provided exceptional help through support to the Desegregation Planning Office and through the development of special media presentations for the community.

In November 1977 the mayor-elect became a key figure in desegregation politics. But again, because of his support and that of the new city government, desegregation did not become a political football in Seattle.

Although the community opponents to desegregation were relatively weak politically, they were adamant in their position and were able to organize a movement to attempt to block the implementation of the plan. Initiative 350, an anti-busing initiative, was successfully presented to the voters state wide. Desegregation was relevant only to Seattle, but the initiative was designed to prevent busing to schools beyond that nearest to the home. A majority of Washington State residents live in small urban, suburban or rural areas and had no need to bus beyond the nearest school. On November 7, 1978, the initiative passed by a two-to-one majority. On June 15, 1979, the initiative was overturned in the federal courts, and the implementation of the plan, which had already begun, continued without interruption. In 1981 the decision of the circuit court declaring Initiative 350 unconstitutional was upheld by the United States Supreme Court.

Community/Civic/Professional Organizations Involved in Desegregation Planning and/or Implementation Support Activities

Active Mexicanos

Ad Hoc Community Group

Ad Hoc Media Education Committee

Advocates for the Orthopedically Handicapped

American Civil Liberties Union

American Friends Service Committee

Anti-Defamation League

Asian American Education Association

Ballard Consortium

Black Professional Educators of Puget Sound

Campus Christian Ministry (University of Washington)

Central Area School Council

Central Area Motivation Program

Church Council of Greater Seattle

Coalition for Quality Integrated Education

Committee for Southeast Seattle Schools

Compensatory Education Parent Advisory Committee

Concerned Parents for Cleveland Community

Concilio for Spanish-Speaking People

District-Wide Advisory Committee for Desegregation

El Centro de la Raza

Filipino Youth Activities, Inc.

Greater Greenwood Community Council

Japanese American Citizens League

Joint Advisory Committee on Education

League of Women Voters

Madrona Community Council

Municipal League of Seattle

National Association for the Advancement of Colored People (Seattle Branch)

National Council of Jewish Women

Office of the Mayor, City of Seattle

Office of Policy Planning, City of Seattle

Parent/Teacher/Student Association (Seattle Council and Local Units)

People Power Coalition

Queen Anne Community Council

Queen Anne/Magnolia Consortium

Rainier Community Action Center

Seattle Chamber of Commerce

Seattle King County Labor Council

Seattle King County Youth Action Council

Seattle Police Department

Seattle Teachers Association

Seattle Urban League

Southeast Education Citizens Committee

Special Education Parent Advisory Committee

Student Action Force on Education

Title VII Parent Advisory Committee

Transportation Advisory Committee

United Indians of All Tribes

U.S. Department of Justice

View Ridge Community Club

Wallingford Community Council

West Seattle Chamber of Commerce

V. Problems and Recommendations

Perhaps Seattle was unique for designing a mandatory desegregation plan without a court order to do so. Yet, the people of the community, and especially the community leaders, place a high value on self-determination.

Each member of the school board, including the one who was opposed to the plan, was committed to resolving the problem without outside interference. In fact, the key element to the entire process was commitment. The difficulty was that this commitment was only verbalized by the board, and for months it was not clear to district personnel nor to the community what the board was actually committed to. Some board members were committed to voluntary only strategies, some to mandatory, and some to a combination of both. The superintendent politically chose to side with those committed to voluntary only strategies. His assumption was that this was where the community strength lay as well. As a result the board and superintendent were often sending conflicting signals to the Desegregation Planning Office, to district administrators, and to the community.

As long as this commitment was unclear, the planning process was, at best, difficult. Many district administrators did not believe that the superintendent intended to desegregate. Many believed that he wanted the issue to go to the courts, which would then remove the political burden from him. Many central office and building administrators did not take the Desegregation Planning Office efforts seriously, and others intentionally undermined the planning process.

Not until the board passed the resolution defining racial isolation and the resolution to eliminate racial imbalance within a specified timeline did district efforts become serious. These resolutions totally clarified the commitments, which were no longer just words. This probably would not have occurred had it not been for the pressure from the ACLU, NAACP, and the Council of Churches of Greater Seattle threatening court action, and for the support of the leadership of the Municipal League, Urban League, Chamber of Commerce, and the mayor.

Thus, commitment was paramount to the development of the Seattle Plan. Commitment to self-determination, commitment of community leadership, written commitment from the board providing the goal and directing the superintendent and district personnel to the accomplishment of the goal, and commitment of the personnel to do the job right.

The Desegregation Planning Office obviously was instrumental to the development and acceptance of the plan. The lead position of this office was originally established as a coordinator with obscure staff functions. Only after considerable challenge and debate was the position elevated to that of director, which was a staff position reporting to the deputy superintendent. In addition to developing a variety of desegregation plans, the director also became responsible for the supervision of the Department of Human Resource Associates, the Ethnic Cultural Heritage staff, and the Human Relations Training Department (nearly a hundred personnel). Several people were assigned to the Desegregation Planning Office for whom no other positions were available. Having only a staff relationship, the Desegregation Planning Office initially had virtually no power or authority and was perceived by many as an enigma. Through the efforts of individuals within the office and the board's clear commitment, the Desegregation Planning Office (DPO) attained exceptional visibility and influence. The director became a part of the superintendent's cabinet and the deputy superintendent's planning team, and became influential in almost all district matters. Since the position was never legitimately given line authority, the reaction of a number of administrators was distrust and resentment. (On one occasion, for example, the DPO planning team worked over a weekend to prepare documents to be presented to the press and the community the following Monday. A budget office staff person, assigned temporarily to the DPO, was directed by his superior to withhold budget information. The information was critical to the outcome of the plan, and DPO staff had to work throughout the night in an attempt to construct the budget data.)

Another phenomenon occurred with the board adoption of the final plan. Psychologically the "ownership" of the plan remained with the Desegregation Planning Office. As the DPO began developing the implementation process with line administrators, it became apparent that the DPO was perceived by the superintendent and others as solely responsible and accountable for the plan. Also, if anything significant should go wrong, termination of the plan and of the DPO was a high probability. The district would then end up in court, and a different plan would eventually be implemented. To prevent this from occurring, the director disbanded the DPO staff and had them reassigned, had the position of director of desegregation eliminated, and dissolved the Desegregation Planning Office. As a result, responsibility for the implementation of the plan was delegated by the superintendent to all line administrators.

Desegregation is a political issue, and the results of both internal and external politics can have a destructive effect upon a school district and the people within. In a district where an official commitment to desegregate has been established, the administrative planning structure and process become of critical importance. In order to accomplish the task, the lead person of the planning office should be appointed as an assistant superintendent with line authority and a reporting relationship with the operations administrator. The office should be staffed with the most highly qualified and committed people available. It should be established at the outset that upon completion of the task, the planning office and the assistant superintendent position will be dissolved and that a separate office will be established with responsibilities for implementation and monitoring.

Finally, in desegregation planning, community knowledge and involvement cannot be overemphasized. In a major social and emotional change such as this, both district personnel and community people need to know what is happening and need to be involved as much as possible in determining the outcome. A continuous flow of information is a necessity.

None of this can be accomplished effectively without a high degree of cooperation among administrators and staff throughout the district. Difficult decisions have to be made almost daily. Many of them are made without any certainty as to their outcome. Many are unpopular. When these decisions are not made, however, the effect is felt throughout the organization. Cooperation is explicitly necessary in order for the decisions to be the best possible at the time.

Notes

1. 1980 student enrollment:
   White - 56.6%   Hispanic - 4.2%
   Black - 21.3%   Native American - 2.9%
   Asian - 9.1%
2. Nancy St. John, *School Desegregation* (New York: Wiley, 1975), p. 95.
3. Ibid, p. 125.
4. *Education Daily,* July 11, 1977, p. 5.
5. *Fulfilling the Letter and Spirit of the Law,* Report of U.S. Commission on Civil Rights, August 1976.
6. The overview of the Seattle Plan and the statement on Education Options are reprinted from *The 1980-81 Seattle Plan, and Educational Opportunity* published by the Seattle Public Schools.

Chapter 9

Desegregation in the Atlanta Public Schools: A Historical Overview

Alonzo A. Crim and Nancy J. Emmons

From 1882 to 1961 the Atlanta Board of Education operated a dual school system. The two systems were defined as a black system and a white system. Statistical evidence and minutes of board meetings from that era indicate that the two systems were distinctly separate all of those years and vastly unequal most of that time. Black people were considered by society at large to be inferior and undeserving of a school system equal to the system maintained for whites. Society perpetuated this social injustice by providing few opportunities for advancement and continual subjugation of an entire segment of humanity.

For eighty-nine years the Atlanta Board of Education chose to mirror society, replete with its racial discrimination and inequity, as a normal course of events. Most black children over the age of ten enrolled in the public schools realized that many of their textbooks came secondhand from the white schools and that these textbooks and other instructional materials contained no black characters, except in stereotypic roles, nor any favorable references to black history and culture. The psychological impact of the dual system on black children was devastating. Black parents were acutely aware that per pupil expenditure in the Atlanta public schools was much lower for black children, that the pupil-teacher ratio was higher, that teachers' salaries were lower, and that the education of black children was the responsibility of the black community with token consideration from benevolent whites. The school system reflected the values and mores of an unjust society and its misguided legal system. Both a dual society and a dual school system were endorsed by the courts until *Brown v. Board of Education of Topeka* in 1954. This landmark Supreme Court decision ruled that separate educational facilities were not equal. The result was a long overdue end to the *Plessy v. Ferguson* era. Separate was declared unequal and in violation of the Fourteenth Amendment. Throughout the country a chain reaction of similar cases gradually forced an end to dual systems one after the other.

The year after the *Brown* decision, black parents in Atlanta began to petition the Board of Education for justice. Attempts to eliminate the dual school system were futile until 1958, when black parents and the National Association for the Advancement of Colored People (NAACP) filed a civil action suit against the Atlanta Board of Education demanding an end to segregated public schools in Atlanta. This suit, first referred to as *Calhoun v. Latimer* and later renamed *Calhoun v. Cook,* followed three frustrating years of negotiations, including at least seven petitions presented to the board by the NAACP in an effort to gain equality for black children.

The court ordered the Board of Education to submit a plan for desegregation. This plan, known as the Atlanta Plan, was approved by the court in 1960. It was drafted in closed meetings by a committee of high-level administrators, board members, and legal advisors with no community, staff, or state and local government involvement. It is difficult, if not impossible, to find the names of the specific people who wrote the Atlanta Plan. Furthermore, no evidence exists that the plan was ever discussed in regular board meetings.

Although the court ordered a transfer of students to achieve integration, the plan listed a complex set of procedures requiring students who requested a transfer to file an application. In addition, the plan established a gradual grade-by-grade approach that would take twelve years to complete. Implementation of the plan began in 1961. However, the Board of Education, concerned about racial unrest and hostility in other cities and at the University of Georgia, wanted to ensure that such incidents would not occur in Atlanta. The black and white communities were organized to assist in paving the way, and the media were asked to cooperate. Only a few carefully selected students in the eleventh and twelfth grades were involved in the initial desegregation. Nine children transferred to four different high schools while the other 100,572 students remained in their former schools. The Atlanta Board of Education believed that this student-assignment plan was adequate for school integration.

In 1965 the court, dissatisfied with the gradual speed, ordered the schools to desegregate all grades *posthaste,* or by 1968. The court further ordered that desegregation of the kindergarten and first grade be accomplished during the 1965-66 school year, the second and third during 1966-67, the fourth and fifth in 1967-68, and the completion of desegregation in all grades by the end of 1968. However, the courts approved of the general procedures for the desegregation as outlined in the Atlanta Plan despite complaints from the plaintiffs that the plan was discriminatory. The Atlanta Board of Education subsequently developed a Voluntary Transfer Program (VTP) which provided for students from schools in which they were in the majority race to transfer to schools in which they were in the minority. This program has been successful in desegregation but has been somewhat disruptive to the "neighborhood schools" concept.

The implementation of desegregation resulted in an exodus of whites from the school system. The racial composition of the system changed drastically from 45 percent black in 1960 to over 90 percent black in 1982. The school system has also witnessed a decline in enrollment of about 30,000 students during those years. Many of the white students who left the system were from higher socioeconomic levels and could afford private school tuition or an expensive move out of the city. In an attempt to counter these moves and to bring white students back into the system, several parent groups formed and activated extensive public relations campaigns. These parent groups, composed primarily of whites, were moderately successful, accounting for the return of several hundred white students to the Atlanta public school system. Another result of the resegregation of the Atlanta schools was a suit brought by a group of black parents who asked the court to consider a merger of the Atlanta system with the predominantly white suburban systems. The court ruled against the plaintiffs in this case. Although whites have been moving back to the inner city during recent years, those who are returning from suburban areas or moving to Atlanta from other states are primarily childless couples and professional single people. Therefore, the "back-to-the-city" movement is not yielding much increase in public school enrollment.

Alternative education programs and magnet schools, which are open to all students systemwide, have been successful in maintaining whites in the public school system. In addition, the Challenge Program (also known as the Program for the Gifted) has, unfortunately, become a status symbol among some white parents who, anxious to have "gifted" children, are enticed to return to the public schools. Favorable media coverage and extensive public relations work have also been helpful. An ambitious program initiated by the superintendent of schools—to bring the Atlanta Public Schools up to the national norm in reading and mathematics by 1985—has resulted in improvements in standardized test scores and in other indices of progress each year. This goal is realistic and underscores the fact that students *can* achieve and that the public schools *do* work. Bringing schools up to the national norm is a systemwide project which has already improved instructional techniques and students' performance in every school.

Historically, education has been the responsibility of state and local governments. No provision was made in the United States Constitution for federal support of public education. The federal government has exercised a "hands-off" policy, except when individual rights are violated as in cases pertaining to civil rights, rights of the handicapped, and equal opportunity. Special projects, mostly in the areas of compensatory education and alternative education, have received support. In relegating the control of the school system to state and local governments, the federal branch has forfeited control of day-to-day operations in school systems. There is no national uniformity of education in this country as there is in most other countries. State control, although greater than federal control, is limited and remote. Local governments are primarily responsible for local school systems. Since local lawmakers are responsible to their constituents, schools tend to reflect the community.

For this reason, educators often advance the notion that a school system is a microcosm of the total community. This is indeed a limited perspective. If a school system were simply a microcosm of society, the class system that now functions to the detriment of some of its citizens and to the advantage of others would be perpetuated by future generations, who would learn inequality and discrimination not only from society, but also at school. Learning classism and racism at school would give these negative values a degree of respect and credence, as children could quickly respond, "It must be all right because I learned it at school."

This is not to say that school is the only place where children learn values. In fact, the home and community are perhaps more influential. However, a certain degree of awe and respect is frequently attributed to educators, especially by parents of children from lower socioeconomic areas.

Since schools have an overwhelming amount of influence on children, a school system must be more than a mirror image of society. It must go one step beyond society and change existing patterns. Schools must actively teach social improvement and lay the groundwork for building a new society, free of class and racial discrimination. One way schools can achieve these goals is to serve as models for children and for society. In this way a school system is not a microcosm of the present society, but may be considered a microcosm of the ideal society. Schools must be symbols of the ideal.

In order to serve as an effective model, a school system must first rectify the inequalities and injustices inherent within the schools themselves. Every child, regardless of race, religion, ethnic background, handicap, or socioeconomic status, must be given an equal opportunity for self-improvement and, in turn, improvement of society.

One may argue that manipulating the school system so that it steps beyond present society is a way of controlling the learning environment, causing it to be less natural. However, there are times when intervention is appropriate to improve humanity, to promote sounder values, and to ensure an equal chance for all.

The "Catch-22" in this philosophy is that a school system cannot operate in a vacuum; schools need the community and the community needs the schools. The relationship is symbiotic. Although society at large comes replete with injustices and inequalities, individuals and groups do exist within communities who believe that children's only chance to change their present status and to fulfill their dreams is through education with the support of the home and the community. These insightful individuals or groups have not lost touch with the philosophy from which sprang the Declaration of Independence, nor have they forgotten the principles behind the "melting pot" syndrome in America. These individuals and groups in the community are believers in public education as the only way to rectify past social injustices and to guarantee that inequalities do not exist in the future.

In the Atlanta Public Schools, staff members refer to this group of citizens as a "community of believers." These believers are a diversified group. They represent all races, religions, ethnic backgrounds, and socioeconomic strata. Believers are parents, politicians, welfare recipients, corporation presidents, factory workers, housewives, ministers, doctors, lawyers, owners of small businesses, executives of large corporations, bankers, members of community groups, and college professors. The common denominator for this "community of believers" is *concern*. Without the faith and support of the "community of believers," public education and all chance of creating equality in society would be destroyed.

In a desegregated school system that is 90 percent black with a predominantly black administration and board of education, the struggle becomes one of classism. Racism, while still important, is now a secondary issue. Now the middle-class schools try to hold on to what they have, and the lower-class schools struggle for equality.

Decreasing enrollment and the Voluntary Transfer Program (VTP) have resulted in closing many schools over the past few years. The majority of schools that have been closed recently are found in lower socioeconomic areas. This is unfortunate, since the school has always been a central focus and a hallmark of stability in poor areas. The fear that the closing of the neighborhood school signals the decay of the community has caused much protest. Some black leaders believe that if the children in a community "stayed at home" rather than participating in the Voluntary Transfer Program, many of these schools would not be closed. It appears that the myth behind the notion that black children learn more by sitting next to white children is about to explode in the black community. If the quality of the school is good, it does not matter where the building is located or how it looks.

The Atlanta Plan is no longer relevant in the Atlanta Public Schools. It merely addressed the issue of desegregation and did not mention socioeconomic factors, learning environment, student achievement, quality of instruction, or preparation for employment. It is a relic from the past and has no practicality in 1982. It served the purpose of satisfying the courts in 1960 and provided a basis for declaring the Atlanta Public Schools a unitary school system. However, it is now clear that a unitary school system and a unitary community go hand in hand. The focus has shifted and the goals have changed since 1960.

The push now in the Atlanta Public Schools is to bring the quality of *every* school up to its potential. A school system should not maintain "good schools" and "bad schools," "rich schools" and "poor schools," "black schools" and "white schools." Programs, materials, and opportunities that are available for one student must be available for *all* students. All schools must provide equal opportunities. Establishing a unitary system is difficult, if not impossible, without a unitary society. Paradoxically, it is also impossible to conceive of a unitary society in the future without teaching equality through example in the public schools.

A unitary public school system is simply one in which equal opportunity is guaranteed for all students, regardless of race, nationality, and socioeconomic status. In a unitary school system *all* schools and *all* students are given equal advantages. There are no inequities of access to equal per pupil expenditure, quality of instruction, abundance of materials, availability of specialized programs, or in extracurricular activities. Dual school systems have been eliminated through legal means. However, some inequities still remain in many systems. The thrust in public education is now toward equality for all while meeting the individual needs of each student through specialized instruction. The Atlanta Public Schools are a leader in this movement.

The Atlanta Public School System serves the inner-city area consisting of 136 square miles and a total population of 425,022. Of this total 287,144 people, or 68 percent, are black and other minorities; 137,878, or 32 percent, are white.

The inner city of Atlanta is surrounded by a suburban area consisting of an additional 1,922 square miles and an additional 1,354,180 people. Of the suburban total 201,993, or 15 percent, are black and other minorities; 1,152,287, or 85 percent, are white. Each of the surrounding suburban areas has its own separate school system.

The April 1982 issue of the *Survey of Current Business* reports that per capita personal income in Georgia for 1980 was $8,041 while per capita income for the Standard Metropolitan Statistical Area (SMSA) that includes Atlanta was $9,041. Since the breakdown in the *Survey of Current Business* is by county, no figures are provided for the inner city of Atlanta. However, almost 85 percent of the students in the Atlanta public schools qualify for free or reduced-price lunches.

The city of Atlanta has become an "international city" and now has a large number of people from varied nationalities. Cultural centers have been established in recent years, and people of common nationalities have been settling together in areas to form more ethnic neighborhoods. The Atlanta Public Schools have responded with a rather extensive bilingual program and the formation of a magnet school for international studies.

The Atlanta Public School System maintains eighty-five elementary schools, ten middle schools, and twenty-two high schools. The total number is 117 schools, which is a reduction of ten elementary schools from the 1981-82 school year. These schools were closed because of decreasing enrollment. The Atlanta Public School System presently has five alternative education programs and six magnet schools. The school system serves 68,611 students (62,716, or 91 percent, black; 5,272, or 8.1 percent, white; 325, or 0.5 percent, Hispanic; and 298, or 0.4 percent, other). The staff breakdown is as follows: 6,438, or 82.6 percent, black; 1,333, or 17.1 percent, white; and 20, or 0.3 percent, other. The total staff is 7,791.

The Atlanta Plan applied only to the inner-city area (or within the city limits), which constitutes all of the Atlanta Public School System. Suburban areas were not included during the original court action and, therefore, were not subject to the requirements of the court concerning the establishment of a unitary system. However, the Atlanta Plan was finally implemented consistently throughout the Atlanta Public School System.

The plan applied only to diversifying racial characteristics of the school population. It did not address socioeconomic issues and classism, which have become more pressing problems in Atlanta. Although the Atlanta Plan did not designate the existence of any racially or ethnically homogeneous schools, the fact that the school system is now over 90 percent black has caused many schools to become totally black. Housing patterns are also responsible for resegregation. Unless housing patterns change or the Atlanta School System merges with predominantly white suburban systems, racially homogeneous schools will continue. However, the push now is to bring the quality of all schools up to the quality of the best school. No school in the system needs to be racially isolated. All students have access to all schools through the Voluntary Transfer Program, alternative education, magnet schools, comprehensive high schools, and special education programs.

All schools in the Atlanta system are comprehensive even though some are more limited in offerings because of factors such as size and student interest. A school may have special programs, including a magnet school within a school, but these programs are components of a larger comprehensive school. At the present time there is no uniform systemwide grade structure. However, the school system is now in the process of shifting to a citywide middle school program, which will result in a uniform grade structure (K to 5, 6 to 8, 9 to 12). This shift is a result of years of study and debate among board members and a demand from the State Department of Education that the Atlanta Public Schools present a uniform organizational plan. The Board of Education has finally resolved the conflict of whether to abolish middle schools or to implement them citywide. However, the middle school debate has always centered on the question of student achievement, rather than on desegregation goals. The equality of a uniform organizational plan is contingent on systemwide quality of instruction rather than on assuring racial quotas.

The Atlanta Public Schools maintain a full range of extracurricular programs. These programs, including athletics, are available in all schools. Equity is achieved in extracurricular activities citywide by providing the same programs and equipment in all schools.

School buildings range in age from one to eighty years old. These buildings are randomly distributed throughout the city. The age and style of the buildings have little effect on the learning process if the quality of instruction and materials is maintained.

Although the system is divided into attendance zones around each school and into three administrative areas, all students have access to all other schools because of special programs and the Voluntary Transfer Program (VTP). Students need only request a transfer for some academic purpose to receive it. Transportation is provided by the school system within home attendance zones as well as to schools outside of home zones for VTP students. Each administrative area covers one-third of the city and represents a racial and socioeconomic mixture of students.

The Atlanta Public Schools are governed by a nine-member elected school board. These members represent various areas in the city, although three are elected at-large. The school board is primarily accountable to the people of Atlanta and secondarily to the state legislature through the State Department of Education and to the City Council. There is little interference from these bodies in academic and financial affairs, except when mandated by the law. Six board members are black; three are white. Five board members are male; four are female. The president of the Board of Education is a white male; the vice-president is a black male. Educational levels of board members range from high school graduates to those with doctorate degrees. Members are ministers, college professors, housewives, and people in business. The policies of the Board of Education have the force of law within the school system.

The chief administrator of the school system is the superintendent. He makes decisions with the help of a cabinet composed mainly of division heads (also called assistant superintendents). Each of the three administrative areas is administered by an area superintendent, who is also a member of the cabinet. The chief administrator of individual schools is the principal. The superintendent and the comptroller are appointed by the Board of Education, and the cabinet members are appointed by the superintendent. All other administrative personnel are appointed by the superintendent after receiving recommendations from the respective cabinet member. The Board of Education must approve all recommendations before appointments are finalized. The superintendent is a black male, the comptroller is a white male. Of the three area superintendents, two are black males, and one is a white female. The two black area superintendents

have white assistant area superintendents, while the white area superintendent has a black assistant area superintendent. The assistant area
superintendents are not members of the cabinet. However, other cabinet
members include a black male associate superintendent, three white male
assistant superintendents (one less than the 1981-82 school year), one black
female assistant superintendent, two black male assistant superintendents, a
black male who serves as a government liaison, and a white male who
represents a liaison with the Atlanta Partnership of Business and Education.
Principals report to the area superintendents who, in turn, report to the
associate superintendent. Some assistant superintendents report to the associate superintendent, while others report directly to the superintendent.

The main divisions of the school system are as follow:

- Administrative Services
- Area I
- Area II
- Area III
- Educational Operations
- Facilities Services
- Fiscal Affairs
- Instructional Planning and Development
- Long-Range Planning and Expanded Services
- Personnel Services
- Research, Evaluation, and Data Processing

The Atlanta Public School System is presently undergoing a reorganization as a result of the retirement of several administrators and support
services staff, school closings, the decrease in enrollment, the shift to
systemwide middle schools, and an increase in the number of magnet
schools. More than fifty-five schools have been closed during the past ten
years with other school closings expected over the next few years.
Therefore, the administrative arrangement will be modified to decrease the
number of promotional positions and to correlate the number of positions
more closely with the decreased enrollment of students.

As a result of the court-ordered desegregation and the implementation of
the Atlanta Plan, the high-level administration was racially "balanced" in
the early 1970s and has remained "balanced." However, the
implementation of this plan abnormally increased the size of the area and
central staffs. Attrition, retirements, and other reasons for departure are
altering the racial ratios.

When the Atlanta Plan was first implemented, there were many in-service
programs for sensitivity training and intergroup relations. However, there is
no longer much need for these workshops, and they are held less frequently.

The workshop focus is now on "back-to-basics" education and introduction to high technology. Under the present administration the attention of the entire school system has turned toward improving student achievement, especially in reading and mathematics.

A statewide testing program, including competency-based education, has put pressure on local school systems to improve the quality of instruction. Students can no longer graduate from high school unless they have passed a statewide minimum competency test. In addition, a systemwide pupil progression plan requires that students master skills in reading and mathematics in one grade before moving on to the next grade. Businesses and parents are demanding that schools produce students who are employable. The Atlanta public schools have responded to that need through staff in-service training, intensified instruction in the basic skills, an end to social promotion, and compensatory programs for students who demonstrate a need not fulfilled by the regular classroom.

For the first time in the history of education, public schools have now established a formal partnership with the private sector. This partnership has even been endorsed by the president of the United States and other government leaders, who have called on private industry to compensate for federal budget cuts. The bottom line from the private sector is that support is available to schools in exchange for productive, skilled citizens to complete the industrial/educational ecosystem.

In the Atlanta Public Schools, this program is known as the Atlanta Partnership of Business and Education, Incorporated. It is defined as "a network of businesses, schools, and people." From this organization has come the Adopt-A-School Project, which is responsible for pairing schools with businesses in a manner similar to the way in which children are paired with parents through an adoption agency. The program has been moderately successful in that some schools have benefited greatly from tutoring services, additional supplies, and part-time employment opportunities while other schools are still struggling to be adopted.

During the 1981-82 school year, fifty schools were adopted. The partnership has established the goal of all schools being adopted by the end of the 1983-1984 school year. In a democratic society business tends to invest in profitable ventures, or those that produce solid returns. Unless the quality of *all* schools equals the quality of the *best* schools, business might view "less than best" as nonprofitable, or a poor investment. Therefore, it is the responsibility of the school system to produce students who require no special accommodations to move into business and industry. In addition, the school system must be very visible with improvements in programs, basic instruction, and achievement test data. Finally, the school system must raise the quality of schools that may not be up to par. The challenge to the businesses is then to provide 100 percent employment for the students.

Some schools appear to be more adoptable than others because of aggressive leadership or specialized programs that appeal to businesses. However, the Atlanta Public School System is working toward equalization of this situation so that the "rich-get-richer" syndrome is not perpetuated in society. In effect, a consciousness raising among businesses seems to be in order for the Adopt-A-School Project to work as intended. However, this effort on the part of the private sector to take some responsibility for public education is well-meaning. Similar partnerships with churches and civic groups have also been successful. Some schools, usually in the predominantly white middle-class areas, have always enjoyed informal benefits from the community and from businesses. Now the time has come to equalize this situation through a formal partnership that includes *all* schools. There should be no "have-not" schools in a unitary public school system.

The Atlanta Partnership of Business and Education is a tax-exempt, nonprofit corporation chartered by the state of Georgia in 1981 with one goal: "To enhance the economic development potential of Atlanta and to improve the standard of living of its people by raising the educational achievement of its citizenry." This partnership forms the basis for the "community of believers." Job placement is perhaps the most important aspect of this program other than the general public relations concept.

The Atlanta Public Schools have always encouraged extensive parent and community involvement. Volunteers are regularly used throughout the individual schools. During the 1981-82 school year, the new parent/teacher conference plan allowed teachers to set aside time during the school day to meet with parents and discuss children's progress. Quarterly reports of volunteer hours spent in each school are submitted to the Board of Education. The Atlanta Public School System is in a position to be constantly monitored by parents, businesses, community members, civic groups, churches, volunteers, media representatives, and staff.

Three employee organizations hold regular discussion sessions with representatives of management. Two organizations represent teachers and paraprofessionals, the Atlanta Association of Educators (AAE) and the Atlanta Federation of Teachers (AFT), while the American Federation of State, County and Municipal Employees (AFSCME) represents classified (or noncertificated) employees. Meetings are held at the request of the employee organizations. The management teams are led by the assistant superintendent for personnel. The organizations present their concerns, which are discussed and debated until a compromise is reached. The management teams then present the compromise to the superintendent, who discusses employee concerns with the cabinet. Problems that require policy changes go before the Board of Education. In addition, elaborate grievance procedures are in place to accommodate employee charges of injustice. The relationship between the employee organizations and management is good. Strikes have not occurred in the Atlanta Public School System since 1973.

The entire school system is about the business of quality education for all students.

In summary, among the several tenets to which the school system ascribes are the following:

- decentralized administration
- development of local initiative
- adherence to standards
- involvement of staff, students, and community
- development of processes and procedures in order to yield specific end-products
- demonstration of initiative and assumption of responsibilities in the discharge of duties
- being visible in manifestations of indices of progress and in monitoring, reviewing, and evaluating
- demonstration of respect for and belief in the other person and in humanity

These and other operational principles promote the development of a "community of believers."

Part IV

ANALYSIS OF MODEL PLANS

Chapter 10

Do Mandatory School Desegregation Plans Foster White Flight?

Charles V. Willie and Michael Fultz

The Supreme Court in *Brown v. Board of Education I* (1954) found that black plaintiffs "by reason of the segregation complained of" were "deprived of the equal protection of laws guaranteed by the Fourteenth Amendment." In *Brown II* (1955), the Court required the predominantly white school-board defendants "to make a prompt and reasonable start" toward fulfilling the personal interests of blacks for "admission to public schools as soon as practicable on a nondiscriminatory basis." The Court ordered this action by white defendants who lost the case because it discovered on the basis of evidence presented, that blacks were educated in segregated schools, and that "segregation of children in public schools solely on the basis of race, even though the physical facilities and other 'tangible' factors may be equal, deprive[s] the children of the minority group of equal educational opportunities."

One could describe the Court decision as "delineating the rights of [the plaintiff black] children" (McGill, 1964:246). As early as 1964, only a decade after the historic decision, Ralph McGill said that some political leaders had "dishonestly distorted it" (McGill, 1964:246). As the years continued, social scientists, education planners, and public administrators joined with politicians to distort further the simple requirement of the Court that the grievances of blacks with respect to segregated education should be redressed.

The Goal Displacement Issue

The distortion took the form of goal displacement. A court order that gave local school authorities primary responsibility for developing school desegregation plans *that protect the rights of blacks* was transformed into a primary responsibility to develop school desegregation plans *that are least offensive to whites.* In this process of goal displacement, the interests of whites became primary and the interests of blacks (which the Court identified as the issue "at stake") became secondary in school desegregation planning.

James Coleman justifies the goal displacement process that has transformed desegregation planning from primary focus on what is good for blacks to what is least offensive to whites. Unless cities that are ordered "to undo the segregation that exists, ordinarily through compulsory busing to achieve racial balance," take cognizance of what is least offensive to whites, Coleman predicts that the outcome "is simple, straightforward, and predictable: the same elements that brought about the segregation in the first place, individual residential and private-school decisions, will do so again. . . ." According to Coleman, "sometimes this process occurs through a rapid evacuation, as in Boston" (Coleman, 1981:187).

Elaborating upon his discussion of the outcome of "severe" remedies, "such as busing [white] children to a different part of the city," Coleman said whites who wish to be in a school district without responsibility for large numbers of black students and who consequently "cannot be found guilty of segregating actions," have a simple strategy in response to compulsory race mixing in public schools: They move their residence "and they do so in large numbers when the 'remedies' imposed are severe" (Coleman, 1981:187-188). Coleman's assertion about white flight has become conventional wisdom. He has been joined in his opinion by several other social scientists such as David Armour who believes "there is ample evidence . . . that Whites do flee desegregation plans that mandatorily assign or bus students to schools outside their neighborhoods" (Armor, 1980:213). Thus, the issue in school desegregation planning has shifted from concern about how best to count blacks in equally on all educational opportunities to concern about how best to avoid driving whites out of the local city school system.

Mandatory Plans Versus Voluntary Plans

School desegregation planners have concentrated on mandatory versus voluntary desegregation plans not so much in terms of what is best for black children educationally as in terms of what is least offensive to whites. Coleman suggests that a mandatory assignment plan like that ordered in Boston results in a rapid evacuation of whites. Despite the characterization of the Boston plan as a comprehensive one that deals with ways of achieving a quality education as well as desegregation, Dentler states that the slogan "Don't let this become another Boston" has "spread from New York City to Los Angeles" and has been used by advocates of every point of view who disregard "the overwhelmingly peaceful and successful implementation of the entire plan" (Dentler and Scott, 1981:x).

In general, mandatory school-desegregation plans are held to contribute to white flight, and voluntary desegregation plans are believed to lessen white flight. Milwaukee has a court-ordered plan that permits students to choose magnet or other preferred schools. This plan has resulted in the desegregation of more than two-thirds of that city's schools and also has been credited with preventing white flight. Thus, many communities have used some but not all features of the Milwaukee plan in their attempts to achieve desegregation.

Two issues that troubled us in the school-desegregation literature were the goal-displacement matter mentioned earlier and the absence of comparative investigations of mandatory versus voluntary plans with respect to the association, if any, between one or the other and white flight. Already a carefully done survey of the association, if any, between voluntary and mandatory desegregation plans and black student achievement has demonstrated the absence of any correlation. After reviewing ninety-three studies, Robert Crain and Rita Mahard concluded that "issues related to voluntary versus mandatory desegregation . . . seem irrelevant. Mandatory plans and voluntary plans show approximately equal achievement gains" (Crain and Mahard, 1982:vi, 33).

We suspect that issues regarding mandatory plans and voluntary plans are unrelated to white flight, too, despite the assertions by Coleman and others. Our suspicion was aroused by reviewing demographic trends in Atlanta, Georgia, for another study (Willie, 1983). That city lost one-fourth to one-third of its total population between 1970 and 1980—a substantial loss; yet, Atlanta had one of the most limited student desegregation plans in the nation, which required little movement of whites. The Atlanta remedy for student desegregation was neither radical nor severe.

If the kind of school desegregation plan implemented by a city is not related to white flight (the avoidance of which, rather than the securing of black student rights, has become the central goal of desegregation planning), school systems can begin to give primary attention to redressing the grievances of children who experienced segregation and discrimination that constituted a denial of equal educational opportunity. This, according to the Supreme Court, is the issue at stake, not what is least offensive to whites. Judge W. Arthur Garrity, Jr., reminded the people of Boston that desegregation planning that displaces that primary goal is inappropriate when he stated that "constitutional principles which mandate duty to desegregate cannot be allowed to yield simply because of disagreement with them" (quoted in Willie, 1978:83).

Data and Method

To determine the association, if any, between mandatory plans and voluntary plans with respect to white flight, Boston and Milwaukee are analyzed. This investigation uses a comparative case study methodology. These two cities, similar in many ways, are good tests of the contribution of one or another desegregation plan to the phenomenon of white flight.

The desegregation plans in both cities were comprehensive. They provide desegregative educational experiences for a substantial number of white, black, and other minority students. However, the Boston Plan emphasizes mandatory student assignments with voluntary enrollment in citywide magnet schools as the secondary feature. The Milwaukee Plan emphasizes voluntary transfers to magnet or other preferred schools, with mandatory assignments as the secondary feature.

Boston and Milwaukee are similar in that both are relatively large cities with populations that exceed one-half million. Both are located in the North. Both were ordered by federal courts to desegregate school student bodies during the 1970s. And both have public school student populations that exceed 50,000.

The racial and ethnic composition of Boston and Milwaukee populations are similar, too. Based on a 1980 count, 70 percent of Boston's and 73 percent of Milwaukee's population is white; 22 percent of Boston's and 23 percent of Milwaukee's population is black; 6 percent of Boston's and 4 percent of Milwaukee's population is Hispanic. Both cities have large white ethnic populations that are predominantly Catholic and that identify with countries in Europe. Boston has many families of Irish and Italian ancestry; Milwaukee has many families of Polish and German ancestry. One-fourth to one-third of the school-going population in both cities enroll in Catholic or other private schools.

Both cities are the locations of major units of a state university. And both cities also have working-class black and working-class white populations that are considerable in size.

Despite these many similarities, Boston and Milwaukee developed comprehensive school desegregation plans that are radically different in primary emphasis—one emphasizing mandatory student assignments and the other emphasizing voluntary transfers. *The question studied is whether the Boston Plan contributed to a more rapid evacuation of whites from the city and public school system than the Milwaukee Plan.* To investigate this question, we analyze changes in total city and public school populations in Boston and Milwaukee before and after court-ordered school desegregation that occurred during the middle 1970s in both cities.

Findings

The school desegregation literature pertaining to white flight asserts that decrease in the number of whites enrolled in public schools is a function of the type of plan implemented. As mentioned above, Coleman (1981) suggested that a rapid evacuation of whites is predictable when a mandatory student-assignment plan such as that of Boston is implemented. For Boston and Milwaukee, we were able to obtain data on the public school population by race the year before implementation of the school desegregation plan, the year of implementation, and for three years thereafter.

The year before plans were implemented whites constituted a majority of the public school students in both Boston and Milwaukee. They remained a majority of all students the first year of desegregation, decreasing from 57 to 52 percent in Boston and 60 to 57 percent in Milwaukee, as seen in Table 10-1A. Three years after desegregation, the white public school population had decreased to 42 percent in Boston and 48 percent in Milwaukee. Although these two cities used different methods to achieve school desegregation, their patterns of decrease in the white public school population were quite similar. A difference of only 6 percentage points between the proportion of whites in Boston and Milwaukee is modest and of little consequence.

A trend analysis, as shown in Table 10-1B, reveals that both Boston and Milwaukee experienced decreases in white public school students before desegregation plans were ordered. Boston lost 16 percent of its white students between 1972 and 1973, and Milwaukee lost 9 percent between 1974 and 1975.

Court-ordered school desegregation began with the implementation of a partial plan in Boston that affected less than a quarter of the city's schools in 1974. Thus, whites in the population who withdrew from city public schools were proportionately fewer the first year of Boston school desegregation than the proportion who withdrew the second year when the comprehensive plan was ordered. After experiencing a high of 17 percent in annual decrease of white students the second year of desegregation (which actually was the first year that the permanent plan was put in place), the declining white population settled into a constant pattern the third and fourth years, decreasing 8 to 10 percent each year; these proportions were lower than the decline in the white public school-going students a year before a remedy was formulated. Thus, the mandatory school desegregation plan for Boston appeared to have influenced the white withdrawal rate from the system for only one year.

The same may be said for Milwaukee and its voluntary transfer desegregation plan. The first year of implementation in 1976 was associated with the highest rate of decline in white public school students of any of the five years under study before or after court-ordered school desegregation. Thereafter the proportion of decrease settled into a constant pattern the next two years and dropped to 8 percent the fourth year, similar to the 9 percent observed in Boston. Moreover, the single year of peak withdrawal of white students in both cities differed less than 5 percentage points, although the plans in the two cities emphasized different approaches to school desegregation.

Boston did not experience a more rapid evacuation of the white student population than did Milwaukee; nor can it be said that the plan in one city caused a pattern of white withdrawal that differed from the pattern manifested in the other city. These data indicate that school desegregation

Table 10-1 White, Black, and Other Minority Population by Percent of Total Public School Population and by Annual Percent of Change, Boston and Milwaukee*

A

Percent of Public School Population Before and After Desegregation

| | Boston | | | | | Milwaukee | | | | |
Race	Yr. before plan	1st yr. of plan	2nd yr. of plan	3rd yr. of plan	4th yr. of plan	Yr. before plan	1st yr. of plan	2nd yr. of plan	3rd yr. of plan	4th yr. of plan
White	57	52	49	45	42	60	57	53	51	48
Black	34	37	39	41	43	34	37	40	42	45
Other	9	11	12	14	15	6	6	7	7	7
Total	100	100	100	100	100	100	100	100	100	100

B

Percent of Annual Change in Students Enrolled

| | Boston | | | | | Milwaukee | | | | |
Race	Yr. before plan	1st yr. of plan	2nd yr. of plan	3rd yr. of plan	4th yr. of plan	Yr. before plan	1st yr. of plan	2nd yr. of plan	3rd yr. of plan	4th yr. of plan
White	−16	− 8	−17	− 8	−10	− 9	−13	−10	−10	− 8
Black	− .7	+ 5	− 5	+ 4	− 3	+ 2	+ .8	+ .2	+ .2	+ 4
Other	+13	+11	+ 6	+ 3	+ 5	+ 2	− .3	+ 1	+ 3	+ 4

*Note: In Boston the first year of court-ordered desegregation was 1974; in Milwaukee it was 1976.

had some effect on the out-migration of white students from the city and from enrollment in public schools, but their decreasing numbers in the central city school systems were not different from the pattern of suburban and rural growth that the total white population has manifested since 1950, as will be discussed later. The beginning of white migration to the suburbs, of course, predates any court-ordered school desegregation.

Between 1970 and 1980, as shown in Table 10-2, Boston and Milwaukee public schools lost 61 and 58 percent, respectively, of their white students.

Table 10-2 Boston and Milwaukee Public School Population by Race, 1970 and 1980

Race	% of Total Public School Population of Boston			% of Total Public School Population of Milwaukee		
	1970	*1980*	*% Change*	*1970*	*1980*	*% Change*
White	64	35	−61	70	44	−58
Black	30	46	+8	26	47	+21
Other	6	19	+119	4	9	+56
Total	100	100		100	100	

Again these figures are similar despite the disparities in their school desegregation plans. The total population decline for these two cities was similar, too. Boston's citywide population was down by 12 percent compared to a loss of 11 percent in Milwaukee. While the initiation of school desegregation may have accelerated the white public school population decline from 3 to 6 percentage points above the average annual percent of decline during a five-year period one year before and three years after the court order in these two cities, even this single year of accelerated decline was not at variance with the ongoing out-migration trend in both cities.

As can be see in Table 10-3, both cities lost approximately one-quarter of their white populations during the decade of the 1970s. Since these losses began before court-ordered desegregation, it would be inappropriate to attribute the impetus for this pattern solely to the constitutional requirement to create unitary systems.

Table 10-3 Boston and Milwaukee Population by Race, 1970 and 1980

Race	Total Population of Boston			Total Population of Milwaukee		
	1970	*1980*	*% Change*	*1970*	*1980*	*% Change*
White	82%	70%	−25	84%	73%	−23
Black	16	22	+21	15	23	+39
Other	2	8	+267	1	4	+228
Total	100	100		100	100	

In fact, as Table 10-4 indicates, white migration to suburban or other areas outside central cities has been a persisting trend since the 1950s. By 1970 the trend had so accelerated that for the first time the decennial census recorded a loss in absolute numbers of whites in central city populations. Thus, as mentioned above, the decreases in total white population as well as public school white population in Boston and in Milwaukee are part of a national trend. Boston and Milwaukee fit into this trend in similar ways.

Table 10-4 U.S. Population by Residence and Race, 1950, 1960, and 1970

Residence and Race	Percent			Percent Change	
	1950	*1960*	*1970*	*1950-60*	*1960-70*
Whites					
In central cities	35	31	27	+6	−1
Suburb and rural	65	69	73	+24	+18
Total	100	100	100		
Blacks					
In central cities	44	53	58	+51	+32
Suburb and rural	56	47	42	+6	+8
Total	100	100	100		

Information for 1980 not available from Census Bureau when published.

Conclusion

Based on this analysis, we conclude that the different school desegregation plans implemented in Boston and in Milwaukee did not result in vastly different shifts in the white population in terms of public school enrollment and central city residence. The decreases that were noted had been in operation before court-ordered school desegregation and, indeed, were part of a national trend that dates back to the midpoint of this century. Thus, mandatory student-assignment or voluntary transfer plans are unrelated to geographic changes of the white population in central cities.

This conclusion is tentative, since it is derived from a comparison of only two cities. If, however, it is confirmed by further investigation, doubt should be cast on the assertions that mandatory student-assignment desegregation plans contribute to white flight. With a clearer understanding of what does and does not contribute to white flight, school desegregation planners may overcome the assumptions that have displaced the primary goal of *Brown I* and *Brown II*—the achievement of equal educational opportunity for minority children.

References

Armor, David
    1980   "White Flight and the Future of School Desegregation," in Walter G.

Stephan and Joe R. Feagin (eds.), *School Desegregation*. New York: Plenum Press, pp. 187-226.

Coleman, James S.
1981   "The Role of Incentives in School Desegregation," Adam Yarmolinsky, Lance Liebman, and Corinne S. Schelling (eds.), *Race and Schooling in the City*. Cambridge, Mass.: Harvard University Press, pp. 182-193.

Crain, Robert L., and Rita E. Mahard
1982   *Desegregation Plans that Raise Black Achievement*. Santa Monica, Calif.: Rand Corporation.

Dentler, Robert A., and Marvin B. Scott
1981   *Schools on Trial*. Cambridge, Mass.: Abt Books.

McGill, Ralph
1964   *The South and the Southerner*. Boston: Little, Brown.

Willie, Charles V.
1978   *The Sociology of Urban Education*. Lexington, Mass. Lexington Books, D. C. Heath.
1983   *Planning Desegregated and Unitary School Systems*. St. Louis, Mo.: Danforth Foundation.

Chapter 11

Community Organization in Seattle for School Desegregation That Is Moral, Ethical, and Fair

Citizen participation and community organization were unique events in the Seattle scene that enabled that city to desegregate its public schools without violence and in a way that was moral, ethical, and fair for minorities as well as the majority. This magnificent story should be understood. It could be repeated elsewhere in the nation. The kind of citizen participation and community organization evident in Seattle is significant because that city approached school desegregation initially in ways that were similar to those in other communities.

There was racism and prejudice in the Seattle community. It was one of the areas in which Japanese-Americans were rounded up and shipped away to relocation camps during World War II. These American citizens of Japanese ancestry were never appropriately compensated for their lost property; nor did other Americans apologize to them and ask for forgiveness for the violation of their constitutional rights.

As blacks and other racial minority groups moved into the community, they, too, experienced discrimination in housing. Many sections of Seattle were racially exclusive. In fact, distinct geographic neighborhoods are a characteristic of Seattle. It even has a more or less closed white ethnic neighborhood—Ballard, the Scandinavian community in the northwest part of the city. The black population is concentrated in the Central Area.

One could even detect a theme of white supremacy in the initial definition of racial imbalance by Seattle school authorities. The school board declared that a school is racially imbalanced "when the combined minority student enrollment in a school exceeds the District-Wide combined minority average by 20 percentage points"; in a racially balanced school "no single minority

Acknowledged with appreciation are interviews on the Seattle experience that were granted by Ann Siqueland, William Maynard, Samuel McKinney, Louise McKinney, C. P. Johnson, Fredie Braxton, and Dorothy Johnson.

enrollment . . . of [a] school [can] exceed 50 percent of the student body" (quoted in Siqueland, 1981:116). According to this definition, no single black or brown racial group could be the predominant population in a racially balanced school, but no limit was placed on the predominant status of whites in racially balanced schools. Clearly an implication of the definition was that it is all right for whites to control learning environments in terms of their numbers but not all right for a single black or brown population to be the majority. This implication may not have emerged into the area of conscious action by the education decision makers. Whether existing at the conscious or unconscious level, the intent of the official definition of racial balance was to foster and facilitate white control.

Even the initial efforts of Seattle to respond to charges of racial discrimination in the schools were hesitant and limited. Seattle did not employ a teacher who identified with the black population until 1947, near the midpoint of this century (Hanawalt and Williams, 1981:6). A voluntary transfer plan that placed the full burden of school desegregation upon black students existed for about a decade but affected not more than 4 percent of public school-going students in any single year (Siqueland, 1981:21). As late as 1977, the National Association for the Advancement of Colored People (NAACP) charged the Seattle school system with continuing to assign faculty to school buildings by race, pursuing the voluntary transfer policy despite its history of failure to desegregate the public schools, and designing plans that could relieve racial imbalance but refusing to implement them (Siqueland, 1981:23-24). Some members of the Seattle community acknowledged that segregation existed in the schools but attributed it to discrimination in housing and not to official action and intent of school authorities. The school superintendent, becoming indignant over the irritating charges and the impatience of minorities, which in his view encroached upon his professional domain, publicly stated that "anyone who wanted him to desegregate Seattle Public Schools with anything but voluntary student transfer strategies would have to take him to court" (quoted in Siqueland, 1981:34). This utterance, these charges, and the decade-old voluntary transfer program that placed the full desegregation burden on blacks and in the end accomplished little diversity in the public schools were not unlike the happenings in other communities throughout the United States. Although Seattle's ultimate response by way of community organization and citizen participation to the requirement of establishing a unitary school system was unique, the city's circumstances and conditions that preceded the citizen action were similar to circumstances and conditions that existed elsewhere. Thus, the way in which Seattle responded is a lesson that could be learned and applied by others.

The community organization that rescued Seattle from violent confrontation over school desegregation was not smooth and conflict-free. Competition between organizations representing minority-group interests surfaced. The majority group represented by such predominantly white associations as the school board, business and religious groups, and special-interest citizens' groups for and against desegregation was not of one mind either.

Seattle emerged from this controversy as a united community because of several factors. At least some members of the majority entertained and responded to the charges of the minorities and did not follow the practice of denying their legitimacy or ignoring them. Minority groups coordinated their varying interests so that their different demands and action strategies were complementary and not contradictory in a self-canceling way. Cleavages in the community among majority-group as well as minority-group members were not reinforcing but were cross-cutting—involving different sectors or populations coalescing around a common concern.

Continuous dialogue and full communication were acceptable and preferred ways of dealing with community issues in Seattle. The community organized itself into a hierarchy of groups ranging from single-interest groups to umbrella, general-concerns groups regarding specific community issues, with the latter groups assuming responsibility for resolving impasses, if any, between the former groups. The community's chief executive officer, the mayor, assumed responsibility for maintaining public order in an ethical way and gave moral leadership to the community process for resolving the school desegregation controversy. These unique community organizational aspects of Seattle differentiated this community from others.

Seattle's minority groups always defined the issues of segregation and discrimination as priority concerns for the total community. They refused to cooperate in their own oppression. Because the minorities in Seattle followed this course of action, they remained an optimistic community; they never became enraged to the point of rioting and destroying their own neighborhoods. A concomitant characteristic of the enraged is loss of the capacity for self-determination, to propose and plan programs for the amelioration of their circumstances. Seattle's minority community never reached this point of despair.

Unlike the situation in many communities where minority plaintiffs in school desegregation cases refuse to propose ways to redress their grievances but rely upon defendant school boards to plan for them, Seattle's minorities were different. The Urban League, a black-oriented group, proposed a triad plan in 1964 and offered it as a way of overcoming segregation of socioeconomic groups in the public schools. The triad plan called for enlarged elementary attendance zones in which schools with dissimilar student bodies would be paired and their student bodies consolidated with one building then serving the consolidated student body for primary grades and the other for intermediate grades. The consolidated student bodies obviously would be more diversified than single student bodies of the former schools. The triad plan of the Urban League was not accepted as presented. However, according to Ann Siqueland, who provided a chronicle of community-wide desegregation planning, the Urban League's plan did become the basis of the desegregation plan eventually adopted by Seattle (Siqueland, 1981:12).

One reason minorities in Seattle did not despair and become enraged is they were not alone. When it became clear that the voluntary transfer plan was not being implemented aggressively, the NAACP was not alone in charging the school board with "adopting a strategy of delay . . . and indefiniteness" (Siqueland, 1981:24). The predominantly white Committee for Quality Integrated Education also prepared a report detailing the numerous issues that the public school system had promised to address but was not addressing (Siqueland, 1981:42). To provide a political base from which to negotiate on the issue of desegregation, the predominantly black Central Area School Council was organized. As the issue of segregated schools broadened from the Central Area to include the Southeast, the predominantly white District-Wide Advisory Committee on Desegregation recognized the need in that community for a negotiating political structure that could overcome feelings of helplessness and assisted in establishing a community-based group called the Committee for Southeast Seattle Schools. When the NAACP threatened to sue the Seattle public schools to force the school authorities to provide meaningful desegregation that was more than the token accomplishments of the voluntary transfer plan, the American Civil Liberties Union, the Church Council of Greater Seattle, and other predominantly white associations promised to join the suit as joint litigants. The minority communities were not alone in Seattle in their movement to achieve an ethical and just solution to the problems of public education. Because of this support, they did not become enraged; they did not despair.

The support the minority communities received from individuals and associations among the majority caused them to feel sufficiently secure to seek the success goal of desegregated education by proposing programs and entering into negotiations despite the risk of failure. There is no success without the risk of failure. But those who distrust all others of dissimilar circumstances as well as their social systems, tend to withdraw in resentment, resist negotiating, and convert their resentment-in-isolation into a sense of rage. This minorities did not do in Seattle because they knew some whites cared, were trustworthy, and were willing to suffer the redemption of minorities by sacrificing dominant-group privileges. Such knowledge contributes to a sense of significance and also to a sense of security that characterized Seattle's minorities.

Thus, the actions of the dominant people of power in a community have a great deal to do with the stress-producing circumstances that subdominants experience and their reactions to such circumstances. As the late Whitney Young, former head of the National Urban League, often pointed out, dominants who prefer to do business with minorities of a less violent persuasion must give them some victories. Otherwise, the leadership of the minorities will pass on to individuals enraged by despair who propose less rational approaches. This is but another illustration of the interdependence that exists between minority and majority communities and a confirmation of the hypothesis set forth by Janice Perlman that a system is balanced precisely to the advantage of some through the explicit exploitation of others (Perlman, 1976:245).

Although several in number, the minority groups in Seattle did not attempt to force a common approach upon each other. They accepted their differences as strategic complements and insured that they would remain that way through continuous communication. Some perceived Asian Americans, for example, as a group that might oppose a desegregation plan. However, they were kept informed about what was happening largely through the Committee for Southeast Seattle Schools, and the Asians were willing to join a lawsuit, if it had been filed (Siqueland, 1981:56). While the NAACP in Seattle was threatening a lawsuit, the Urban League developed a desegregation plan and worked with others in the community for adoption of a modification of it without a court order. While in 1962 the NAACP accepted the Voluntary Racial Transfer plan that placed the greater burden on blacks to achieve desegregation, the black-oriented Central Area School Council endorsed the Seattle Plan in 1977 only because of its "fixed assignments . . . equity of movement" provisions among other features. The NAACP did not endorse this plan but served as a watchdog to see if it was implemented as promised. Earlier, the Black United Clergy for Action had endorsed desegregation of the schools but had not called for "full integration," preferring a plan that recognized the "maintenance of ethnic identity" (Siqueland, 1981:20). Because the various minority groups played several roles, one group could sit at the conference table and bargain for benefits while another could threaten legal action or a boycott. Indeed, a successful boycott of the Central Area school was carried out by blacks in 1966 (Siqueland, 1981:12). Despite these differences in style of operating, some coordination of black community groups was achieved through efforts of the Urban League; black community groups, using different tactics, were able to maintain a united position on school desegregation as a goal. Moreover, minority groups were coordinated with others through participation in two combined majority-minority umbrella groups—the District-Wide Advisory Committee on Desegregation and the No-Name Committee.

Because differences within the minority community existed and were acknowledged, the majority could not do business with a handpicked leader and ignore all others. The Seattle minority communities were not monolithic structures that could be taken for granted. While the absence of a unified approach may have weakened the minority community in negotiations with the majority, its diversity served as a form of protection. No single individual or group could curry favor from the community at large by offering to deliver minority votes for or against specific proposals.

Minority-group members of the community initiated school desegregation activity by refusing to cooperate in their own oppression. But the ultimate outcome depended upon the response of the majority. Would it stand pat and defend its privileges or repent for transgressions against subdominants and make the sacrifices that are necessary to suffer the redemption of subdominant out-groups from deficiencies that are functions of the actions of the dominant in-group?

Seattle, unlike most communities, recognized dual school systems within a single community that provided unequal opportunities for minorities as moral and ethical issues. Self-interest was still a motivating factor for the remedial actions taken by the majority. But the actions undertaken were for the purpose of fulfilling majority-group members' moral and ethical self-interest rather than their economic or political self-interest. Thus, the definition of the desegregation situation is important in determining outcomes. For example, school desegregation defined as an economic phenomenon is not likely to have outcomes that involve the suffering of financial loss by the dominant group; and school desegregation defined as a political phenomenon is not likely to have outcomes that involve the sacrificing of power by the dominant group. Such outcomes are possible, however, when desegregation is defined as a moral or ethical phenomenon as Seattle identified it.

One reason Seattle defined school desegregation as moral and ethical is the prominent role played by the community's religious leadership in framing the issue and proposals for resolution. As stated by one citizen, "the Seattle plan came about when the black clergy and the Church Council began to take a real serious look at things and began to do something about the situation." Specifically, the Council of Churches of Greater Seattle formed a task force on Racial Justice in Education (Siqueland, 1981:20). While some might emphasize the efforts of associations in other institutional sectors as significant in initiating action, clearly the religious groups were central in alerting the community that change was necessary.

Before the religious groups became involved, the school board viewed desegregation largely "as a by-product of quality education" (Siqueland, 1981:12). One school board member who was first elected on a platform against mandatory student assignments to achieve desegregation defeated an anti-busing candidate in a reelection bid after voting in favor of the Seattle Plan and its mandatory features. This board member said, eventually "a majority of the Board" saw school desegregation "more as a moral question than as an education question" (Siqueland, 1981:26).

Phase I, the middle school desegregation plan, was "the first mandatory effort initiated in Seattle" and stimulated so much opposition and anger among some citizens that a possibility existed that the majority of the school board who favored desegregation would be defeated. So deeply had the issue been implanted in moral ideals, however, that the superintendent who implemented Phase I resigned in the early 1970s as "a personal sacrifice" to increase the likelihood that "individuals supportive of desegregation would be elected to the School Board, thereby insuring the continuation of Seattle's desegregation effort" (Siqueland, 1981:31). In other words, the superintendent offered himself as a sacrificial scapegoat upon whom the anger over mandatory school desegregation could be heaped, leaving other education authorities less blameworthy in the mind of the public. And the school desegregation effort did continue, although slowed somewhat by the fear engendered by the enormity of the sacrifice required by a supportive dominant-group member.

The very act of defining desegregation as a moral issue also probably contributed to the peaceful and nonviolent way it was implemented. "The school district desegregated all of its racially imbalanced schools in three years without one incident of violence" (Siqueland, 1981:185). This idea that a moral solution contributes to nonviolence is in opposition to one that identifies morality as a source of human activity that fans the passions of people and stimulates irrationality. Actually, economic, educational, and political interests are passionately adhered to as much as religious interest of a moral nature.

The benefit, then, of defining an issue as one that is moral is the flexibility that morality generates in the search for solutions. Moral self-interest is less fixed and less segregating, than, for example, economic or political self-interest. Similar moral self-interests may be found among liberal and conservative political groups. Members of affluent and poor economic groups may also share common interests that are moral. Morality cuts across other group boundaries and can function to unify, while self-interest defined along political, economic, and even educational lines tends to differentiate the people and set them against each other.

"In seeking victory for the individual, one has to seek victory for the group; and in seeking victory for the oppressed group, one has to seek victory for those who formerly were the oppressors. The inclusive approach is what [Martin Luther] King [Jr.] called the double victory" (Willie, 1981:10). In *The Ivory and Ebony Towers,* I point out that "the double victory is achieved when there is mutual fulfillment. There is no victor and vanquished but a synthesis that consists of the old parts related to each other in a new way." All of this is to say that, "the justice that blacks seek is a justice for whites as well as for blacks." And I concluded that "the double victory in education uplifts whites as well as blacks" (Willie, 1981:10). The double victory, of course, is a moral solution.

Several decades ago, sociologist Edward Ross discussed the benefit of crosscutting cleavages in the community. He said, "every species of social conflict interferes with every other species in society . . . save only when lines of cleavages coincide; in which case they reinforce one another. . . . A society, therefore, which is ridden by a dozen oppositions along lines running in every direction may actually be in less danger of being torn with violence or falling to pieces than one split along just one line" (Ross, 1920, quoted in Axelrod, 1970:159). More recently, a similar observation was made by Robert Dahl: "If all the cleavages occur along the same lines, if the same people hold opposing positions in one dispute after another, then the severity of conflicts is likely to increase" (Dahl, 1967, quoted in Axelrod, 1970:159). Based on these observations and his own analysis, Robert Axelrod arrived at this conclusion: "If the cleavages [in a community] are crosscutting, relatively little conflictful behavior is expected" (Axelrod, 1970:159).

By defining school desegregation as a moral issue in Seattle, the issue cuts across several cleavages. The search for a solution that was moral, ethical, and fair united blacks and whites in the various church groups and people in different neighborhoods so much that a white school board member from the conservative West Seattle area, who was elected on a nonmandatory-student-assignment platform when school desegregation was defined as an education issue only, could vote for an equitable plan involving mandatory student assignments after school desegregation was defined as a moral and ethical issue that should be solved in an equitable way. The moral issue effectively cut across racial and geographic interests in a way that enabled the school board member to be reelected. Other examples can be given of how the search for a moral solution unites people previously separated into opposing interest groups. Thus, politics and religion, for example, are different orders of interest in society and have different functions. Power interests tend to divide the people, and moral interests tend to unite them. Power interests contribute to reinforce cleavages, and moral interests tend to cut across them. The definition of school desegregation as a moral issue is one reason that it occurred in Seattle without a major event of violence. In other communities throughout the nation, religious groups are notable by their absence in the school desegregation controversy. Without their central participation, school desegregation usually is defined as an educational, economic, or political issue around which reinforcing cleavages are formed.

Another reason Seattle approached and moved through its school desegregation crisis with fewer harmful effects than exhibited in other communities may be attributed to the skilled way the community organized its groups into a coordinated hierarchy. As pointed out in another study,

conflicting interests, whether in the voluntary, governmental, economic, educational, or religious sector of the community, are inevitable in a free society. This means that communities must develop mediating structures to deal with impasses when they occur. The third party is a necessity in a community that is increasing in its complexity and must rely more and more on formal rather than informal ways of acting. It is to each institution's advantage to structure in its own mediating instruments. . . . Otherwise, the system must await a crisis between two or more of its components; then some organization on a trial and error basis may come forward and try to help the contending parties resolve their differences. . . .The third party is a necessary function in local community organization increasingly characterized by groups clustered into power coalitions in conflict with each other. . . .It is well to plan for ways to facilitate third party intervention before the need arises. (Willie, 1966:40)

Seattle had a plethora of special-interest groups concerned with school desegregation that could have generated much conflict and canceled out the efforts of each. While its various community groups were not always in agreement, this did not happen. The community planning process never reached an impasse because of the strategic way umbrella, general-concern groups were organized. They helped resolve differences between competing special-interest groups that were affiliated with them by serving as channels of communication and, when necessary, as settings in which negotiations could take place. Prior to 1975, an umbrella group that had worked with the school administration to assist with desegregation efforts was the Coalition for Quality Integrated Education. It brought together three ad hoc groups which had formed to support Phase I of the Seattle Plan (Siqueland, 1981:40). In 1975 the District-Wide Advisory Committee on Desegregation (DWAC) was reorganized and its charter extended so that it might advise the school board and the office of the superintendent. DWAC "included representatives from community councils, school advisory groups, and citywide community organizations" (Siqueland, 1981:43). DWAC has been described as "provid[ing] a base on which several individuals representing several organizations could begin to construct a framework of ideas within which a unified community approach to desegregation could be developed" (Siqueland, 1981:44). As a way of continuing to build trust through regular dialogue another umbrella group was formed in 1977. It was called the No-Name Committee precisely because it did not have a name. This group brought together the NAACP, the ACLU, and downtown groups such as the Chamber of Commerce, the Municipal League, and the Office of the Mayor. Representatives of DWAC participated in No-Name Committee sessions, too (Siqueland, 1981:131). All of these umbrella groups provided valuable and viable communication links.

The final unique development in Seattle that differentiated its approach from that of other cities is the deep involvement of the mayor and the executive structure of city government in school desegregation. By 1969 Marilyn Gittell reported that "urban mayors had removed themselves from the educational arena" because "mayors are not likely to gain political advantage from school issues" (Gittell, 1971:156, 142). Seattle demonstrates, however, that mayors are likely to gain a safe community where public order prevails when they place the power and prestige of the highest elective office in the community behind a school desegregation plan that is moral, ethical, and fair. Although the Seattle experience is not repeated as often as it should be, the United States Commission on Civil Rights found that "where officials . . . have given their support, the process of desegregating the schools has tended to go relatively smoothly" (U.S. commission on Civil Rights, 1976, quoted in Siqueland, 1981:105). The process proceeded this way in Seattle.

Early in 1977, the mayor of Seattle decided that the school board should assume responsibility for desegregating the public schools rather than waiting for a federal court order. The mayor believed that with sufficient support from business and civic leaders the school board could be persuaded to develop and implement a meaningful desegregation plan. To show support, the mayor proposed that a letter be sent to the school board signed by him and board presidents of the Chamber of Commerce, the Municipal League, and the Urban League. Within a period of ten days the three groups and the mayor agreed on the contents of the letter. The letter was a positive endorsement of desegregation as a way of helping children adjust to a pluralistic society, and it struck an optimistic note that the flight of the middle class from the city was not likely to result from school desegregation if the board maintained its commitment to provide quality education and citizens remained involved in desegregation planning. Many credit the letter that the mayor urged the civic leaders to prepare in support of school desegregation as contributing to a turning point in school desegregation efforts. There was no precedent in any community for a joint letter like that received by the Seattle public schools and certainly no precedent for such a letter signed by the mayor.

June 8, 1977, less than a month after the school board received the letter, it passed a resolution which defined racial imbalance and set a timetable for its elimination. In effect, the school board followed the letter's suggestion and came to a firm decision to eliminate segregation in Seattle public schools without a court order (Siqueland, 1981:104-119). By the fall of 1980, only one school exceeded the cutoff point for a racially imbalanced school (Hanawalt and Williams, 1981:40).

Seattle is a place where community members were genuinely involved in school desegregation planning, and their involvement made a difference. Minority-group members decided to cease cooperating in their own oppression and confronted the community with the need to change. Majority-group members responded by defining school desegregation as a moral and ethical issue as well as one having to do with quality education. This definition of the situation united the people by cutting across racial, geographic, and other cleavages. Finally, the support rallied in favor of school desegregation by the mayor provided a positive endorsement and an optimistic outlook. All of this contributed to a peaceful and nonviolent school desegregation experience in a pluralistic community and in this nation's most prominent city of the Northwest.

References

Axelrod, Robert
  1970   *Conflict of Interest*. Chicago: Markham Publishing.
Gittell, Marilyn
  1971   "Education: The Decentralization-Community Control Controversy,"
          in Jewel Bellush and Stephen M. David (eds.), *Race and Politics in New
          York City*. New York: Praeger, pp. 134-163.
Hanawalt, Frank, and Robert L. Williams
  1981   *The History of Desegregation in Seattle Public Schools, 1954-1981*.
          Seattle, Wash.: Seattle Public Schools.
Perlman, Janice E.
  1976   *The Myth of Marginality*. Berkeley, Calif.: University of California
          Press.
Siqueland, Ann L.
  1981   *Without a Court Order*. Seattle, Wash.: Madrona Publishers.
Willie, Charles V.
  1966   "The Evolution of a Community Art Museum," *Event* 6 (Summer):
          23-41.
  1981   *The Ivory and Ebony Towers*. Lexington, Mass.: Lexington Books,
          D. C. Heath.

Chapter 12

Generosity and Justice— The Goals of Atlanta's Unitary School System Where Blacks Are In Charge

When the full history of school desegregation is written, said sociologists S. M. Miller and Pamela Roby, it will reveal that the United States sent its children forth to deal with the problem of racial segregation that adults had created (Miller, 1968:18). This may be the approach of most communities in this nation, but it is not the approach that Atlanta used. The Atlanta, Georgia, black community pressed for and won desegregation of the teaching and administrative staff while the number of students deliberately moved from one setting to another to achieve desegregation was limited. How and why the black community focused on achieving faculty and staff desegregation as basic in a unitary public school system is a unique Atlanta story that should be examined in depth. General features of the desegregation effort and its rationale will be discussed in this essay.

In the early 1970s, at the height of the desegregation effort in Atlanta, a total of 16,000 students were transferred in a mandatory way by rezoning local school districts. Even of this relatively small number, only 4,000 were transferred to accomplish more desegregation. They represented about 4 percent of the total citywide student enrollment of approximately 111,000 young people in the public schools (Ecke, 1972:420). The remaining 12,000 were transferred to schools where the enrollment was predominantly of the race of the newly assigned student.

Before 1970, Atlanta's black parents had petitioned for and the school board had tried a number of desegregative devices that achieved little or limited student desegregation. According to Superintendent Alonzo Crim, "the next year after the *Brown* decision [that rendered deliberate segregation in public education illegal], black parents in Atlanta began to petition the Board of Education for justice." However, he said "attempts

The author acknowledges with appreciation interviews granted by Alonzo Crim, Benjamin Mays, J. Y. Moreland and Walter Bell.

to eliminate the dual school system were futile until 1958, when black parents and the National Association for the Advancement of Colored People (NAACP) filed a civil action suit against the Atlanta Board of Education'' (Crim and Emmons, 1983). The trial date was set for 1959.

A presentment by the Fulton County Grand Jury (the county in which Atlanta is located) demonstrated as well as any document why little movement had occurred in responding to the petition of blacks to desegregate the schools. According to historian Melvin Ecke "public opinion . . . was definitely opposed to desegregating the schools'' (Ecke, 1972:346). And the presentment that was intended as a conciliatory gesture by calling for the formation of biracial committees of temperate-thinking leaders in both races, also asserted that whites would not do anything that was repugnant to them. Specifically, the presentment said that "In the history of the white English-speaking race, never has there been imposed upon them for long, a statute or a way of life from without, which is fundamentally objectionable to a majority of the citizens'' (quoted in Ecke, 1972:353).

The presentment also reflected the sentiments of the predominantly white school board. When the NAACP petitioned the Atlanta schools to desegregate in accordance with the *Brown* decision of the Supreme Court, the school board responded that it would obey the law. However, the board planned to fulfill only the letter of the law, not the spirit, and in its own time. The black school board member who participated in these deliberations was elected in 1954. Repeatedly, he stated his belief that the board was acting in good faith, although it did not respond to the NAACP's 1953 petition to desegregate the schools until 1957 and did not officially discuss for the record the NAACP's 1958 court suit against the board for desegregation until November 1959. The issue of desegregation was treated as less pressing than other matters. While the black member of the school board was claiming good-faith efforts on the part of his other board colleagues, the actions of the education authorities clearly indicated that they intended to follow "every conceivable channel of the court process'' and to seek "every legal means possible'' to delay desegregation (Ecke, 1972:347).

Examples of board action to meet only the letter of the law were the series of hesitating steps that it took after the Federal District Court, in *Calhoun v. Latimer* (1959), gave its decision. The court found that racial segregation did indeed exist in the Atlanta Public School System and that such segregation was a violation of the Fourteenth Amendment constitutional rights of the black plaintiffs.

Responding to requirements of the court order, the Atlanta public schools developed a plan to desegregate gradually, one grade a year, beginning with the twelfth grade. Carefully screened black students who applied for enrollment in a predominantly white school had to meet eighteen criteria of an elaborate process. The first year of court-ordered desegregation was 1961 and involved only nine students in grades 12 and 11. The number of black student transfers which the elaborate screening process let through was miniscule, and the official policy of the school board was not to give reasons for denying transfer requests (Ecke, 1972:366). According to the plan implemented in 1961, from that date eleven years would be required to desegregate the Atlanta public schools.

The plan was a way of delaying the implementation of justice for black petitioners; those sufficiently courageous to request a transfer had no guarantee they would be reassigned to a desegregated school. Meanwhile double sessions continued in some overcrowded black schools. For example, the E. R. Carter School had been on double sessions from 1919 to 1963 (Ecke, 1972:375-376). Moreover, no Reserve Officer Training Corps (ROTC) unit existed in any black school in Atlanta until one was placed at Washington High School in 1963.

The United States Court of Appeals in 1963 ordered the Atlanta schools to abandon the grade-a-year timetable and the elaborate screening plan. Consequently, in 1964 the school board assigned all entering high school students to the school of their choice. Moreover, students already enrolled could transfer to any high school they wished if space was available and the school was geographically near the student's residence.

In 1964 the NAACP turned its attention to faculty desegregation, too. Supported by the National Council of Human Rights, the local NAACP chapter "requested the Board to assign black teachers and counselors to high schools to which substantial numbers of black students had transferred" (Ecke, 1972:386). Meanwhile, the court that same year urged the board to make a diligent study of ways by which acceleration of student desegregation might be obtained. As a token action toward this goal, the Atlanta school board in 1965 desegregated a white elementary school— Kirkwood—which was underutilized. Blacks in the area who had attended overcrowded black schools were sent to Kirkwood. This was the first effort toward desegregating elementary education in any meaningful way.

The accelerated desegregation plan prepared by the board in 1964 and ordered by the court for the 1965-66 school year proposed full integration of the sixth and seventh grades by the fall of 1968. Having gone this far, the school board in 1965 agreed that black students in all grade levels could petition for enrollment in a desegregated school, and by 1966 the board agreed that the pupil's preference and the availability of space would be the sole criteria determining the approval of requests for transfers (Ecke, 1972:388).

Probably the NAACP requested desegregation of the teaching staff in 1964 not only because of exasperation with the slow movement toward student desegregation, but also because it sensed that efforts were under way to make it more difficult for black teachers to qualify for local school employment, probably as a penalty for supporting desegregation of students. The board voted in 1961 that the National Teacher Examination would be used as part of the selection process for new teachers and that the required score for candidates eligible for hiring should be set at 425 on the common portion of the test and 43 on the optional portion (ECKE, 1972:369). The board earlier had discussed using this screening instrument but had not required it. Experience in other communities has revealed that as many as eight out of ten minority teachers who took this test could fail it. South Carolina has had this experience with the National Teacher Examination. At any rate, the board refused to entertain the 1964 request to desegregate teachers, stating that it would be improper to consider the matter while the original case of *Calhoun v. Latimer* was on appeal to the Supreme Court.

The adopted resolution of the school board that from 1965 on "pupils in every grade from kindergarten through the twelfth could request a school assignment when room was available at a school to which they wished to transfer" (Ecke, 1972:388) was not necessarily an affirmative action in favor of desegregation. The burden for requesting a transfer rested solely upon the initiative of blacks. This school board policy was not proactive but reactive — continuing the 1958 policy of using every legal means to delay desegregation (Ecke, 1972:347). The 1965 board policy merely laid an opportunity before black students but, operationally, did nothing to foster use of it.

To focus their concerns more, to gain consensus, and to provide an organized channel for communicating with the black community which the elected black school board member was unable to provide, a group of blacks called the Summit Leadership Conference was organized. The cochairman of this group was a black executive of an insurance company with headquarters in Atlanta. This group presented a petition to the school board in 1965 that dealt with specific issues. Among the issues raised were (1) the continuing dissatisfaction with double sessions in overcrowded black schools, (2) the absence of texts that presented a proper perspective on race, (3) the need for more black teachers on the faculty of the vocational-technical school, (4) the assignment of more black principals to all schools, especially schools with more than 60 percent black students, (5) the promotion of two or three blacks to head schoolwide departments in central administration, and (6) the promotion of a black person to the role of first associate superintendent. This list of concerns definitely was upping the ante. It is a principle in organizational behavior that when little demands are ignored, the petitioners will escalate their requirement and ask for more, not less. This happened in Atlanta. The request ten years earlier to desegregate the students had been so thoroughly resisted that blacks increased their demands to include desegregating the faculty and the administrative staff as well as the student body of the school system.

Although not an explicit demand in 1965, the Summit Leadership Conference informed the school board that "[it saw] no reason why the chief administrator should not be Negro" (Ecke, 1972:404). In due time this concern became a demand to be fulfilled along with the others made earlier, which were ignored as long as possible.

A school board that in 1961 would respond to a court order to desegregate by placing only nine black students in predominantly white schools had to integrate 35,000 blacks in predominantly white schools in 1967. A school board that would not entertain a request in 1964 to assign black teachers and counselors to high schools to which substantial numbers of black students had transferred had to desegregate more than 50 percent of the school faculties and the central administrative staff by 1967. The Summit Leadership Conference insisted on the promotion of a black professional to the position of assistant or associate superintendent, so that someone of their race would be present to participate in the formulation of policy and personnel recommendations. Finally, the Summit Leadership Conference insisted that local black-controlled banking institutions should be used as depositories for some school system funds. This demand was implemented in 1970 (Ecke, 1972:404).

The organized pressure of blacks came from several sources within the black community, including the NAACP, which continued to press legally for more student desegregation but also from the Summit Leadership Conference consisting of several black business executives and others who pressed for faculty and administrative staff desegregation. Observers of these times have credited Atlanta's business community with playing "a key role" in creating "good local race relations during the 1960s" (Walker, 1982:8A). The Summit Leadership Conference led by a black business executive could speak directly to white business executives. When the business executives became involved, the dilatory tactics of the board of education tended to cease.

Dan Sweat, president of Central Atlanta Progress, said "the stakes were too high [in the 1960s] to allow the city to be torn apart by racial violence." The "businessmen," he said, "began making the necessary deals with the black community" (quoted by Walker, 1982:8A). By 1969, the board no longer was reactive, claiming that it had no responsibility to move affirmatively to achieve desegregation. In fact by 1969 it sought a grant from the federal government "to formulate, verify, implement, evaluate, and disseminate workable solutions to school desegregation" (Ecke, 1972:418). The grant proposal was funded the summer of 1970.

Meanwhile the first black elected to the school board—a higher education administrator—died in 1964. For many years he was the only black member participating in board deliberations on school desegregation. Earning the respect and admiration of his fellow white board members, the first elected black member began to lose credibility with his constituents. He "could have been disruptive, but wasn't" said historian Melvin Ecke (1972:405). There is some indication that he may have been too conciliatory. Be that as it may, by 1969 the Atlanta school board had begun to recognize that the black community could not be represented by a single person or a single group. Moreover, the white community was beginning to realize that it could not move at its own pace with little if any consideration for the interests and timetable of blacks. This realization was heightened not only by the escalated demands of the Summit Leadership Conference, but also by the increasing proportion of blacks in the public school population. Their number had risen beyond a majority of all students by 1969. Also in that year black educator Benjamin E. Mays, president emeritus of predominantly black Morehouse College and one of Atlanta's most distinguished black citizens, was elected to the board. In 1970 Mays also was elected president of the board. His election signaled the end of dilatory tactics. The goal of Mays, according to historian Melvin Ecke, was "to bring unity to the Board and to take the lead in moving the school system toward becoming a completely unitary one" (Ecke, 1972:418).

Almost immediately after Mays took office, the federal courts issued new orders that took into consideration the escalated demands of the plaintiff class. This time, the school board developed a good-faith plan in reality to comply with the court order. The freedom-of-choice plan that placed the full burden for achieving desegregation upon blacks and their initiatives was abolished. Students of a majority racial group in any school were allowed to transfer to another school in which members of their racial group were the minority. School district lines were rezoned to increase desegregation. This rezoning, however, affected only about 16 percent of the students. The school board was parsimonious in rezoning to avoid large outlays for purchasing or contracting for buses to transport students to and from school. Moreover, the courts also required desegregation of the faculty so that the racial ratio of faculty in each school would be the same as the systemwide ratios at the elementary, middle school, and high school levels. The school system complied with this order by transferring 800 teachers; by then, a majority of all teachers in the Atlanta schools was black.

Indeed, the blacks in Atlanta were able to retain a high number of teachers because of their earlier demand that the staff in central administration should be desegregated. As a result, a black professional was retained as one of the personnel administrators and was able to prevent racial subterfuge that tends to bar blacks from seeping into the hiring process.

The large proportion of blacks in the teaching and administrative staff of Atlanta schools not only provided mentors and role models for black students, it guaranteed that a fair share of the wealth of Atlanta generated by the public school system remains in black families. This is an important outcome of any desegregation program. Assuming an annual median salary of about $20,000 for about 6,500 black and Hispanic professional staff in public schools in 1982, a public school system would pay approximately one-eighth of a billion dollars to such families each year. Indirectly, a high proportion of blacks employed by a public school system has an impact on the education of children in the community in that the employees have the resources necessary to support higher education for their offspring.

Communication between the racial populations by way of formal and informal groups was at a high level and was effective in 1969. The court sought to maintain the forward progress that this communication had achieved by appointing in 1970 an Interracial Committee to assist the board in an advisory capacity to make plans for further desegregation.

The affirmative response to all sectors of the community by the school board under the leadership of its new president was so effective that the court permitted the defendant school board, the black plaintiffs, and the community to work out a consensus proposal that it could order as a final decree in 1973, declaring that Atlanta had achieved a unitary school system.

The school board in consultation with the Interracial Committee that represented the court, the Summit Leadership Conference and the NAACP that represented the black community, and the business and political leaders in the white community agreed that the time was now ripe to meet the demand hinted at in 1965 by the Summit Leadership Conference. The next superintendent of schools was to be black. Although by 1970 close to two-thirds of the students in the Atlanta public schools were black, the black leaders promised whites 50 percent of the administrative positions in the consensus proposal. This deal represents an action of generosity on the part of the black community toward whites that is a model for the rest of the nation. There is no record elsewhere of a community in which a majority of the students are white that has reserved at least half of the administrative staff positions for blacks or other minorities. Also, no other school system has employed as many black teachers and has desegregated the faculty of schools and the central administrative staff as thoroughly as Atlanta has. The student desegregation plan continued to be a modest one. It required little movement of whites to achieve desegregation, since their numbers had dwindled to less than one-third of all public school students in Atlanta. However, black students were assigned to all predominantly white schools so that, in most instances, they represented at least one-third of a school's student population. This plan, of course, permitted many schools to remain all black. Thus, the Atlanta consensus agreements on school desegregation that were ordered by the court are unique.

Alonzo Crim, the first black superintendent of schools in Atlanta, has led that system for a decade. Meanwhile, the first black president of the school board who presided over the hiring of the first black chief administrator served three terms and did not seek reelection. The spirit of generosity that prevailed during the past decade has continued. When Mays stepped down as president of the school board, it elevated a white member to that office, even though the board consisted of six black and three white members and could have elected another black as the presiding officer.

By 1982 the Atlanta public school system consisted of 117 schools, had 68,611 students (of whom 91 percent are black), and employed a professional staff of 7,791 (17 percent of whom are white). These data also indicate a unique arrangement. While a professional staff of a big-city school system four-fifths black is unusual, no other big-city school system in the United States has awarded the minority component of its public school population a proportion of professional positions that is twice as large as that racial population's proportion of public school students. White students in the Atlanta public schools are 8 percent of all students; as such, they are the minority. But white adults occupy 17 percent of all professional staff positions. I know of no big city in America where blacks are the minority and whites are in control that has hired blacks in teaching and administrative positions at a rate twice as great as the rate of black students in the total school system. Both in its school board electoral practice and in its public school employment policy, Atlanta has manifested an affirmative response of generosity and justice that is new and unique in the United States during these concluding decades of the twentieth century. This policy and this practice are worthy of emulation by communities where whites are in charge as well as by other urban communities controlled by blacks.

There is evidence that the Atlanta school board and school administration, consisting of the kinds of individuals mentioned with their commitment to generosity and justice, are beginning to deal with new issues in public education as required of a unitary school system. In addition to facilitating racial diversity, the chief administrator in Atlanta has identified a new goal for a unitary public school system: guaranteeing equal opportunity for all students regardless of socioeconomic status.

In 1980 the administration of the Atlanta public schools developed a five-year plan that focused on academic achievement. By 1985 the superintendent promised that Atlanta public school student test scores in reading and mathematics would be at or above the national norm. In the second year of the plan, 48 percent of the elementary school students had reached the 1985 goal. The central administration hopes to increase the proportion of students achieving at or above the national norm for each grade level each year. Standards are established annually for all grades. Teachers not performing adequately are invited to participate in the reading academy for teachers—an in-service educational program staffed by specialists in the system.

Currently, about half of the graduates of Atlanta public schools continue their education in postsecondary schools. The goal of the administration is to increase this number by 5 percent each year.

Moreover, the Atlanta public schools plan to begin instruction early by working with about 300 public and private day-care centers. Also the public schools continue to invite parent and citizen participation. The goal is to increase a citywide Parent-Teacher Association membership of 10,000 (in a school system of 68,000 to 69,000 students) to 15,000 during the course of a single year. The Atlanta public school system is serious in its desire to work with parents and to connect with the home.

The public school system is also serious in its concern about the community. It has a good track record of working with community groups as revealed during the 1970 decade. The linkage with the business community that, in the words of the president of Central Atlanta Progress, "saw [Atlanta] through that stormy era" of desegregation (quoted by Walker, 1982:8A), has continued. The administration has set as a goal an increase of fifty a year in the number of businesses that adopt individual schools and provide supplies, tutors, and part-time employment opportunities for students. And the school system would like to develop in a single year, if possible, at least 700 more part-time jobs for its students (Crim, 1982). The Atlanta schools are attempting to remove socioeconomic barriers that impede the progress of students. As stated by the superintendent, "In a desegregated school system that is 90 percent black . . . the struggle becomes one of classism" (Crim, 1983).

A tangible memorial of school-community relations in Atlanta is the John F. Kennedy School and Community Center. A dozen or more city, county, state, and federal agencies helped plan the facility. It includes a middle school that can accommodate up to 1,000 students, comprehensive day care for preschool-age children, activity centers for older people, housing, shelter workshops for handicapped individuals, and other services for all age levels (Ecke, 1972:443). The school and community center opened in 1971. The Atlanta schools can turn toward the community without fear of usurpation of authority because professional administrators have a clear conception of the nature of this interrelation. According to the superintendent, the community identifies *what* it would like the schools to accomplish, and the school staff has the responsibility to determine *how* programs will be implemented.

In the edition of his book *Social Theory and Social Structure* issued in 1968, the year in which Martin Luther King, Jr., died, sociologist Robert Merton said that it is frequently the case that the nonconforming minority represents the basic values of the society better than the conforming majority (Merton, 1968:421). Although a majority of the public school population in Atlanta, blacks are a minority of all students in the United States. Nationally, then, the Atlanta experience is of inestimable value in demonstrating how to achieve consensus among formerly antagonistic groups. In Atlanta, a national minority population is in charge of a major urban area, the preeminent city of the South. There, it is demonstrating how others in charge elsewhere should act for the joint welfare of majority and minority populations. In Atlanta, Georgia, blacks who are in control appear to be achieving a double victory—one for themselves as well as one for whites, and a victory for the poor as well as a victory for the affluent. Atlanta is in the process of implementing the proposition that in a nation in which blacks and poor people are subdominant populations in terms of power, ultimately one helps whites only by helping blacks and one helps the affluent only when the interests and concerns of the poor are fulfilled. What is happening in Atlanta represents the basic values of generosity and justice professed by this nation. Atlanta began to follow this course only a decade ago. Now it is time to begin to evaluate the outcome, for the purpose of determining what is unique to Atlanta and what can be adapted to other settings.

One clear conclusion is that social change in Atlanta has been a cooperative venture between blacks and whites, between young people and adults, and between poor people and those who are affluent. In public school education, blacks in Atlanta did not send forth their children alone to undo segregation and to deal with discrimination. Black teachers and administrators went with and before to desegregate the public schools and to achieve a unitary system that accommodates the needs of all.

References

Atlanta Public Schools
    1982   *Proposed Operating Budget, June 1, 1982-June 30, 1983.*
Crim, Alonzo A.
    1982   "School Opening Address." Presented by the superintendent to the
            faculty of the Atlanta Public Schools (Aug.).
Crim, Alonzo A., and Nancy J. Emmons
    1983   "Desegregation in the Atlanta Public Schools: A Historical Overview,"
            in C. V. Willie, *Planning Desegregated and Unitary School Systems.* St.
            Louis, Mo.: Danforth Foundation.
Ecke, Melvin W.
    1972   *From Ivy Street to Kennedy Center.* Atlanta, Ga.: Atlanta Board of
            Education.
Merton, Robert K.
    1968   *Social Theory and Social Structure.* New York: Free Press.
Miller, S. M. and Pamela Roby
    1968   "Education and Redistribution: The Limits of a Strategy," *Integrated
            Education* 6 (Sept.-Oct.) pp. 13-18.
Walker, Tom
    1982   "Black, Business Leaders' Team Work Hailed," *The Atlanta
            Constitution* (Aug. 31).

Part V

SUMMARY AND CONCLUSION

Chapter 13

Comparative Analysis of Model School Desegregation Plans

Charles V. Willie and Michael Fultz

Educational Advancement and Racial Diversity: The Twofold Goal

In an earlier chapter it was mentioned that education planners associated with racial minority populations tend to emphasize educational opportunities while majority planners are largely concerned with ways of achieving racial diversity as the basic goal of desegregation. Analysis of the four model plans presented in this study reveals that both educational advancement and student-body diversity are essential in an ideal plan for a unitary public school system. A plan that emphasizes one aspect of the twofold goal but ignores the other is incomplete and cannot achieve meaningful desegregation for white, black, and other minority students to the greatest extent practicable.

Plans designed to enhance educational experiences as well as interracial contacts tend to require desegregation for majority as well as minority students. But those that focus either on student-body diversity or educational opportunities but not on both tend to achieve substantially more desegregation for one racial population than for another.

The 1973 Atlanta Plan, for example, did not include an educational component but prescribed a minimum black enrollment of 30 percent in all schools. In effect, this plan provided desegregative experiences for whites but left many blacks in racially isolated schools.

The Seattle Plan vacillated between a voluntary transfer program and then mandatory student assignments; also used were some citywide magnet schools and magnet add-on programs within regular schools, but they were few in number and their potential impact on desegregation has not been fully determined. It is fair to say that the educational component in the Seattle Plan is modest. Finally, the Seattle Plan emphasized fixed student assignments but retained the voluntary transfer options and a small number of special schools. Essentially, the Seattle Plan is a student-assignment plan to achieve diversity that mandates a desegregative experience for blacks in that minority enrollment for a single black or brown group may not exceed 50 percent of the student body in a specific school, but no upper limit is given for white enrollment in city schools. The Seattle Plan was designed to desegregate predominantly black schools and left some white schools in a racially isolated state.

The Boston and Milwaukee plans provided desegregative experiences for a substantial number of black and white students. They achieved these because the plans emphasized both educational advancement and student diversity. The special educational opportunities in desegregated learning environments of both plans were available to volunteers who left their neighborhood schools. Students who did not volunteer were assigned to schools in ways that contributed to racial balance.

Differences between the Boston Plan and the Milwaukee Plan have to do with aspects of the twofold goal of desegregation, and which goal is emphasized as primary or secondary. The Boston Plan emphasized mandatory assignments for 70 to 80 percent of the public school students. They were assigned to eight districts, each of which encompassed racially heterogeneous populations. Voluntary enrollment in desegregated citywide magnet schools was the secondary desegregative device that affected from 20 to 30 percent of all Boston public school students. In Milwaukee voluntary transfer to magnet or other preferred schools was the primary desegregative strategy and mandated assignments the secondary method. Milwaukee desegregated about 20 to 30 percent of its students through its primary method of specialty and other preferred schools. This proportion is similar to that for Boston students enrolled in magnet schools.

The methods of desegregation used in Boston and Milwaukee were effective. Boston desegregated about 80 percent of its schools for whites, blacks, and other minorities, using mandatory assignments and voluntary transfer. Before the court-ordered plan, about 80 percent of Boston schools were segregated. All desegregated Boston schools had to have student bodies with racial compositions similar to the racial makeup of their local district and could vary only by specified percentages above or below the district percentage. While a desegregated school in Milwaukee could not have more than 60 percent blacks or Hispanics in the student body, no school could have a minority population less than 25 percent. All-white schools were not permitted in the Milwaukee plan. Thus, Milwaukee, like Boston, provided desegregative experiences for black and white students. It moved from segregation in approximately 90 percent of its schools before the court-ordered plan to the present when most schools are desegregated.

The conclusion from this analysis is that an ideal school desegregation plan should be sufficiently comprehensive to embrace the twofold goal of a unitary school system—educational advancement and racial diversity.

Under this condition, effective desegregative experiences can be provided for all racial groups. Those who suggest that school desegregation should limit concern to formulas for race mixing only are clearly wrong. Such plans tend to affect one racial group more than another and provide less interracial contact.

If mandatory student assignments to achieve diversity are the primary feature of a plan, then opportunities for voluntary participation in special educational experiences should be made available as a secondary feature. If such educational experiences are the primary feature, then mandatory student assignments are necessary as a secondary approach. The two features complement each other. One without the other is incomplete.

Of the four communities studied, Boston and Milwaukee had comprehensive desegregation plans: Atlanta and Seattle had plans that were less than comprehensive. One may wonder whether a comprehensive plan, beneficial in terms of education and racial and cultural contacts, had negative demographic consequences. Our study reveals that Milwaukee and Boston lost 11 to 12 percent of their total populations between 1970 and 1980 and that Atlanta with a less comprehensive plan lost 29 percent while Seattle also with a less comprehensive plan lost only 7 percent. Apparently population losses in large central cities are due to factors other than the comprehensiveness of a school desegregation plan. They would appear to be more closely associated with the racial composition of total city population. In fact, a rank correlation for the four cities reveals a perfect indirect association between the proportion of population loss for the total community during the decade and the proportion of combined blacks, Hispanics, and other nonwhite minorities. The 1970 nonwhite population in Boston and Milwaukee were similar, 18.2 percent and 15.6 percent, respectively; the overall decade loss in total population for these cities also was similar (12 and 11 percent). Seattle, which had the lowest percentage loss in total population during the decade, had a 1970 nonwhite population of only 12.6 percent; and Atlanta, which had the highest percentage loss during the sample period, had a 1970 nonwhite population of 51.6 percent. Based on this analysis, one cannot claim that limited school desegregation plans contribute to population stability and that comprehensive plans contribute to greater population losses in urban communities.

The assets of freedom of choice and mandatory assignments in achieving meaningful school desegregation have been discussed in previous chapters. Here, we mention some of the liabilities to facilitate a more informed decision regarding which aspect of the twofold goal of a unitary school system should be emphasized as the primary desegregation strategy. Among liabilities encountered with voluntary transfer programs are these: the expense of recruiting volunteers; insuring an appropriate match between volunteers and openings within grade levels; student uncertainty regarding space availability in preferred schools; unwieldy school bus routes. Fixed student assignments by subdistricts or attendance zones have the obvious liability of denying freedom of choice. With shifts in the population, fixed attendance zones may lose their heterogeneity in time and become resegregated; this, too, is a liability. While the voluntary transfer or freedom-of-choice plan has more liabilities than one based on mandatory assignments, all liabilities may be minimized through appropriate planning.

Although both Milwaukee and Boston are identified as having comprehensive school desegregation plans, Boston clearly had the most comprehensive design of all four cities in this study. It gave full consideration to educational as well as racial-balance issues. The burden of physical movement to achieve a desegregated education was shared in a more equitable way among all races in the Boston Plan, compared with the other cities. These facts lead us to the conclusion that the fairest way to meet both constitutional requirements and educational needs in a unitary public school system is to assign students to specific schools but permit enrollment in other preferred schools if the freedom of choice will contribute to racial desegregation. This means that the local educational authority must retain the prerogative for making final assignments, including the decision of whether or not to honor a student's preference to enroll in a school other than the one assigned. This prerogative is retained so that it may be exercised by a school board for the public good and the achievement of both contributive and distributive justice.

Varying Definitions of Desegregation

The term "racial imbalance" as embodied in desegregation planning is perhaps the key concept in the entire complex enterprise. How this term is defined determines how racial populations are recruited or assigned to schools under either voluntary or involuntary desegregation plans, and this, in turn, determines where, and often how, children are educated. How the term is defined also often reveals certain underlying assumptions in the desegregation planning process and which racial population shall prevail in determining the social climate at individual schools.

To recapitulate the plans under consideration: (1) Boston in 1975 had a citywide student enrollment which was 52% white, 36% black and 12% other minority. "Racial imbalance" was determined such that the racial make-up of each school within the eight individual Community Districts—excluding East Boston—should not vary more than 25% from its district's ratio. The Madison Park Community District, for example, had an individual district racial make-up of 40% white student enrollment, 35% black enrollment and 25% other minority; a single school, therefore, might be 15% white, and 85% black and other minority and still, under the guidelines, be racially balanced. On the other extreme, Hyde Park Community District had an individual district racial make-up of 61% white enrollment, 35% black enrollment and 4% other minority; a single school in this district, therefore, might be 86% white and 14% black and other minority and still be racially balanced. In other words, as "racial imbalance" is defined in the Boston desegregation plan, all-white and all-black schools would be at variance with the plan; white enrollment levels might range from 15 to 86% in any individual school while the combined black and other minority enrollment might range from 14 to 85%. Boston could accommodate such variable racial make-up in its definition of racial imbalance because, as Robert Dentler has noted, the planning in this city was "explicit in enabling diverse ratios [favoring no racial population] as an antidote to the specious assumption made by some planners that majority white schools are a precondition for desegregation."

(2) Seattle, in 1977, had a citywide enrollment composed of 65.3% white students, 18.3% black students and 16.4% other minorities. "Racial imbalance" was defined as

The situation that exists when the combined minority student enrollment in a school exceeds the [overall] District-wide combined minority average by 20 percentage points, provided that the single minority enrollment (as defined by current federal categories) of no school will exceed 50% of the student body.

Thus, under this definition, all-black schools are forbidden but all-white schools are permissible. Furthermore, the plan explicitly states that if the enrollment of a single black or brown racial population exceeds 50%, that school is in noncompliance.

(3) Milwaukee, in 1975, had a citywide student enrollment which was 60.1% white, 34.4% black and 4.5% other minority. "Racial imbalance" was defined by the court in 1976 as existing in any school falling outside the range of 25 to 45% black enrollment; this was modified in 1977 to a 25 to 50% black enrollment range, and was again modified in a 1979 settlement plan to a 25 to 60% black enrollment range for elementary and junior high schools, and a 20-60% black student range in high schools. Thus, in Milwaukee, all-white and all-black schools are prohibited. The highest white enrollment permissible is 75% to 80%, while at least for three years under the court orders no school could have had a predominantly minority enrollment. In the event a school deviated from these racial ratio guidelines and became more or less a one-race school, Milwaukee guaranteed students in such a school a desegregated education in a diversified setting at their request.

(4) Atlanta, in 1974, had a citywide school-going enrollment which was 83% black and 17% white. A baseline was set under the 1973 Settlement Plan such that each school must have a minimum black student enrollment of 30%, although a few schools that were "stable and integrated" had black enrollments as low as 20%. Furthermore, under the settlement white

students could only be transferred into schools where the resulting enrollment would be 30% white. This definition, or standard, leaves open the possibility of all-black schools but would overcome all-white schools.

What can be said, then, regarding these varying definitions and standards of racial imbalance? In three of the four plans, all-white and all-black schools are explicitly prohibited; all-white schools are permissible in Seattle, while all-black schools are permissible in Atlanta. In Seattle and under the original desegregation order in Milwaukee, the combined minority enrollment—that is, the combined total of black, Hispanic, and other minority students—could not exceed 50 percent of the enrollment in any individual school or that school was defined as "racially imbalanced." In Boston and Atlanta, on the other hand, schools with a combined minority enrollment over 50 percent are allowed and are not by definition, racially imbalanced. Boston, it should be noted, clearly had the most variable standard—the one most flexible in adapting to the racial makeup of the local community in which the school is situated.

One is inclined to suspect that both Seattle and Milwaukee (intentionally or unintentionally) initially adopted plans that assumed that the educational and social environments of desegregated schools are enhanced in those instances in which white students are the prevailing or dominant population. The 1976 version of the Milwaukee plan stated, for example, that "the *psychological guarantee* of not having to attend a school that is predominantly minority will tend to stabilize the population of the city" (emphasis added). This assumption guided the desegregation effort in Milwaukee between 1976 and 1979. It is important to note that the racial makeup of Boston schools was not vastly dissimilar from enrollment levels in Seattle and Milwaukee; yet, that city not only adopted the most comprehensive desegregation plan, but also implemented the most flexible standard for racial imbalance. It is also significant that, intentional or unintentional, the race relations assumptions that guided the initial Milwaukee and Seattle plans are characteristic of what many social analysts have described as institutional racism. (In 1979 the Milwaukee Plan was changed to accommodate some schools that might have a majority student body of blacks, Hispanics, and other groups not classified as white.) The roots of such assumptions are deeply embedded in our society. It is incumbent upon those involved in desegregation planning to examine the assumptions that will exert such tremendous influence upon our future generations.

On the basis of this analysis, we conclude that the racial percentages used in defining desegregation should favor neither the majority nor the minority population. Moreover, we believe that it is inappropriate to develop a plan that proscribes blacks, Hispanics, Asian Americans, and Native Americans from being the majority of the student body in any school. The plans should provide flexible guidelines that ensure racial diversity and should permit the clustering combinations of racial and ethnic groups so that the minority component is not less than 20 percent of the student body in any school. This minimum proportion is needed to provide a critical mass that will have an educative and social impact upon the learning environment. Finally, we believe that a school system should guarantee a desegregated education for all of its students; any student in a racially isolated school should have the privilege of requesting a transfer to a more diversified setting.

State and Local Planning: Prescribed and Proscribed Actions

The plans analyzed in this study demonstrate the need to relate state and local planning as complementary functions in achieving unitary, desegregated public school systems. Although it may be the highest authority, state government should limit direct participation in local affairs but should have the authority to monitor local operations, give needed assistance, and provide sanctions and incentives—financial, legal, and otherwise—when necessary. The Boston and Milwaukee plans benefited from involvement of state government in school desegregation in ways like those mentioned above. The Seattle Plan and its implementation was hampered by the harassment of state government through a statewide referendum against busing that attempted to invalidate the method used to achieve desegregation. The Seattle School Board appealed the issue to the Supreme Court and won, thus gaining freedom to continue the implementation of its plan. Atlanta experienced a state government that was remote, that neither assisted nor interfered with its plan but more or less ignored the city and its school desegregation struggle.

The Seattle experience is not unlike that of several cities in Virginia shortly after the *Brown* decision. Massive resistance to court-ordered school desegregation was legislated as state public law and was implemented until declared unconstitutional in 1959. The governor was authorized to usurp the authority of local boards of education for the purpose of closing any school in Virginia that attempted to desegregate its student body. The centerpiece of the massive resistance laws was one that required the state education agency to handle pupil assignments in all local communities. Such assignments clearly are equity activities that are beyond the competence of the state; they are handled best at the local level. By direct intervention in what should have been a local arrangement, the state made a mess of things including the closing of public schools. Public opinion surveys revealed that most of the population of Norfolk and Arlington, for example, were against desegregation but would have arrived at an equitable decision, accommodating some race mixing to keep their schools open. They were prohibited from taking this action concerning the distribution and use of local educational resources by a higher authority that should have limited its involvement to matters of access and participation in education. When pupil assignment and other activities concerning the distribution and use of local resources were returned to local authorities, most chose desegregation. Their opinion at that time was that both race mixing and the closing of schools were evils, but race mixing was the lesser of the two (Lubel, 1966:103).

Even when state government is supportive of school desegregation but inappropriately involves itself in a community for the purpose of making local equity decisions, it contributes to a confused situation. The Phase I student-assignment plan for Boston incorporated in the 1974 order of Federal District Court Judge W. Arthur Garrity, Jr., was developed by the Bureau of Equal Educational Opportunity of the Massachusetts State Education Department. The state-prepared plan for Boston was partial, not comprehensive. Some but not all sections of the city were affected. A substantial proportion of the city's schools were left in a segregated state. The outcome was great bitterness on the part of blacks and whites in the affected communities, which consisted largely of working-class people. Their opinion was that the state-sponsored partial desegregation plan was arbitrary, capricious, and inequitable (Willie, 1978:82).

While acceptance of a comprehensive plan proposed by a panel of four court-appointed masters and two court-appointed experts was not unanimous, the Boston community embraced it as more equitable. The plan was proposed by six individuals who were residents of the local metropolitan area and who identified with local Irish American, Jewish American, black American, and white Anglo-Saxon populations. While not appointed as official representatives, the masters and experts negotiated with each other and brought to their joint decisions the knowledge and wisdom of the racial and cultural groups with which they were affiliated. Equitable decisions have a better opportunity of emerging from diversified local groups such as the court-appointed masters and experts. The court modified and ordered the comprehensive plan proposed by these individuals, described and discussed by Dentler in chapter 6.

The state agency in Massachusetts stepped in to fill a void in local planning created by the Boston School Committee, which refused to prepare a desegregation plan and which informed the court that it would do only what it was ordered to do. A brief plan for Boston school desegregation was submitted to the court by the plaintiffs. It did not contain an educational component, and the masters and experts described it as inadequate. Despite the good intentions of the state agency in Massachusetts, it usurped a local equity function—that of assigning students to schools in a way that is fair. In the end, state intervention as a local planner had a negative outcome.

Community Adaptation to School Desegregation

Community involvement in school desegregation planning has been advocated as beneficial to the process and its outcomes. There is evidence from the four communities analyzed in this study that community involvement, for example, tends to lessen the violence with which school desegregation plans are received and also tends to promote their acceptance.

Violence was a recurrent experience in and around the Boston schools from 1975 to 1979, after the court order to desegregate. Although about 90 percent of the violence occurred in and around only four high school buildings, it was severe and resulted in serious injuries (Dentler and Scott, 1981:66).

Milwaukee, a city similar to Boston in many respects, adapted to school desegregation more or less peacefully. There were no massive rallies. A black protest group concerned about the inequitable burden placed upon its children to use transportation to and from school staged a limited boycott for a limited period of time. One incident of rock-throwing by whites at a bus loaded with black students was reported, and whites were attacked one day in a South Side high school by a group of blacks who roamed the halls. There was no recurrence of incidents like these. In general, the police presence in school desegregation planning and implementation was minimal in Milwaukee (Barndt, Janka, and Rose, 1981:257-258).

Similarities between Boston and Milwaukee are their common experience of comprehensive court-ordered school desegregation plans, their relatively large white, working-class populations with European ethnic heritages, their segregated housing patterns by racial and ethnic group, and their proportions of blacks in the total city population. Despite these important likenesses, there were remarkable differences in the way these two communities adapted to court-ordered school desegregation. Particularly significant was the minimal level of violence in Milwaukee, compared with Boston. This difference may have a great deal to do with variations in patterns of community organization in these two cities.

The role played by city and school authorities is an appropriate beginning point for this analysis. Robin Williams and Margaret Ryan found that "in general a clear-cut policy, administered with understanding but also with resolution, seems to have been most effective in accomplishing desegregation with a minimum of difficulty. [Moreover, they found that] long-drawn-out efforts and fluctuating policies appear to have maximized confusion and resistance" (Williams and Ryan, 1954:242). Finally, they pointed out that school desegregation "seemed to be successful where the administration and the board kept control of the situation" (Williams and Ryan, 1954:242-243).

Boston conformed to the second finding of Williams and Ryan. Ralph Smith's case study of the struggle to desegregate the Boston schools confirmed the assessment of the United States Commission on Civil Rights that a "crisis of civic responsibility" existed (quoted in Smith, 1978:98). Smith found "the absence of meaningful political leadership and effective support from the religious, intellectual, and business leaders." This in turn, he said, "undermined community support for the desegregation effort" (Smith, 1978:98). The school committee was described as recalcitrant; it refused to submit a desegregation plan to the court. Several school superintendents who tried to cooperate with the court were not reappointed or were dismissed (Smith, 1978:105).

Despite its recalcitrance, the Boston School Committee fingered the mayor and told the court, "the mayor had become increasingly vocal . . . and had moved from constructive criticism to obstruction of the federal court order" (Smith, 1978:65). At the same time, the school committee described the mayor as "a 'leading political and community figure' whose statements and actions are accorded widespread attention" (Smith, 1978:65). Meanwhile, the mayor said he would uphold the law but then confessed that he was "powerless to implement the decision" (Smith, 1978:53). Vague and evasive statements were what the community heard from the mayor. Moreover, he joined the school committee in appealing the federal court order. Meanwhile, without interference from the chief administrator of the city, the Police Patrolmen's Association let it be known that its members "would not gratuitously enforce any part of [the school desegregation court order] not made explicit" and publicly announced that "it would tell its members that there were circumstances in which they were not compelled to obey their superiors." This announcement clearly was a challenge to court authority and was so disturbing that "Judge Garrity met in closed session with the attorney serving as legal counsel to the police association . . . [to] 'clarify' the legal and ethical issues" (Smith, 1978:63). The legislative branch of city government, the Boston City Council, permitted anti-busing groups to hold regular weekly meetings rallying support against school desegregation in the council's executive hearing room at City Hall (Smith, 1978:57).

Judge Garrity told the Boston defendants and parties to the case that constitutional principles which mandate duty to desegregate cannot be allowed to yield simply because of disagreement with them. Not until the end of the second year of court-ordered desegregation did the mayor explain this fact to the citizens of Boston. In June 1976 the mayor said in a televised speech, "any who tell you . . . that violent resistance will succeed . . . mislead you." However, the mayor did not tell the people of Boston this "until it was too late to avoid the violence caused by those who thought that they could resist a court order if they disagreed with it" (Willie, 1978:82-83). The violence in Boston undoubtedly was a by-product of the absence of forthright support by government officials and other community leaders for the court order. The absence of support from such individuals undermined community faith in efforts to achieve equality and equity in public education by way of school desegregation. It was not the comprehensiveness of the court order as claimed by some people that stimulated violent resistance in Boston. It was the absence of community leadership in favor of lawful authority that unleashed the passions of people who opposed desegregation. Boston is an example of a city without a clear-cut policy pertaining to desegregation administered with resolution. Evasion and vacillation by public authorities generated uncertainty and confusion about school desegregation in the community at large and contributed to some of the difficulties experienced.

The Milwaukee, Seattle, and Atlanta experiences of peaceful school desegregation demonstrate that communities can accept radical change such as race mixing in the public schools without violence when there is affirmative political and other public leadership in favor and supportive of the change. Like Boston's, Milwaukee's plan was comprehensive, but plans implemented in the other two cities required less dislocation. Nevertheless, all three cities peacefully adapted to the school desegregation process in a way that differed from the Boston experience.

The school board in Milwaukee has been described as "conservative-moderate." However, "all of its members promised compliance with the [school] desegregation order, although the conservative members pushed for the least amount of compliance possible" (Barndt, Janka, and Rose, 1981:246). The new superintendent, hired only six months before the desegregation court order was issued, took advantage of his "honeymoon period with board members" and developed a broad concept of specialty schools desegregated by voluntary transfers but backed up by a mandatory student-assignment plan as the primary desegregative device. He touted this plan as a way of revitalizing the quality of education within the total system. This concept was popular and received support from all sectors of the community.

Moreover, the school superintendent and his staff organized the entire community into eighteen planning leagues or planning associations. Each league or association was racially diversified and consisted of people from inner-city, middle-ring, and outer-ring neighborhoods. Citizens' leagues and associations were urged to assist the school system in planning for enhanced quality in desegregated schools for their respective areas. Giving advice and consent to the desegregation planning by the administrative staff of the school system was a Committee of 100, a school-sponsored parents' group.

In effect, the Milwaukee school authorities organized the community in support of school desegregation before opposition could organize against it. The media and the court responded favorably to the community organizational effort. People who participated in planning sessions also became such strong advocates of the desegregation effort that some board members who wanted to limit desegregation to a minimum found themselves the targets of much public criticism.

With wide-ranging community support from parents and other citizens, the superintendent was able to proceed with little harassment. Other city authorities and the police kept a low profile in school desegregation issues; neither opposing nor rendering extraordinary support, they were more or less neutral but did not telegraph negative signals to the citizens as the Boston officials had done. Milwaukee is an example of a city that successfully desegregated the public schools with a comprehensive plan, community support, and little or no violence because the administration kept control of the situation by initiating action and cultivating goodwill.

Seattle and Atlanta also experienced extensive community support for school desegregation, coming largely from the community power structures in these two cities as opposed to the grass-roots approval that Milwaukee mustered. The Seattle community leaders who supported school desegregation have been described as "a group of community elites who through their respected and influential organizations formed a close network in order to communicate, bargain, and compromise with one another." They were Seattle's "solid middle road reform community leaders": lawyers, businessmen, civic leaders, and university professors connected with such organizations as the District-Wide Advisory Committee for Desegregation, the Municipal League, the Urban League, the Council of Churches, the Chamber of Commerce, the superintendent's office, and the mayor's office. The superintendent was hired and asked to devise a plan to desegregate the city's schools. However, the school board was not of a common mind as to how this should be done; some favored a voluntary, freedom-of-choice approach while others believed that mandatory student assignments would be necessary. All wanted to keep Seattle free of court jurisdiction and orders. The president of the school board and others were greatly encouraged to move ahead with dispatch and develop a program of mandatory student assignments while retaining some magnet programs for voluntary enrollment after receiving a letter commending the board for its efforts and pledging support for desegregation by the joint signatories that included the mayor, the president of the Municipal League, the president of the Urban League, and the president of the Chamber of Commerce (Hart-Nibbrig, 1978:32-33). As an observer of the Seattle scene, Nand Hart-Nibbrig said, the importance of that letter cannot be overstressed (Hart-Nibbrig, 1978:32).

Atlanta is a Sunbelt community with extensive economic development under way. Moreover, it has been described "as a center of culture and commerce for the whole southeastern region." According to Barbara Jackson, "the black and white community leadership knew that the school issue had to be resolved." Leaders of both races, she said, "feared the economic consequences of racial turmoil." The black and white leaders agreed that a negotiated settlement was possible because of the dialogue that had already occurred in a biracial committee created in 1970 under the leadership of the executive director of the Atlanta Urban League. This committee had advised the school board on further planning for school desegregation. Jackson credits this dialogue between "influential . . . blacks within the schools and in the city . . . [and] whites [as] an integral part of the . . . working toward a peaceful beginning [of a negotiated settlement]'' (Jackson, 1978:47).

The leadership group among blacks, according to Jackson, consisted of ''a black middle class whose economic position came from banking, insurance, and construction, as well as higher education.'' She said, this group of blacks is ''comfortable with the white economic and political leaders'' (Jackson, 1981:212).

The Atlanta Plan ordered by the court emerged from negotiation between such blacks and whites in the city power structure. It included a modest student-assignment plan that did not achieve citywide desegregation, a small majority-to-minority transfer program that involved less than 5 percent of all students, a plan for staff desegregation, and a plan for desegregation of the administration. The Atlanta school system had been dominated by whites for many years, even after its student body had become majority black. Thus, the administration-desegregation component of the Atlanta Plan was its most significant feature. Half of the appointments to the administrative staff were to be blacks and half whites. Although not a part of the court-ordered plan, the settlement agreement stipulated that the superintendent would be black. This unofficial but negotiated arrangement was honored; indeed all aspects of the negotiated settlement were implemented without a hitch. Thus, the Atlanta Plan largely dealt with the transfer of power and authority among the city's racial populations. With this business taken care of, the community leaders said, ''attention could be turned from the courts to the educational needs of children'' (Jackson, 1978:48).

Regardless of whether community support is derived from the grass roots or from the power structure, it is effective in the achievement of peaceful school desegregation as seen in this analysis. However, school desegregation leadership by some authority figure in the community would appear to be necessary even when widespread grass-roots support has been cultivated.

The absence of sanctions and support of school desegregation from leaders of institutions and associations and the presence of opposition by political officials is sure to generate fear and uncertainty in the community. Where fear and uncertainty reign and are cultivated by political leaders, the potential of violence is ever present. Ralph McGill explained that ''If the power structure could damn the courts and describe their actions as illegal, then the man who wished to dynamite or burn . . . a school felt himself approved'' (McGill, 1964:248). Thus, we conclude that community leadership style rather than the type and kind of school desegregation plan has much to do with whether a community adapts to race mixing in the public schools in a peaceful or a violent way.

Whether a school desegregation plan is comprehensive or limited appears to be a function of how it emerges—through conflict or consensus. Boston had a recalcitrant school board, and conflict or capitulation were the only routes available. Actually "the battle to desegregate the Boston schools, begun in the eighteenth century, flared up again in the nineteenth and continued, if at a somewhat lower pitch during the twentieth century" (Smith, 1978:34). The antecedent to the present controversy began in 1961 when the local chapter of the National Association for the Advancement of Colored People (NAACP) asked the Massachusetts Commission Against Discrimination to determine if there was discrimination by race in the distribution and education of Boston students. The Commission made a finding in favor of the school board. NAACP meetings with the School Committee were always disappointing. Boston ignored the Racial Imbalance Act passed in 1965. The State Department of Education took the School Committee to court to force it to obey the Racial Imbalance Law but was frustrated with the outcome. Moreover, Boston managed to get the law modified and weakened. Finally in 1971 the local NAACP enlisted the aid of the Harvard Center for Law and Education and filed a complaint in the United States District Court in 1972. The court made a finding against the Boston School Committee in 1974 and ordered a partial desegregation plan in 1974 and a comprehensive plan in 1975.

The School Committee was so recalcitrant that the court had to retain its own planning staff and retain jurisdiction for ten years. It issued hundreds of additional orders to implement the plan. Because of the reluctance of Boston to plan its own future, the future was planned for Boston by a panel of court-appointed masters and experts. Their plan, modified by the court and ordered, was one of the most comprehensive desegregation plans in the nation.

Atlanta, on the other hand, took matters into its own hands. Its black and white citizens negotiated a settlement, which the court ordered as a settlement plan or consent decree. In the past, Atlanta had ignored its minority population and had operated a dual school system, separate for black and white racial populations and unequal. Response to all attempts to eliminate discrimination were unsympathetic until the NAACP filed suit in 1958. The court ordered desegregation in 1961. The Atlanta school system began a gradual approach to desegregation with a few carefully selected black students in the eleventh and twelfth grades. In 1965 the court ordered that all grades be desegregated by 1968. The freedom-of-choice plan to accomplish this was ineffective and was replaced in 1970 with a court-ordered majority-to-minority transfer plan; also in 1970, the faculty was desegregated. The majority-to-minority plan was deficient and was supplemented with the 1973 court-ordered settlement plan that increased desegregation by redrawing some attendance zones but also transferred decision-making power from white administrators to black administrators in the office of the superintendent. By 1974 the court had significantly reduced its oversight function in the Atlanta case, largely because the school system had responded favorably during the past decade and a half each time there was a challenge.

The Atlanta School Board was not as recalcitrant as the Boston School Committee. Thus, the court-ordered desegregation was less pervasive and comprehensive, since it came about through negotiation and consensus and was not imposed by external authority.

Both conflict and conciliation are appropriate ways to bring about change. The conclusion derived from this analysis, however, is that change resulting from conflict tends to be more pervasive than change resulting from consensus. In the end, those who resist change ultimately may have to accommodate more than those who make meaningful and timely responses to each circumstance of challenge.

The Milwaukee situation also illustrates how pervasive change comes about to the recalcitrant who are forced to act. The Milwaukee Plan, however, was less comprehensive precisely because the superintendent seized the initiative from the moderate to conservative school board and enabled Milwaukee to plan its own future. When a community plans for itself, it seems to do so in a less grand scale than when others not responsible for implemention do the planning. Thus, the superintendent in Milwaukee dampened the conflict strategy and turned school desegregation planning into a consensus operation. In the end, the community emerged as a more harmonious unit, but the desegregative outcomes were less comprehensive than those in Boston.

In Seattle the desegregative outcomes were less comprehensive than those in Milwaukee largely because the Seattle community established coalitions and other groups that involved Asians, blacks, and whites and negotiated a solution to the school desegregation issue without the polemical conflict and coercion of court intervention. One reason Seattle worked hard at developing and maintaining a consensus strategy was the threat of a lawsuit by the NAACP. The Seattle community felt good about what it had accomplished. But the desegregative outcomes obviously were less comprehensive.

Atlanta already has been analyzed but is mentioned again in this comparative analysis of all four communities. While the NAACP filed suit in 1958, the school board was not intractable. A positive response, even if only a token response, was made to each order of the court. Moreover, the school board racially diversified its membership as early as 1953, chose a respected black educator for its president in 1969, and consented to be advised on future desegregation planning by a biracial community group in 1970. Finally, the attorneys of record for the plaintiffs joined the consensus process and participated in negotiating the settlement plan ordered by the court. Other than the transfer of power over the school system and the integration of faculty, the desegregative outcomes in Atlanta were less than those in the other two communities that experienced more conflict.

A peaceful settlement, though less pervasive, has some merit. The community emerges less scarred from the initial desegregative encounter and better able to plan cooperatively for the future with less bitterness to overcome. Atlanta appears to be doing precisely that. It is fair to say that the educational aspects of the Atlanta Plan still are in an inchoate stage. Daily attendance in schools has increased to 93 percent, and the dropout rate is less than 6 percent. Annual educational goals now are formulated for the total system (Crim, 1981:153).

The conflict approach can be initiated by a militant minority or a reactionary majority. It has a winner-take-all quality to it. If one wins, one gets more than one asked for (remember the plaintiffs' plan in the Boston case did not have an educational component in it); but if one loses, one gets less or even nothing. In the consensus approach the winner gets something but not as much as he or she wanted and the losers never are wiped out. One approach is not recommended over the other. Both approaches have value. Which should be used depends upon the situations and circumstances.

Unique Features of Community Plans

We conclude this analysis by discussing aspects of the characteristics of desegregation plans that are unique to each community but which may be of value to others.

The Atlanta Plan focused initially on desegregating the administrative and teaching staff. An equal number of blacks and whites were to hold administrative positions, and the office of the superintendent was designated to be filled by a black professional. The teaching staff was also majority black and distributed throughout all schools. It would appear that Atlanta decided to deal first with adults in achieving a desegregated and unitary school system. This approach differs from that in most plans, which emphasized student desegregation. According to Jackson, "there is some evidence in Atlanta that the black leadership is beginning to make a difference" (Jackson, 1981:212). A southern city that has experienced the brutality of racial discrimination for years, Atlanta is a community where blacks were concerned about decision-making power and authority.

Boston is a community that has had a long tradition of promoting its gifted students and ignoring those who are classified as disadvantaged for one reason or another. The Boston Latin School that sends a high proportion of its students on to college and other postsecondary education is the oldest public high school in the nation and one of the most prestigious in the city. It requires an examination for admission. Boston is a community that has sanctioned exclusive arrangements that have had negative impacts upon racial minority populations and others not identified as mainstream students.

The comprehensive school desegregation plan ordered by the court for Boston was designed to change these arrangements, so that the system would become more inclusive and responsive to all students. This is precisely what happened. After court-ordered desegregation, the proportion of students with special needs who received services in Boston was 15 percent. This proportion was double that of any other city in this study. Moreover, Boston provided bilingual education for 8 percent of its students, while the other three cities provided this kind of special education for not more than 2 percent, despite the presence of population groups for whom English is a second language. Thus, the comprehensive school desegregation plan in Boston emphasized the inclusion of students who had been left out of the mainstream in the past.

The unique contribution of Milwaukee and Seattle to school desegregation planning was their extensive involvement of the community. Milwaukee achieved substantial grass-roots participation through school-sponsored citizens' leagues and associations. Seattle involved existing organizations and mobilized elites in the power structure. Both methods of community organization were effective. In different ways, the citizens in these two communities worked on behalf of school desegregation to achieve a consensus supportive of affirmative action by public school administrators. This consensus seems to have been associated with the greater acceptance of school desegregation in Seattle and Milwaukee and the absence of violent resistance. These communities were able to use a consensus planning model because the school administrators gave assertive leadership in defining problems and possible remedies and therefore remained in charge of the planning process.

References

Barndt, Michael, Rick Janka, and Harold Rose
  1981   "Milwaukee, Wisconsin: Mobilization for School and Community Cooperation," in Charles V. Willie and Susan L. Greenblatt (eds.), *Community Politics and Educational Change*. New York: Longman, pp. 237-259.
Crim, Alonzo A.
  1981   "A Community Believer," *Daedalus* 110 (Fall): 145-162.
Dentler, Robert, and Marvin Scott
  1981   *Schools on Trial.* Cambridge, Mass.: Abt Books.
Department of Health, Education, and Welfare, Office of Civil Rights
  1970   *Directory of Public Elementary and Secondary Schools in Selected Districts,* Washington, D.C.: U.S. Government Printing Office.
Hart-Nibbrig, Nand
  1979   "Policies of School Desegregation in Seattle," *Integrated Education* 17 (Jan.-April), pp. 27-28.
Jackson, Barbara L.
  1978   "Desegregation: Atlanta Style," *Theory into Practice* 17 (Feb.): 43-53.
  1981   "Urban School Desegregation from a Black Perspective," in Adam Yarmolinski, Lance Liebman, and Corinne S. Schelling (eds.), *Race and Schooling in the City*. Cambridge, Mass.: Harvard University Press, pp. 204-216.

Lubell, Samuel
   1966   *Black and White.* New York: Harper.
McGill, Ralph
   1964   *The South and the Southerner.* Boston, Mass.: Little, Brown and
           Company.
Milwaukee Public Schools
   1976   "First Draft: Comprehensive Plan for Increasing Educational
           Opportunities and Improving Racial Balance in Milwaukee Public
           Schools."
Smith, Ralph R.
   1978   "Two Centuries and Twenty-Four Months: A Chronicle of the Struggle
           to Desegregate the Boston Public Schools," in Howard I. Kalodner and
           James F. Fishman (eds.), *Limits of Justice.* Cambridge, Mass.:
           Ballinger.
Williams, Robin, and Margaret Ryan
   1954   *Schools in Transition.* Chapel Hill, N.C.: University of North Carolina
           Press.
Willie, Charles Vert
   1978   *The Sociology of Urban Education.* Lexington, Mass.: Lexington
           Books, D. C. Heath.

Appendix

Outline for the Preparation of an Essay on a Systemwide Model Plan for a Unitary Public School System

Introduction

The instructions given to authors of the school desegregation plans analyzed in this book are presented. By reviewing these, the reader may understand the perspective from which these cases were written and why selected materials were included. Ralph McGill, in his book *The South and the Southerner* (1964), said that "the careful . . . phrasing of the [*Brown*] decision [of the Supreme Court] . . . anticipated that the knowledge and skills of educators . . . and of social [scientists] would assume direction of the process of desegregation." This did not happen. Through the middle years of the 1960s, most school desegregation plans were created "not by educators but by political office-holders and lawyers" (p. 249). Recently, this situation has been changing. Courts and local school authorities have increasingly sought the advice of educational planners and applied social scientists in fashioning plans. Such plans are for the purpose of eliminating the inequities of duality in educational services for different racial and ethnic populations and promoting a unitary experience for all students within a common public school system.

In this project, the basic features of a series of systemwide, model school desegregation or unitary plans are described. These plans demonstrate alternative ways of achieving a unitary system in which educational resources are available to the various population groups in equitable ways. Your plan should provide information in the following six categories.

Basic Information

1. *A description of the educational and desegregational goals and assumptions, if any, of your plan for a unitary public school system.*

Mention assumptions about the association, if any, between racial and ethnic segregation, desegregation, or integration, and learning environments. Does your plan include any assumptions about learning environments and variations in composition of student bodies by socioeconomic status? If so, please indicate. Indicate assumptions about the effects, if any, of varying ratios of racial and of ethnic populations upon affective as well as cognitive learning. What are your assumptions regarding optimum conditions for learning? Are racial and ethnic characteristics of a learning environment associated with any of these optimum conditions?

Indicate the basic goals that your plan attempts to achieve. Are these goals influenced by any particular characteristics of the community and its history, or the school-age population? Have these goals been implemented effectively elsewhere, or are they specific to a particular kind of community such as the one you will describe? If, for any reason, the goals of your plan are applicable to particular settings only, please indicate why this is so.

2. *A brief description of the kind of community for which your plan for a unitary public school system is most applicable.*

Indicate the size of community in terms of geographic area in square miles, total population and that of major racial and ethnic groups, including the percentage of minority- and majority-group members in the total population. Historic circumstances, the economic base of the community including the socioeconomic mixture of the total population, unique geographic features of a community, and other environmental characteristics, if any, that condition the design and implementation of your plan may be mentioned. Describe also the size of the school-age population, its racial and ethnic mixture, the proportion enrolled in public schools, the size of the public school system, including the number of comprehensive and special or magnet schools at elementary and secondary levels for which your plan is applicable.

3. *A description of the scope of your plan for a unitary public school system in terms of geographic area, population groups, and grade levels included.*

Does your plan apply to a portion of a civil district (or jurisdiction), a total civil district (or jurisdiction), or multiple civil districts (or jurisdictions)? (In other words, is your plan applicable only to part of the city, the total city, or city and suburban areas?) If the plan is applicable to only part of a civil district, indicate why some sectors are included and others excluded. Please indicate why your plan covers only a portion of a civil district, a total district, or multiple districts.

Is your plan concerned only with diversifying the student body of schools in terms of the racial and ethnic characteristics of the school-age population? Is the scope of your plan-design to provide a unitary system for groups of varying socioeconomic status levels? Is your plan concerned with diversifying student bodies in terms of racial and ethnic characteristics only, enhancing educational opportunities for all students only, or both? Why does your plan focus on population diversity only, educational enhancement only, or both?

Is your plan concerned with all students, including kindergarten, the lower grades of elementary school, the upper grades of elementary school, middle school or junior high school, and high school? Or is your plan concerned only with certain age levels of the student population? Specify, if only certain age levels are included. Explain why your plan involves all school-age people or is limited to selected age levels. If the plan is applicable to selected age levels, indicate why some were included and others excluded.

Does your plan permit the existence of any racially or ethnically isolated or homogeneous schools? What proportion of the elementary schools, middle schools, or junior high schools, and high schools are racially isolated, and what proportion are desegregated? What proportion of the various racial and ethnic students and what proportion of majority students are enrolled in homogeneous or racially isolated schools and heterogeneous or desegregated schools? If some schools in your plan will continue to be racially isolated, explain why the plan accommodates such schools. Also, explain the educational assumptions that support programs in both desegregated and racially isolated schools. Does your plan provide for desegregated educational or extracurricular experiences for minority and majority students enrolled in racially homogeneous or isolated schools? If so, what are these experiences, where and how often during the week do they occur, and how many minority and majority students in the homogeneous schools participate in them? Is the desegregation experience for students in racially isolated schools voluntary or mandatory for minority and majority students in such schools? What are the assumptions on which the desegregated experience is based?

4. *A description of how your plan will achieve equity for racial and ethnic groups in the availability of educational programs, extracurricular programs, school building facilities, student assignment, and transportation.*

With reference to educational programs, is there a uniform grade structure that is systemwide? Are all elementary and secondary schools comprehensive schools? If not, what proportion of the schools at various grade levels are special schools (that is, vocational, magnet, selective, population-specific such as, for example, for handicapped or foreign language populations), and what proportion are comprehensive? Why are some schools special and others comprehensive? How are special and comprehensive schools distributed by geographic areas (including central-city or peripheral-area locations, and racial and ethnic neighborhoods)? What educational assumptions underlie the development of a unitary school system with some comprehensive and some special schools? How does your plan guarantee equity in the distribution of the school-age population by race and ethnicity between and within comprehensive and special schools at elementary and secondary school levels? Are the educational programs in your plan designed to achieve a unitary system for students of various socioeconomic groups?

With reference to extracurricular programs, is there a full range of athletic and other student activities in all elementary and secondary schools in your plan? If athletic and other student activities are selectively maintained in some but not all schools at a particular grade level, how do you determine the range and kinds of extracurricular activities that are appropriate for various schools? Is there a geographic pattern associated with the differential range and kinds of extracurricular programs available in schools? How are students distributed in terms of race and ethnicity between schools with different ranges and kinds of extracurricular programs? How does your plan achieve equity in distribution of extracurricular programs between schools? How does your plan achieve equity in extracurricular participation by various racial and ethnic groups? What educational and other assumptions about learning underlie the development and support of extracurricular programs in your plan? Are the extracurricular programs in your plan designed to achieve a unitary system for students of various socioeconomic status levels?

With reference to school building facilities, give the age range and style of buildings for elementary and secondary schools. In number and proportion what is the variation in building capacity for elementary and secondary schools? Are buildings of various ages, styles, and capacities randomly distributed geographically or concentrated in particular areas? If there is concentration of selected facilities, describe the location for various concentrations including racial and ethnic characteristics of the concentration settings. How does your plan achieve equity in the distribution of various racial and ethnic groups between school buildings of varying ages, styles, and student capacities? What educational assumptions underlie the uses made of various school building facilities in your plan? Is your building facilities plan designed to achieve equity for students of varying socioeconomic status levels?

With reference to student assignments and transportation, does your plan organize the system into several attendance zones or is there a single, systemwide attendance zone? What is the rationale for the pattern of attendance zones or the single zone in your system? What guidelines were followed in establishing several attendance zones or a single attendance zone? If there are several attendance zones, how many are there and what is the distribution of racial, ethnic, and socioeconomic groups within and between the various zones? Is student enrollment in schools within attendance zones and in schools outside attendance zones voluntary, mandatory, or both? What circumstances are associated with voluntary choice, mandatory assignment, or both? If there are multiple attendance zones, under what conditions may a student enroll in a zone that is different from the one in which he or she lives? How many and what proportion of students in your plan require transportation to go to and from school within attendance zones and outside attendance zones? What mode of transportation do they use, what proportion travel varying distances, and why? How does your student-assignment and transportation plan achieve equity for racial and ethnic groups? Does your student-assignment and transportation plan design achieve a unitary system for students of varying socioeconomic status levels?

5. *A description of the policy-making and the policy-implementing associations, and the procedure for recruiting and maintaining a diversified faculty and professional staff in your plan for a unitary public school system.*

With reference to the policy-making association, are your schools governed by a school board (committee), or the elected legislative body for the total civil district or jurisdiction? If governed by a school board (committee), is it relatively independent or completely accountable to the legislative and executive authority of the total civil district or jurisdiction? Do policies of the school authorities in your system have the force of law, or must they be ratified by the legislative and executive authority of the total district or jurisdiction? Are members of the governing body for the schools elected at large, by single-member districts, by a combination of single-member districts and at large, or appointed? If appointed, by whom are they appointed? How many and what proportion of school board members are associated with racial and ethnic groups and with the majority population? How many and what proportion are male and female? How does the method of election or appointment to the school governing body guarantee diversity and equity of representation for racial and ethnic populations? Does the method of electing or appointing members to the governing body for the schools attempt to achieve diversity in the socioeconomic status levels of decision makers?

With reference to the policy-implementing association, what title, authority, and responsibility does the chief administrative officer of the schools bear? By whom is this officer appointed, for what period of time is the appointment, and how may this officer be dismissed? Is the chief administrative officer who must implement your plan the same chief administrator who participated in the initial design of the plan? What are the major central administrative units of the school system by name and function? What rank, authority, and responsibility do individuals have who supervise the work of these units? How are central administrative officers recruited? By whom are the officers of administrative units recommended, appointed, and dismissed? What is the term of office, if any, of officers of central administrative units for the schools? Who is the chief administrative officer in a school building by title of office, and what is the scope of authority and responsibility of this officer? How are school building chief administrative officers recommended, appointed, and removed? Who in central administration and what unit or units in name and function have primary authority and responsibility for implementing the plan to achieve a unitary school system? What is the total number of central administrative officers? What proportions of central administrators are representatives of the various racial and ethnic groups and the majority group in the community?

With reference to local facilities, how many and what proportion of school building chief administrators (and at what level, elementary or secondary school) are representatives of the various racial and ethnic populations and of the majority population? How many and what proportion of racial and ethnic minority-group chief administrators and of majority-group chief administrators are in charge of facilities in which most of the students are of a population group different from their own? How does your plan achieve equity for racial and ethnic minorities in the recruitment and appointment of central administrators and in the recruitment and appointment of school building chief administrators? How many and what is the proportion of racial and ethnic group members in the faculty and other staff positions of the system in local facilities? How many and what proportion of racial and ethnic minority-group teachers and staff and majority-group teachers and staff are located in schools in which most of the students are not members of their population group? How are racial and ethnic minority-group teachers and staff and majority-group teachers and staff recruited and assigned to schools? How does your plan achieve equity for racial and ethnic groups in the appointment and retention of central administrative staff, school building chief officers, faculty, and other personnel? Are there any educational assumptions on which your affirmative action plan is based for achieving racial diversity in faculty and staff?

With reference to preparation of professional personnel, does your plan provide for in-service education or external education pertaining to skills in intergroup relations? Does the plan provide incentives that encourage professional personnel to participate in programs designed to enhance their knowledge, skills and competence in handling race- or ethnic-related issues in the learning environment? What is the frequency of and range of participation in such programs?

6. *A description of school-community relations aspects of your plan for a unitary public school system.*

Are parents invited to contribute directly to the education of children as paid school aides, as volunteers, as observers in classrooms, or advisors in extracurricular activities? Indicate the number and kinds of parent associations prescribed in your plan, and whether they are school-specific, neighborhood-based, or systemwide. Indicate the range of their responsibilities and whether they have official or advisory authority. How do parent associations recruit their members and finance their activities? Indicate the educational assumptions on which the involvement of parents is based and how your plan achieves equity in parent participation for racial and ethnic groups.

What linkages, if any, does your plan encourage between schools, business and labor institutions, museums and other institutions of the humanities, health-welfare-social service institutions, religious institutions, and governmental institutions? Does the plan provide for building-specific, neighborhood-based, or systemwide linkages between schools and other community institutions? Are such linkages between schools and community institutions for the purpose of providing advice, support, or direct services? What is the formal or informal procedure for the development, maintenance or coordination, and dissolution of linkages between schools and other community institutions? Indicate the educational assumptions on which linkages between schools and other community institutions are based and how such linkages benefit in an equitable way minority-group and majority-group students.

To oversee implementation of a unitary school system, does your plan provide for a community monitoring group other than the board of education? If so, how large is the group, and what community interests are represented on it? By whom is the monitoring group appointed, to whom does it report, and what is the source of its authority? How does your plan achieve racial and ethnic diversity in the composition of the monitoring group?

Conclusion

By presenting information on your plan according to the outline, a comparative analysis of different plans is possible. Your plan may contain unique features not mentioned in this outline. Please elaborate upon such features in the appropriate category or under a new category that you may add. Do not limit your discussion to the issues mentioned in the outline. Do not hesitate to explain your plan fully. This is your opportunity to tell not only what should be done in a good desegregation or unitary plan for public schools but also why.

Your plan was selected for this project because it more or less attempted to achieve equity among the pluralistic populations of elementary and secondary schools, encouraged interaction between minority-group and majority-group populations in extracurricular activities, tried to overcome the liabilities of rigid tracking practices, recognized the fundamental role of teachers in achieving an equitable or unitary school system, attempted to achieve diversity in the administrative and teaching staff of schools, gave attention to the recruitment of effective leaders in charge of school buildings, developed ways for teachers to enhance their skills and general competence in intergroup relations, and tried to implement a curriculum with multicultural concerns. These were the criteria used in selecting schools for this project. The school system for which your plan was designed may not fully meet all of the criteria listed. But your plan deals with a substantial proportion of the issues raised and merits full documentation for others to review.

You may wish to end the discussion of your plan by indicating, based on experience, changes, if any, that would enhance your plan. Also you may indicate circumstances that can interfere with the full implementation of a unitary plan. Please point out opportunities as well as problems of which planners for unitary public school systems should be aware.

While your plan obviously was developed for a particular community, it should be described in a way that will help others see its applicability to other communities. Remember that the goal of this project is to provide models that may be adapted to other communities.

Selected Bibliography

Alston, Jon P., and Ben M. Crouch. "White Acceptance of Three Degrees of School Desegregation." *Phylon* 39 (September 1978): 216-224.

American Civil Liberties Union. *School Desegregation Organizer's Manual.* New York: American Civil Liberties Union, 1978.

Aldridge, D. P. "Litigation and Education of Blacks: Another Look at the U.S. School Desegregation." *Phylon* 39 (September 1978): 216-224.

Anrig, Gregory R. "State Leadership in School Desegregation." In *School Desegregation and the State Government*, ed. National Project and Task Force on Desegregation Strategies. Denver, Colo.: Education Commission of the States, 1979.

Arewa, O. "Cultural Bias in Standardized Testing: An Anthropological View." *The Negro Educational Review* 28 (1977): 153-171.

Axelrod, Robert. *Conflict of Interest.* Chicago: Markham Publishing, 1970.

Badillo, H. "Bilingual Education." *Integrated Education* 13 (1975): 166-167.

Banks, James A. *Teaching Strategies for Ethnic Studies.* Boston: Allyn and Bacon, 1975.

Bash, J. H. *Effective Teaching in the Desegregated School.* Bloomington, Ind.: Phi Delta Kappa Educational Foundation, 1973.

Beck, William, and Glenn M. Linden. "Anglo and Minority Perceptions of Success in Dallas School Desegregation." *Phi Delta Kappan* 60 (January 1979): 378-382.

Beck, William, Glenn M. Linden, and M. E. Siegel. "Identifying School Desegregation Leadership Styles." *Journal of Negro Education* 49 (1980): 115-133.

Bell, Derrick A., ed. *Shades of Brown: New Perspectives on School Desegregation.* New York: Teachers College Press, 1980.

Biggs, Carroll W. "School Districts Merge to Desegregate, Smoothly." *Journal of Educational Communication* 3 (1979): 4-9.

Blackwell, James E. *The Black Community.* New York: Dodd, Mead, 1975.

_____. *The Participation of Blacks in Graduate and Professional Schools: An Assessment.* Atlanta, Ga.: Southern Educational Foundation, 1977.

222 Selected Bibliography

Blaustein, A. P., and C. Clyde Ferguson, Jr. "Desegregation and the Law." *Harvard Educational Review* 28 (1958): 163-168.

Blumenberg, Eleanor. "The New Yellow Peril (Facts and Fictions about School Busing." *Journal of Intergroup Relations* 2 (Summer 1973): 33-45.

Bosma, Boyd. "The Role of Teachers in School Desegregation." *Integrated Education* 15 (November-December 1977): 106-111.

Broh, Anthony C., and William T. Trent. *Qualitative Literature and Expert Opinion on School Desegregation.* Nashville, Tenn.: Center for Education and Human Development Policy, Institute for Public Policy Studies, Vanderbilt University, 1981.

Bullock, Charles S. "The Coming of School Desegregation: A Before and After Study of Black and White Student Perceptions." *Social Science Quarterly* 54 (June 1973): 132-138.

Campbell, A., and S. Hatchett. "The Impact of School Desegregation: An Investigation of Three Mediating Variables." *Youth and Society* 9 (1977): 79-111.

Candoli, I. C. "An Urban Superintendent Looks at School Desegregation." *Theory into Practice* 17 (February 1978): 17-22.

Carol, Lila N. "Court-Mandated Citizen Participation in School Desegregation." *Phi Delta Kappan* 59 (November 1977): 171-173.

Carter, David G. "The Case Against Separated Schools." *Clearing House* 51 (November 1977): 125-130.

Clark, Kenneth B. "Alternative Public School Systems." *Harvard Educational Review* 38 (1968): 100-113.

Cohen, David, and Barbara Neufeld. "The Failure of High School and the Progress of Education." *Daedalus* 110 (Summer 1981): 69-89.

Cohen, E., M. Lockhead, and M. Lohman. "Center for Interracial Cooperation: A Field Experiment." *Sociology of Education* 52 (1979): 47-58.

Coleman, W. G. "Schools, Housing, Jobs, Transportation: Interlocking Metropolitan Problems." *The Urban Review* 10 (1978): 92-107.

Crain, Robert L., and R. Mahard. "Desegregation and Black Achievement: A Review of the Research." *Law and Contemporary Problems* 42 (1978): 17-56.

Crain, Robert L., R. Mahard, and R. E. Narot. *Making Desegregation Work: How Schools Create Social Climates.* Cambridge, Mass.: Ballinger, 1981.

Crim, Alonzo A. "A Community of Believers." *Daedalus* 110 (Fall 1981): 145-162.

Cronin, Joseph M. "The State and School Desegregation." *Theory into Practice* 17 (1978): 3-11.

Cunningham, George K., et al. "The Impact of Court-Ordered Desegregation on Student Enrollment Patterns (White Flight)." *Journal of Education* 160 (May 1978): 36-45.

Davis, Arthur, Jr. "New Paths in Thinking About School Integration." *Kappa Delta Pi Record* 17 (October 1980): 8-10.

Dentler, Robert A. "Desegregation Planning and Implementation in Boston." *Theory into Practice* 17 (1978): 72-77.

Dentler, Robert A., and Marvin B. Scott. *Schools on Trial.* Cambridge, Mass.: Abt Books, 1981.

Dodson, Dann W. "What Is Quality Education?" *Negro Educational Review* 25 (January 1974): 5-17.

Doughty, J. J. "Diminishing the Opportunity for Resegregation." *Theory into Practice* 17 (1978): 1-90.

Drury, D. W. "Black Self-Esteem and Desegregated Schools." *Sociology of Education* 53 (1980): 88-103.

Dunaway, David King. "Desegregation and City Hall: The Mayor's Role in the School." *Integrated Education* 15 (1977): 3-9.

_____, and Leonard C. Beckum. "The Mayor's Influence in Urban School Desegregation." *Phi Delta Kappan* 58 (March 1977): 553-556.

Durham, Joseph T. "Sense and Nonsense About Busing." *Journal of Negro Education* 42 (Summer 1973): 322-335.

Ecke, Melvin W. *From Ivy Street to Kennedy Center.* Atlanta, Ga.: Atlanta Board of Education, 1972

Edmonds, Ronald. "Desegregation Planning and Educational Equity." *Theory into Practice* 17 (Fall 1978): 12-16.

_____. "Some Schools Work and More Can." *Social Policy* 9 (1979): 28-32.

_____. "You Can Get Hurt Waiting for the Bus." *Journal of Intergroup Relations* 2 (October 1972): 13-23.

Entin, David. "Standard Planning Techniques for Desegregation." *Integrated Education* 11 (March-April 1973): 43-53.

Falk, W. W. "Mobility Attitudes of Segregated and Desegregated Black Youth." *Journal of Negro Education* 47 (1978): 132-142.

Farley, Reynolds. "Is Coleman Right?" *Social Policy* 6 (January-February 1976): 14-23.

_____, S. Bianchi, and D. Colosanto. "Barriers to the Racial Integration of Neighborhoods." *Sociology of Education* 53 (1980): 123-139.

Foster, Gordon. "Desegregating Urban Schools: A Review of Techniques." *Harvard Educational Review* 43 (1973): 5-36.

_____. "Trends in Inter-district Remedies." *NOLPE School Law Journal* 8 (1979): 145-153.

Fridie, S. "Black Teachers Inside Predominantly White Schools: An Identification of Their Problems." *High School Journal* 58 (1975): 323-325.

Friedman, Helen, and Harold Friedman. "Letter from Malmo, Sweden." *Integrated Education* 13 (January-February 1975): 14-16.

Friedman, Murray, et al., eds. *New Perspectives on School Integration.* (Philadelphia: Fortress Press, 1979.

George, Pamela. "The Competency Controversy." *Southern Exposure* 7 (May 1979): 114-118.

Giles, M. W., and D. S. Gatlin. "Mass-level Compliance with Public Policy: The Case of School Desegregation." *Journal of Politics* 42 (1980): 722-746.

Gittell, Marilyn. "Education: The Decentralization-Community Control Controversy." In *Race and Politics in New York City,* ed. Jewel Bellush and Stephen M. David. New York: Praeger, 1971, pp. 134-163.

Gordon, Edmund W. "The Political Economics of Effective Schooling." In *Equality of Educational Opportunity,* ed. La Mar P. Miller and Edmund W. Gordon. New York: AMS Press, 1974.

———, and Adelaide Jablonsky. "Compensatory Education in the Equalization of Educational Opportunity." *Journal of Negro Education* (Summer 1968).

Griffore, Robert J., et al. "Lansing, Michigan." *Integrated Education* 15 (November-December 1977): 28-32.

Harris, Ian M. "The Citizens Committee in Milwaukee." *Integrated Education* 16 (July-August 1978): 35-41.

Hawley, W. D. "Getting the Facts Straight about the Effect of School Desegregation." *Educational Leadership* 36 (1979): 314-321.

Hawley, Willis D., et al. *Strategies for Effective Desegregation: A Synthesis of Findings.* Nashville, Tenn.: Center for Education and Human Development Policy, Institute for Public Policy Studies, Vanderbilt University, 1981.

Holman, Ben. "Desegregation and the Community Relations Service." *Integrated Education* 13 (January-February 1975): 27:29.

Hooker, Clifford P. "Unresolved Legal Issues in School Desegregation Litigation." *NOLPE School Law Journal* 8 (1979): 221-236.

Hughes, L. W., W. M. Gordon, and L. W. Hillman. *Desegregating America's Schools.* New York: Longman, 1980.

Inbar, Dan E. "The Paradox of Feasible Planning: The Case of Israel." *Comparative Educational Review* 25 (February 1981): 13-27.

Jefferson, Arthur. "Detroit's Educational Renaissance." *Crisis* 86 (March 1979): 87-94.

Jones, R. S. "Racial Patterns and School District Policy." *Urban Education* 12 (1977): 297-312.

Kalodner, Howard I., and James Fishman, eds. *Limits of Justice.* Cambridge, Mass.: Ballinger, 1978.

Kapenzi, Geoffrey. "The Metropolitan Council for Educational Opportunity: An Evaluation." *Negro Educational Review* 25 (October 1974): 203-207.

Kirp, David, D. Fine, and S. Angelides. "Desegregation, Politics, and the Courts: Race and Schooling Policy in Richmond, California." *American Journal of Education* 88 (1979): 32-82.

Kluger, Richard. *Simple Justice.* New York: Vintage Books, 1977

Levin, Betsy, and Willis D. Hawley, eds. *The Courts, Social Science, and School Desegregation.* New Brunswick, N.J.: Transaction Books, 1977.

Levine, Daniel U. "Difference between Segregated and Desegregated Settings." *Journal of Negro Education* 39 (1970): 139-147.

Levine, Daniel U., and Eugene F. Eubansk. "Attracting Nonminority Students to Magnet Neighborhoods." *Integrated Education* 18 (January-August 1980): 52-58.

Levinsohn, Florence, and B. D. Wright, eds. *School Desegregation: Shadow and Substance.* Chicago: University of Chicago Press, 1976.

Lewis, R. G., and Nancy St. John. "Contribution of Cross-Racial Friendship to Minority Group Achievement in Desegregated Classrooms." *Sociometry* 37 (1974): 79-91.

McGill, Ralph. *The South and the Southerner.* Boston: Little, Brown and Co., 1964.

Mack, R. W. *Our Children's Burden: Studies of Integration in Nine American Communities.* New York: Random House, 1968.

Marshall, Kim. "The Making of a Magnet School: A Personal Account of the Journey from Chaos to Quality." *Journal of Education* 160 (May 1978): 19-35.

Marshall, Thurgood, and Roy Wilkins. "Interpretation of Supreme Court Decision and the NAACP Program." *Crisis* 86 (June-July 1979): 205-209.

Maynor, W., and W. G. Katzenmeyer. "Academic Performance and School Integration: A Multi-ethnic Analysis." *Journal of Negro Education* 43 (1974): 30-38.

Mercer, W. A. *Teaching in the Desegregated School.* New York: Vantage Press, 1971.

Miller, S. M. and Pamela Roby. "Education and Redistribution: The Limits of a Strategy." *Integrated Education* 6 (September-October 1968), pp. 13-18.

Mills, Roger. "Justice Delayed and Denied—HEW and Northern School Desegregation." *Civil Rights Digest* 7 (February 1974): 10-21.

Milstein, Mike M., and Paul A. Lafornara. "Internal Change Teams in Urban School Districts: The Buffalo Experience." *Group and Organizational Studies* 6 (March 1981): 96-113.

Mondale, Walter F. "Busing in Perspective: Forward or Reverse?" *New Republic* 166 (March 4, 1972): 16-19.

Monti, Daniel J., and James H. Laue. "Implementing Desegregation Plans: The Social Scientist as Intervenor." *Education and Urban Society* 9 (May 1977): 369-384.

Newman, Dorothy K., et al. *Protest, Politics, and Prosperity: Black Americans and White Institutions: 1940-75.* New York: Pantheon Books, 1978.

Ogbu, John U. "School Desegregation in Racially Stratified Communities—A Problem on Congruence." *Anthropology and Education Quarterly* 9 (Winter 1978): 290-292.

Ollie, Bert W., Jr. "Racine." *Integrated Education* 15 (November-December 1977): 24-27.

Orfield, Gary. "How to Make Desegregation Work: The Adaptation of Schools to Their Newly-Integrated Student Bodies." *Law and Contemporary Problems* 39 (1975): 314-340.

_____. *Must We Bus?* Washington, D.C.: Brookings Institution, 1978.

Ornstein, Allan C., and Glen Thompson. "Desegregation of Schools Enrolling 50,000 + Students: A Status Report." *Illinois Schools Journal* 57 (Winter 1977-78): 40-48.

Pettigrew, Thomas. "The Cold Structural Inducement to Integration." *Urban Review* 8 (Summer 1975): 137-144.

Phi Delta Kappa. *Why Do Some Urban Schools Succeed?* Bloomington, Ind.: Phi Delta Kappa, 1980.

Polsby, D. D. "The Desegregation of School Systems: Where the Courts Are Headed." *Urban Review* 10 (1978): 136-148.

Raffel, Jeffrey A. "Political Dilemmas of Bussing: A Case Study of Inter-district Metropolitan School Desegregation." *Urban Education* 11 (January 1977): 375-396.

Rist, Ray C. *Desegregated Schools: Appraisal of an American Experiment.* New York: Academic Press, 1979.

————. "School Integration: Ideology, Methodology, and National Policy." *School Review* 84 (May 1976): 417-430.

————. "Sorting Out the Issues and Trends of School Desegregation." *USA Today* 107 (November 1978): 45-47.

Rodgers, H. R., Jr., and C. S. Bullock. "School Desegregation: Success and Failure." *Journal of Negro Education* 43 (1974): 139-154.

Roos, Peter D. "Bilingual Education: The Hispanic Response to Unequal Educational Opportunity." *Law and Contemporary Problems* 42 (1978): 111-140.

Rosenbaum, James E., and Stefan Presser. "Voluntary Racial Integration in a Magnet School." *School Review* 86 (February 1978): 156-186.

Rosenberg, M., and R. Simmons. *Black and White Self-esteem: The Urban School Child.* Washington, D.C.: American Sociological Association, 1971.

Rossell, Christine H. "Magnet Schools as a Desegregation Tool: The Importance of Contextual Factors in Explaining Their Success." *Urban Education* 14 (October 1979): 303-320.

————. "School Desegregation and White Flight." *Political Science Quarterly* 90 (1975): 675-695.

————. "The Effect of Community Leadership and the Mass Media on Public Behavior." *Theory into Practice* 8 (1978): 131-139.

————, et al. *A Review of the Empirical Research on Desegregation.* Nashville, Tenn.: Center for Education and Human Development Policy, Institute for Policy Studies, Vanderbilt University, 1981.

Rutter, Michael, et al. *Fifteen Thousand Hours.* Cambridge, Mass.: Harvard University Press, 1979.

Schafft, Gretchen E. "White Children in a Majority Black School: Together Yet Separate." *Integrated Education* 14 (July-August 1976): 3-7.

Schofield, Janet W., and H. A. Sagar. "Peer Interaction Patterns in an Integrated Middle School." *Sociometry* 40 (1977): 130-138.

Siqueland, Ann L. *Without a Court Order.* Seattle, Wash.: Madrona Publishers, 1981.

Smith, A. Wade. "Racial Tolerance as a Function of Group Position." *American Sociological Review* 46 (October 1981): 558-573.

Smith, Charles U. "Race Relations and the New Agenda for Higher Education." *Phi Delta Kappan* 46 (May 1965).

Sobol, Marion Gross, and William M. Beck. "Phenomonological Influences in Minority Attitudes Toward School Desegregation."*Urban Review* 12 (Spring 1980): 31-41.

Sommerville, Joseph C. "Leadership for Successful School Desegregation." *Educational Leadership* 37 (May 1980): 622-626.

Stephan, Walter G., and D. Rosenfield. "Effect of Desegregation on Racial Attitudes." *Journal of Personality and Social Psychology* 36 (1978): 795-804.

————, and D. Rosenfield. "Effect of Desegregation on Racial Attitudes." *Journal of Personality and Social Psychology* 36 (1978): 795-804.

Stinchcombe, Arthur L., et al. "Is There a Racial Tipping Point in Changing Schools?" *Journal of Social Issues* 25 (January 1969): 127-136.

Taeuber, Karl E. "Demographic Perspective on Metropolitan School Desegregation." *Urban Review* 10 (Summer 1978): 71-81.

Taylor, Howard F. "IQ Heritability: A Checklist of Methodological Fallacies." *Journal of Afro-American Issues* 4 (Winter 1976): 35-49.

_____. "Quantitative Racism: A Partial Documentation." *Journal of Afro-American Issues* 3 (Winter 1975): 19-42.

Taylor, William L. "Metropolitan Remedies for Public School Discrimination: The Neglected Option." *Urban Review* 10 (Summer 1978): 184-192.

Teele, James E. *Evaluating School Busing: A Case Study of Boston's Operation Exodus.* New York: Praeger, 1973.

Thomas, Gail E., ed. *Black Students in Higher Education.* Westport, Conn.: Greenwood Press, 1981.

_____. "Puritans, Indians, and the Concept of Race." *New England Quarterly* 48 (March 1975): 3-27.

_____. *Race and Sex Effects on Access to College.* Baltimore, Md.: Center for Social Organization of Schools, Johns Hopkins University, 1977.

Troiker, R. "Research Evidence for the Effectiveness of Bilingual Education." *NABE Journal* 3 (1978): 13-24.

U.S. Civil Rights Commission. *Fulfilling the Letter and Spirit of the Law: Desegregation of the Nation's Public Schools.* Washington, D.C.: Government Printing Office, 1976.

_____. *Racial Isolation in the Public Schools.* Washington, D.C.: U.S. Government Printing Office, 1967.

_____. *Reviewing a Decade of School Desegregation, 1966-1975.* Washington, D.C.: U.S. Government Printing Office, 1977.

_____. *With All Deliberate Speed: 1954-19??.* Washington, D.C.: U.S. Government Printing Office, 1981.

Useem, Elizabeth L. "Correlates of White Student Attitudes Towards a Voluntary Busing Program." *Education and Urban Society* 8 (August 1976): 441-476.

VanFleet, Alanson A. "Student Transportation Costs Following Desegregation." *Integrated Education* 15 (November-December 1977): 75-77.

Vergon, Charles B. *Desegregation Strategies and the Courts.* Nashville, Tenn.: Center for Education and Human Development Policy, Institute for Public Policy Studies, Vanderbilt University, 1981.

Weinberg, Meyer. "The Relationship between School Desegregation and Academic Achievement: A Review of the Research." *Law and Contemporary Problems* 39 (Spring 1975): 240-270.

Williams, Robin, and Margaret Ryan. *Schools in Transition.* Chapel Hill, N.C.: University of North Carolina Press, 1954.

Willie, Charles V. *Black Students at White Colleges.* New York: Praeger, 1972.

_____. "Desegregation in Big-City School Systems." *Educational Forum* 47 (Fall 1982): 83-96.

_____. *The Ivory and Ebony Towers.* Lexington, Mass.: Lexington Books, D. C. Heath, 1981.

_____. *Race, Ethnicity and Socioeconomic Status.* Bayside, N.Y.: General Hall, 1983.

_____. "Racial Balance or Quality Education." *School Review* 84 (May 1976): 313-325.

_____. *The Sociology of Urban Education.* Lexington, Mass.: Lexington Books, D. C. Heath, 1978.

————, and Susan L. Greenblatt (eds.). *Community Politics and Educational Change: Ten School Systems Under Court Order.* New York: Longman, 1981.

Wise, Michael B. *Desegregation in Education: A Directory of Reported Federal Decisions.* Notre Dame, Ind.: Center for Civil Rights, University of Notre Dame Law School, 1977.

Wurdock, C. "Public School Resegregation after Desegregation: Some Preliminary Findings." *Sociological Focus* 12 (1979): 263-274.

Yarmolinsky, Adam, Lance Liebman, and Corinne S. Schelling, eds. *Race and Schooling in the City.* Cambridge, Mass.: Harvard University Press, 1981.

Zirkel, Perry. *A Digest of Supreme Court Decisions Affecting Education.* Bloomington, Ind.: Phi Delta Kappa, 1978.

Index

assignment in, 150; Voluntary Transfer Program (VTP), 150-51, 153, 155, 156, 209
Axelrod, Robert, 31, 37, 180

Barbee, Lloyd, 81
Bell, Derrick, 44, 46, 60
Bennett, David A., 81-118
Bilingual programs, 60, 84; in Atlanta, 154-55; in Boston, 69, 213; in Milwaukee, 99; in Seattle, 131, 138, 140, 142
Black United Clergy for Action, 177
Boston, x, 15, 18-20, 21-22, 24, 36, 42, 46, 52, 70, 164, 206; Boston School Committee (BSC), ix, 35, 59, 64, 65, 70-78, 204, 206, 210, 211; Children's Defense Fund, 78; City Countil, 206. Colleges: Boston College, 62; Boston State College, 62; Boston Teachers College, 62. Department of Implementation (DI), 72; description of, 62-65, 166; Harvard Center for Law and Education, 210; Home and School Association, 51, 74; Hyde Park Community District, 200-201; Madison Park Community District, 200; METCO Program, 65, 71; population of, 166-67, 169, 170, 199; public school development, 62, 64; Racial-Ethnic Student Councils, 70; school-community relations, 74-76. Schools: Boston Latin School, 69, 212; Boston Technical High School, 64; East Boston High School, 65; English High School, 64; Hernandez School, 69; Latin Academy, 69; South Boston High School, 69. Violence in, ix, 205, 206
Boston Plan, 59-80, 204; absence of community leadership for, 206-7; busing, 63, 68, 70; Citywide Coordinating Committee, 74; Citywide Parents Advisory Council (CPAC), 74, 75; compared to Milwaukee Plan, 165-70, 198; comprehensive, 199, 200; deficiencies of, 77-78; District Advisory Councils, 74; educational

concerns of, 76, 198, 212; Elective Racial-Ethnic Parent Councils (REPCs), 74, 75; goals and assumptions, 59-62; involvement of state government, 203; magnet schools, 64, 65, 66, 67, 68, 70, 76, 166, 198; Master Parents Advisory Committee (MPAC), 74-75; pairings of colleges, businesses, and agencies, 75-76; policy making and staffing, 71-74; resistance to, 209-10; scope of, 65-68; Voluntary Transfer Program, 198
Bottomly, Forbes, 119
Boycotts, 177, 205
Brookover, W. E., 94
Brophy, J. E., 94
Bureau of Equal Educational Opportunity, 204
Busing, 7, 12, 30, 47, 65, 101, 121, 164; exemption from, 52; in Boston, 63, 68, 70; in Milwaukee, 106, 110; in Seattle, 136-37, 139, 144, 178; two-way, 70

California, 8
Census, U.S. Bureau of the, 4-5, 11
Center for Education and Human Development Policy (Vanderbilt University, 31, 45, 51
Charne, Irvin, 113
Cheng, Charles, 47
Chesler, Mark, 48
Civil Rights Act, 7, 29-30, 41, 42
Civil rights movement, 5, 7
Civil Rights, Office of, 127
Civil Rights, U.S. Commission on, 4, 11, 17, 31, 41, 49, 53, 126, 182, 205
Cohen, David, 12
Cohen, Michael, ix, x
Coleman, James, 164, 165, 166
Coles, Robert, 52
Colorado, 8, 9
Colton, David, 60
Community involvement in desegregation, 204-12, 219-20; in Atlanta, 207-8; in Boston, 74-76, 206-7; in Milwaukee, 207-8, 213; in Seattle, 146-48, 174-82, 208, 213

About the Contributors

David A. Bennett, Ph.D., is the deputy superintendent of the Milwaukee Public Schools. He was responsible for both the design and implementation of the Milwaukee desegregation plan in response to a 1976 federal district court order. A Phi Beta Kappa graduate of the University of Iowa, Bennett began as a researcher in the Milwaukee school system in 1970. He was general assistant to the superintendent of schools in 1976, when he was given the responsibility to direct staff and community planning and write the desegregation plan. Since 1976 he has served the school system as its deputy superintendent and is responsible for its day-to-day operation. In addition, he monitors the desegregation implementation and modifies it through a systemwide, yearly planning approach. Bennett worked directly with state legislators in the development of Wisconsin's Chapter 220 seminal legislation providing fiscal incentives for the voluntary participation of urban and suburban school districts in the improvement of metropolitan racial balancing.

Alonzo A. Crim, Ed.D., has been the superintendent of the Atlanta Public Schools more than ten years. Before going to Atlanta, he served as superintendent of the Compton Unified School System, Compton, California, for four years. Crim was born in Chicago, Illinois. He attended the Chicago Public Schools and graduated from Crane Technical High School. He received his bachelor of arts degree from Roosevelt College in Chicago in 1950 and his master of arts degree from the University of Chicago in 1956. He has served in several positions in the Chicago Public Schools: elementary school teacher, principal of the Whittier Elementary School, principal of the Hilliard Adult Education Center, principal of the Wendell Phillips High School, and district superintendent. He received his doctorate in education from Harvard University in 1969.

Robert A. Dentler, Ph.D., is professor of sociology, University of Massachusetts in Boston, and is a former senior sociologist at ABT Associates, Inc., Cambridge, Massachusetts. He has served as dean of education and university professor of education and sociology at Boston University, as professor of sociology and education, Teachers College, Columbia University, and as director of the Center for Urban Education, a regional laboratory. He has researched and planned school desegregation approaches in thirteen cities. Most recently, he has served as a court-appointed expert in the Boston schools case, where he has advised Judge W. Arthur Garrity, Jr., for eight years, and in the St. Louis schools case. The author and coauthor of many books in applied sociology, his most recent book is *University on Trial.*

Nancy J. Emmons, Ed.S., is a research assistant in the Division of Research, Evaluation, and Data Processing of the Atlanta Public Schools. She has previously served as a school psychologist and as a high school English teacher. Emmons has been active in the National Anti-Klan Network, the National Education Association (NEA), the National Association for the Advancement of Colored People (NAACP), the Atlanta University Consortium Chapter of Phi Delta Kappa, and the United Youth Adult Conference (UYAC). Emmons edits a systemwide newsletter, which provides information on all programs within the school system. She is a member of the superintendent's Discussion Teams, which negotiate with employee organizations, and has recently been involved in research on desegregation and resegregation in the Atlanta schools in preparation for the twentieth anniversary of the desegregation of the Atlanta schools.

Michael Fultz is a candidate for a doctoral degree at the Harvard Graduate School of Education. He is interested in the history of education of black Americans and has recently completed a paper on "The Early Writings of Horace Mann Bond, 1924-1939."

William Maynard, Ed.D., worked as a teacher, vice-principal, and principal of Cleveland High School in Seattle prior to taking the position of director of desegregation. As a result of his work in developing the Seattle Plan, he received a Citation of Merit from the Seattle School Board of Directors. He was also selected by *Time* magazine and the Seattle Chamber of Commerce as a "Newsmaker of Tomorrow." In recent years Maynard has coauthored two books, *School Climate Improvement: A Challenge to Administrators* (Phi Delta Kappa) and *School Climate: A Guide For Practitioners* (CADRE Publications Center). He has worked as a consultant throughout the United States and Canada and has conducted numerous seminars for the Association for Supervision and Curriculum Development and the National Association of Secondary School Principals.

Charles V. Willie, Ph.D., is professor of education and urban studies, Harvard Graduate School of Education. He was a court-appointed master in the Boston school desegregation case and an expert witness in desegregation cases in Dallas and Denver. He also testified in the North Carolina higher education desegregation case. A past president of the Eastern Sociological Society, he is also a former member of the Council of the American Sociological Association and the Board of Directors of the Social Science Research Council. He also served on the President's Commission on Mental Health. Among his published books on education and school desegregation are *Black Students at White Colleges, Black Colleges in America, The Sociology of Urban Education, Community Politics and Educational Change,* and *The Ivory and Ebony Towers.* A Morehouse College graduate, he received a Ph.D. degree in sociology from Syracuse University.